THE POLITICS OF CYBER-SECURITY

By combining theoretical discussions with real-world examples, *The Politics of Cyber-Security* offers readers valuable insights into the role of cyber-security in the realm of international politics. In the face of persistent challenges stemming from the exploitation of global cyberspace, cyber-security has risen to the forefront of both national and international political priorities. Understanding the intricacies and dynamics of cyber-security, particularly its connections to conflict and international order, has never been more essential. This book provides the contextual framework and fundamental concepts necessary to comprehend the interplay between technological opportunities and political constraints. Crafted to resonate with a diverse audience, including undergraduate and postgraduate students, researchers, course instructors, policymakers, and professionals, it aims to bridge gaps and foster understanding across various backgrounds and interests.

Myriam Dunn Cavelty is Senior Scientist and Deputy Head of Research and Teaching at the Center for Security Studies (CSS), ETH Zurich. She is the author of *Cyber-Security and Threat Politics: US Efforts to Secure the Information Age* (Routledge 2008) and many other articles and books on the politics of cyber-security.

International Studies Intensives

Series Editors: Shareen Hertel and Michael J. Butler

Series Description

International Studies Intensives (ISI) is a book series that springs from the desire to keep students engaged in the world around them. ISI books are meant to offer an intensive introduction to subjects often left out of the curriculum. Our authors are from a range of disciplines and employ many different methodological approaches to teaching about international issues. Yet each and every ISI book packs a wealth of information into a small space, and does so in ways that students find compelling and instructors find useful. ISI books are relatively short, visually attractive, and affordably priced. Examination/inspection copies for course adoption may be requested from the Webpage of any book in the series. Book proposals for the series should be directed to the co-editors: *shareen.hertel@uconn.edu* and *mbutler@clarku.edu*.

Recent Books in the Series:

All the World's a Stage
The Theater of Political Simulations
Hemda Ben-Yehuda

Human Rights and Justice for All
Demanding Dignity in the United States and Around the World
Carrie Booth Walling

The Politics of Cyber-Security
Myriam Dunn Cavelty

THE POLITICS OF CYBER-SECURITY

Myriam Dunn Cavelty

Routledge
Taylor & Francis Group

NEW YORK AND LONDON

Designed cover image: Getty/Andriy Onufriyenko

First published 2025
by Routledge
605 Third Avenue, New York, NY 10158

and by Routledge
4 Park Square, Milton Park, Abingdon, Oxon, OX14 4RN

Routledge is an imprint of the Taylor & Francis Group, an informa business

© 2025 Taylor & Francis

Library of Congress Cataloging-in-Publication Data
A catalog record for this title has been requested

ISBN: 978-1-032-80489-7 (hbk)
ISBN: 978-0-367-89598-3 (pbk)
ISBN: 978-1-003-49708-0 (ebk)

DOI: 10.4324/9781003497080

Typeset in Sabon
by Apex CoVantage, LLC

CONTENTS

TABLES, FIGURES, AND INFO BOXES

ABBREVIATIONS

AI	Artificial Intelligence
APTs	Advanced Persistent Threats
ARPANET	Advanced Research Projects Agency Network
ASEAN	Association of Southeast Asian Nations
CCC	Chaos Computer Club in Germany
CCDCOE	The NATO Cooperative Cyber Defence Centre of Excellence
CERT	Computer Emergency Response Team
CFAA	Computer Fraud and Abuse Act in the US
CIA (agency)	Central Intelligence Agency
CIA (triad)	Confidentiality, Integrity, and Availability
CIP	Critical Infrastructure Protection
CISRTs	Computer Security Incident Response Teams
CNO	Computer Network Operations
COT	Council on Foreign Relations' "Cyber Operations Tracker"
DARPA	Defense Advanced Research Projects Agency in the US
DCID	Dyadic Cyber Incident and Campaign Data
DDoS	Distributed Denial of Service
DNC	Democratic National Committee in the US
DNS	Domain Name System
DoD	The US Department of Defense
EuRepoC	European Repository of Cyber Incidents
FBI	Federal Bureau of Investigation in the US
FSB	Federal Security Service in Russia

GCHQ	Government Communications Headquarters
GCSC	Global Commission on the Stability of Cyberspace
GRU	Chief Intelligence Office in Russia
ICCPR	International Covenant on Civil and Political Rights
ICTs	Information and Communication Technologies
IDS	Intrusion Detection System
IGF	Internet Governance Forum
IHL	International Humanitarian Law
InfOps	Information Operations
IoT	Internet of Things
IR	International Relations
ISIS	The Islamic State of Iraq and Syria
ITU	International Telecommunication Union
MAD	Mutually Assured Destruction
ML	Machine Learning
NASA	The National Aeronautics and Space Administration in the US
NSA	The National Security Agency in the US
OEWG	The Open-Ended Working Group
PCCIP	The President's Commission on Critical Infrastructure Protection
PoA	Programme of Action
RaaS	Ransomware-as-a-service
RAT	Remote Administration Tool
RMA	Revolution in Military Affairs
ROI	Return on Investment
SCADA	Supervisory Control and Data Acquisition
TTPs	Tactics, Techniques, and Procedures
UN	United Nations
UNGGE	The United Nations Group of Governmental Experts (on Developments in the Field of Information and Communications Technologies in the Context of International Security)
US	The United States of America
US DOJ	The US Department of Justice
USCYBERCOM	The US Cyber Command
VEP	Vulnerabilities Equities Process
WSIS	World Summit on the Information Society

ACKNOWLEDGMENTS

With gratitude, I extend my heartfelt thanks to my husband and my daughter, my two cats, and my Xoloitzcuintle. Their unwavering support, encouragement, and understanding have been my rock, and their belief in me has been my anchor—especially my essentially hairless dog, who never judged my writing skills, but is always deliriously happy to see me. The countless walks we have taken together not only provided a much-needed break from the screen but also served as moments of clarity where ideas were unleashed in lieu of the dog. His enthusiasm for each walk mirrored my own for this project, and for that, I am truly thankful.

I also want to express my sincere appreciation to the Center for Security Studies at ETH Zürich, led by the indomitable Andy Wenger. The resources, facilities, and academic environment provided by the Center were indispensable for the successful completion of this work. Thanks to my colleagues, my caffeine-fueled writing marathons had the perfect backdrop of intellectual stimulation. Who could wish for more than a place of work you want to return to daily because everything there is welcoming and inspiring!

Special shout-outs go to my cyber-colleagues: Miguel Gomez, Lennart Maschmeyer, and Max Smeets. Their constructive feedback, lively discussions, and the shared coffees and lunches kept me going. I feel fortunate to have met such brilliant colleagues whose passion for cyber-security politics matches their wit. Our stimulating co-teaching experiences enriched our collaboration, influencing the depth and direction of my arguments.

A tip of the hat also to my non-cyber-colleagues who bravely waded into the first solid draft of the manuscript: Michiel Foulon, Sara Hellmüller,

Stephen Herzog, Sarah Kostenbader, Dominika Kunertova, Enzo Nussio, and Nina Silove. Your willingness to engage with the sometimes-perplexing world of cyber-talk is a testament to your adventurous spirits.

A special nod to those who added a dash of nonintellectual stimulation: Bruno Barbieri (my favorite Italian), Levi Ackerman, Spike Spiegel, and Gojo Satoru. Manowar and Metallica are ever-reliable constants; Jag Panzer deserves a mention for the best live concert ever; while Ungfell, Metamorphosis, and Satyricon set the perfect mood, mood-dependent of course.

To everyone who has been part of this journey, whether directly or indirectly, your support has been as integral to the success of this book as Ctrl+C and Ctrl+V are to copying and pasting. This is dedicated to all the "good cybers" out there—may your analyses be insightful, your passwords secure, your memes always on point, your policy recommendations impactful, and your collaborations at the intersection of technology and politics contribute to a better digitalized world.

1

AN INTRODUCTION TO THE POLITICS OF CYBER-SECURITY

In June 2017, a seemingly routine software update sent ripples of disruption across the globe. Someone had compromised the software's update mechanism, allowing them to distribute a malware to users who downloaded and installed the infected update. This is the story of NotPetya, the costliest cyber-attack the world has seen to date.

The epicenter of the attack was Ukraine, a country already grappling with political tensions after Russia's annexation of Crimea in 2014. The malware's release was timed to coincide with Constitution Day, a Ukrainian public holiday commemorating the signing of the post-Soviet Ukrainian constitution. From Ukraine, NotPetya swiftly spread to networks around the globe. Taking advantage of a known vulnerability in Microsoft's Windows operating system, the malware encrypted files on unpatched computers, rendering them inaccessible. Paying the demanded ransom proved futile. The true intent of the malware—a Wiper—was to erase data irreversibly (Fayi 2018). As a result, multinational corporations struggled to recover, supply chains were disrupted, and critical services ground to a halt. The financial losses resulting from NotPetya are estimated at over US$10 billion (Greenberg 2018).

The staggering impact of incidents like NotPetya can, in part, be attributed to companies' negligence in cyber-security practices, as patches addressing the exploited vulnerability were left unapplied since March 2017. However, the incident not only underscores the potentially far-reaching impact of individual corporate practices on a global scale but it also lays bare the dual-use nature of computer vulnerabilities. The exploit that was used—EternalBlue—was stolen from the United States' National Security

DOI: 10.4324/9781003497080-1

Agency (NSA) and leaked by a hacker group known as "The Shadow Brokers" a few months prior to the attack. This not only highlights the risk of such capabilities falling into the wrong hands but also emphasizes the delicate balance governments face in deciding whether to disclose strategically valuable vulnerabilities for general cyber-security improvement or to keep them secret for potential offensive purposes against adversaries (Dunn Cavelty and Egloff 2019).

Not least, NotPetya had a significant international security link. A few months after the incident, public attribution linked the malware to a Russian state-sponsored hacker group known as "Sandworm," operating within GRU, the Main Intelligence Directorate in Russia (Greenberg 2019). While the exact intentions behind the malware's spread beyond Ukraine remain unclear, the group evidently and recklessly risked the consequences of massive collateral damage. In the aftermath of other destructive and disruptive computer intrusions by the same group, the US Department of Justice (DOJ) took legal action by indicting six Russian military intelligence officers in 2020 (US DoJ 2020).

NotPetya is just one of many politically motivated cyber-attacks the world has been confronted with in the last decade. As an illustrative example, it demonstrates how the interconnected fabric of ubiquitous digital systems bridges technical vulnerabilities to the well-being of individuals and the security of nations. Reflecting the ongoing challenge posed by the exploitation of global cyberspace by both state and non-state actors, cyber-security has emerged as a paramount concern on both national and international political agendas. Consequently, comprehending the essence and dynamics of cyber-security and its intricate connections with conflict and international order has never been more crucial. Yet, despite this urgency, public awareness of this complex and dynamic issue remains basic (Stevens 2023). By combining theoretical and conceptual discussions with real-world examples, this book provides the essential context and concepts for understanding how the evolving cyber-threat landscape shapes global politics and vice versa.

BOX 1.1   KEY VOCABULARY

The beginning of this chapter used terminology that is essential for confidently navigating the realm of cyber-security politics. While many of these key terms originate in the information security community and have a technical flavor, they are equally employed by practitioners and scholars in the cyber-security field. Familiarity with the nuances of this vocabulary is fundamental for effective communication, collaboration, decision-making, and addressing the multifaceted challenges posed by cyber-threats in today's interconnected world.

Cyber-attack: A deliberate, malicious action that seeks to compromise the confidentiality, integrity, or availability of computer systems, networks, or digital information.

Cyber-incident: Any observable or suspected event in the digital domain that has the potential to compromise the security of information systems, networks, or digital data.

Cyber-operation: A coordinated and planned set of activities conducted in the digital domain for a specific purpose.

Malware: Short for malicious software, it refers to any software specifically designed to harm, exploit, or compromise computer systems, networks, or users.

Vulnerability: A weakness or flaw in a system, network, application, or process that could be exploited by attackers to compromise the security of the system.

Exploit: A piece of software, a sequence of commands, or a technique designed to take advantage of a specific vulnerability in a computer system, network, or application.

Patch: A piece of code or software update designed to fix, improve, or update a computer program or its supporting data.

Cyber-capabilities: The resources, skills, and technologies that enable entities, such as government agencies or military organizations, to conduct cyber-operations for defensive or offensive purposes.

This introductory chapter situates cyber-security as an issue in international politics and will clarify the scope of the book, the conceptual framework that guides the deliberations, and the structure.

Cyber-Security as an Issue of International Politics

In their essence, the challenges arising from cyber-security are not new. Throughout history, society has consistently confronted the task of reconciling the benefits offered by technological progress with the inherent risks that accompany all technological innovations. This dilemma becomes especially apparent in the realm of digitalization. Across the globe, societies are increasingly embracing mobile devices, the Internet of Things (IoT), cloud-based technologies, self-learning algorithms, and big data analytics to varying extents. The collective aspiration is that this "digital transformation" can yield a range of benefits, such as improved operational performance, enhanced value creation, and increased efficiency (Vial 2019). However, digital technologies come with a series of risks that permeate more and more aspects of our lives as digitalization deepens. Due to technical design legacies, economic factors, and political influences that often tolerate vulnerabilities in software and hardware, these technological artifacts can be exploited for economic, criminal, or political purposes. As the collection and intentional exchange of data intensify to optimize processes, and our reliance on digital media to shape our opinions and worldviews grows, the ease of monitoring and influencing human subjects escalates as well (Clarke 2016).

In the face of perceived security threats, a political response is soon to follow. The escalating economic and political ramifications linked to cyber-incidents have spurred actors across government, business, and civil society domains to actively prioritize security within the digital realm. This pursuit takes the form of dedicated policies, streamlined processes, best practices, and the development of more robust security solutions and products to manage the risk (Bayuk et al. 2012). A significant aspect of these measures lies in their technical nature, as computer networks and the data transmitted or stored within them are the primary targets of threats. Consequently, efforts are directed toward bolstering technical defenses, fortifying network security, and implementing advanced technologies to mitigate vulnerabilities. Besides, organizational measures play a crucial role in combating the insecurity of the digital environment. These include the adoption of standardized risk management processes, ensuring proper governance structures, promoting a culture of security awareness, and fostering a proactive approach toward cyber-security within organizations (Tropina and Callanan 2015).

Unlike the many volumes that delve into technical and organizational aspects of cyber-security, this book takes a distinct approach by focusing on the intersection of threats and responses within the realm of *international (security) politics*. By adopting this focus, the book naturally finds its disciplinary home in the field of International Relations (IR) and Security Studies as one of its prominent subfields. There has been a noticeable expansion in both literature and educational courses focused on cyber-security since approximately 2018 (Gorwa and Smeets 2019; Herr et al. 2020). However, the escalation of socially pertinent yet underexplored questions at the crossroads of digital technologies and national and international security is outpacing this growth. This dynamic realm is poised to remain a salient topic for years to come, making the investment of time in acquiring in-depth knowledge about cyber-security at the confluence of policy and politics highly worthwhile. As the demand for experts who can articulate with depth and authority on the interplay between digital transformation, security challenges, and their social consequences continues to rise, the importance of cultivating expertise in this field becomes increasingly evident.

Interactions: The Relationship Between Technologies and Politics

The study of cyber-security as a pivotal aspect of security politics has remained a niche topic when compared to other issues in the field of IR for many years. A fundamental reason for this lies in the discipline's reluctance to view technologies as more than mere material objects or capabilities of state and non-state actors (McCarthy 2018: 2). By regarding technologies as the primary driving forces behind change and transformation in the international system (Fritsch 2014: 116), they are attributed an independent "power" that exists outside of social interactions. This analytical fallacy, commonly known as "technological determinism," assumes that technologies unilaterally propel social change without any influence from society on their development, form, and utilization (Herrera 2003; Mayer et al. 2014). This perspective, which was particularly prevalent in writings from the 1990s to the early 2000s, whether overly optimistic or pessimistic, imbues the political discourse with a sense of inevitability. It is exemplified by statements like "digital technologies bring equality" or "digital technologies have fundamentally altered society," or the notion that it is only a matter of "when, not if" we will witness a large-scale digital catastrophe. Paradoxically, this perspective renders the technologies themselves academically uninteresting, thereby discouraging a thorough examination of their form and the diverse ways they exert influence.

The notion of monolithic, black-boxed technologies that passively impose fundamental change upon society does a great disservice to both scholarly work and policy engagement and development. From a scholarly perspective, it becomes impossible to explain why the same technology yields different effects in various contexts or why it is utilized in diverse ways by different actors in different locations. In the realm of cyber-security politics, the most crucial question revolves around understanding the political actions and reactions made possible by digital technologies. It is imperative to comprehend who develops these technologies, in what manner, and who holds the power to shape their use at any given point in time. This knowledge forms a vital piece of the puzzle. For policymakers and those involved in shaping policies, it would be concerning if technology governance were solely determined by the technologies themselves, rather than being influenced by the social and political factors that shape their design and usage. Recognizing that the use and governance of technologies are intertwined with broader social and political dynamics is essential for effective policy formulation and decision-making. Failing to account for these factors could have dire consequences for the development of appropriate and effective technology policies.

The approach this book takes in analyzing technology ultimately revolves around identifying whose actions or interventions can produce specific effects in different situations. As highlighted by Leese and Hoijtink in their edited volume on technology and agency, "humans and technologies mutually *enable each other* to generate an impact in the world" (Leese and Hoijtink 2019: 2, emphasis added). In this perspective, agency is not an inherent attribute of an entity but emerges through *socio-political interactions* (Leese and Hoijtink 2019: 3; cf. Jackson and Nexon 1999). In other words, technologies do not autonomously bring about change, nor do they possess the power to act independently without humans utilizing them in specific ways. Instead, their relevant impact is intricately intertwined within contextualized and contingent contexts.

Simultaneously, we must also avoid the mistake of disregarding the technological path-dependencies and constraining factors that exist at the interface of technologies and human life. Technologies are not isolated entities but are influenced by and, in turn, shape the broader system and its constituent elements, becoming embedded within intricate global socio-technical systems (Fritsch 2014: 116). In this regard, Sheila Jasanoff's concept of "co-production" becomes relevant, emphasizing the concurrent processes through which modern societies develop their epistemic and normative understandings of the world (Jasanoff 2004). Consequently, scholars and policymakers should refrain from adopting oversimplified conceptualizations of these interactions merely for the sake of convenience. Instead, they should always strive to place the dynamics of co-shaping at the core of their deliberations. Recognizing the reciprocal relationship between technologies and society, and acknowledging how they mutually influence and transform each other, is crucial for comprehensive and nuanced analyses of the complex interplay between technology and human affairs.

The Interaction in Practice: Pertinent Examples From Cyber-Security

Cyber-security serves as a compelling example of why adopting a more complex and interactive perspective is necessary to comprehend the dynamic relationship between human actors and technologies. During the design phase of technologies, the intentions, norms, and values of developers shape the artifacts, imposing certain restrictions on their use while enabling other possibilities. However, as technologies diffuse and become widely adopted, they acquire diverse meanings and purposes that may diverge from the original intentions of the developers (Matthewman 2011).

A pertinent illustration of this phenomenon is the Internet, which has undergone a remarkable evolution from its origins as the Advanced Research Projects Agency Network (ARPANET). Initially designed to facilitate optimized information exchange between universities and research laboratories involved in the US Department of Defense (DoD) research, the early focus was not on security. Information systems were hosted on large proprietary machines with limited connections to other computers. The network designers envisioned computers as a means of communication among trusted groups of experts, resulting in an open (and unencrypted) network that prioritized robustness and survivability over confidentiality (Libicki 2000; Leiner et al. 2009). However, as the internet interacted with various private and public entities over the subsequent years, it expanded far beyond the scope envisioned in the 1970s, in terms of both its size and functionality. It has transformed into an immense socio-technical system for information exchange, generating massive amounts of data amounting to hundreds of zettabytes today. Nevertheless, at its core, this networking technology remains fundamentally insecure due to its historical origins.

This example underscores the significance of considering the interplay between human actions, intentions, and the evolving nature of technologies. It highlights the ways in which technologies can surpass their initial designs, acquiring new functions and vulnerabilities as they interact with different social actors and institutions. Understanding the insecurities and risks that arise from this historical trajectory is necessary for developing effective cyber-security measures in the present digital landscape.

Another example highlighting the importance of focusing on interactions is the contingent process of innovation, diffusion, and application of technologies, which is crucial for understanding their impact (Krause 2019). One can examine the cat-and-mouse game between attackers and defenders as an illustration, demonstrating how human actors drive the exploitation of technological vulnerabilities. This, in turn, leads to the development of new technical, organizational, and even political countermeasures. As a result, new risks and opportunities emerge for attackers, creating a feedback loop between technological possibilities and human innovation.

Yet another example of this dynamic pertains to the changes observed in the public attribution behavior of states (Rid and Buchanan 2015; Egloff 2020). Initially, the "attribution problem" (Lupovici 2016) was widely recognized as one of the significant challenges in cyber-security. It was argued that states would be vulnerable to cyber-attacks because they lacked the ability to identify the responsible actors and subsequently respond with appropriate measures. At that time, this technological determinist perspective suggested that traditional strategic concepts such as deterrence would become invalidated (Lindsay 2015; Baliga et al. 2020), potentially leading to severe consequences for the balance of power. However, what transpired was a significant investment by the United States, arguably the world's leading cyber-power (International Institute for Strategic Studies 2021), in enhancing their attribution (and response) capabilities. This was achieved through collaboration with the private sector, which responded to the profitable opportunity by establishing dedicated companies focused on "threat intelligence" and attribution (Work 2020). As a result, the cost-benefit calculations for attackers had to undergo fundamental changes in recent years.

This example emphasizes the interplay between technological advancements, human agency, and the evolution of cyber-security dynamics. It demonstrates how the pursuit of technological innovation, combined with human responses and countermeasures, generates a complex and evolving landscape of risks and opportunities. Understanding these interactions is vital for comprehending the dynamics of cyber-threats and developing effective strategies to mitigate them.

Last, the influence of power structures on the desirability and shaping of technology is an essential consideration in contemporary cyber-security debates. History has shown that great power politics and technological races are deeply interconnected (Buzan and Hansen 2009). Today, cyber-security should be viewed as an issue that emerged not only due to technological developments but also because of strategic choices made within a broader context. Historical examples, such as the space race, highlight how visions and strategic aspirations fueled the United States' drive for the development and deployment of innovative technologies. It becomes evident that cyberspace is not solely a product of human creation but, to a significant extent, shaped by states and their strategic interests (International Institute for Strategic Studies 2015: 17; Price 2018; Buchanan 2020). In the field of cyber-security politics, economic and security considerations are intricately intertwined, making it challenging to separate the two.

Whose History, Whose Focus?

This book aims to shift the perspective on cyber-security from a narrow focus on digital technologies to a broader understanding of its socio-political embeddedness. While digital technologies serve as the foundation for cyber-security challenges and solutions, it is crucial to recognize that their usage and misuse are shaped by human actors within specific social and political contexts. The decisions made by individuals and organizations, in conjunction with digital technologies, determine the nature and outcomes of cyber-security dynamics. The book is written from a meta-theoretical position that does not take the objective existence of security threats in the cyber-realm for granted. Rather than just existing, so the general take in this book, all security issues are socially constructed through practices in which different actors mobilize diverse power resources to establish their views. The same happens in the case of the countermeasures that get established as "the best."

By focusing on how cyber-security became a security political issue in socio-political contexts and how the issue has changed throughout the year, this book has a macro-historical foundation. Indeed, a focus on history and the past more generally can help to inoculate us against seeing all technology-related issues as fundamentally, even radically new, which is a recurring problem in the policy debate (Healey 2013). There are three caveats with regard to using history to draw lessons for the present, however, which are of relevance for this book. The first is about the embeddedness of historical events. The second is about the focus, and the third is about the "visibility." First, when looking at the past, we must ensure we never lose our awareness of the immediate contexts that shaped it. In hindsight, historical narratives may appear to us as a straight trajectory that almost inevitably arrives at a certain point in time. Instead, we should attempt not (only) to focus on the outcomes of historical processes but also stay attentive to "controversial stages" in between (Sismondo 2010: 121). History, in that view, is a process of contingent struggles instead of a smooth and linear progression that reveals "disputes, the special interests, vital concerns, and hidden assumptions of various actors" (Nelkin 1992: vii).

Second, we must be aware that dominant histories crowd out alternative histories. Dominant histories are the histories of the most powerful, the "winners" of the struggles and controversies. In international relations, this is with no exception the history of the "hegemons" or the "colonizers." The important point raised by post-colonialism and critical IR is that the silencing of alternative perspectives is a form of "epistemic violence" (Brunner 2021). When engaging with the impact of dominant cyber-security conceptualizations and knowledge in different parts of the world, we need to be sensitive to how dominant (Western) ways of framing the issue interact with local power structures and needs, sometimes in violent ways (see also Dwyer et al. 2022). This is especially apparent when cyber-security is fused with military or intelligence activities but also works in much more subtle ways through the type of devices we use, and the way information is exchanged (Powers and Jablonski 2015).

Third, and closely connected, dominant histories are usually the most "visible" histories. This visibility is not solely a matter of recognition; it is intricately tied to the power dynamics of knowledge creation and dissemination. The term "epistemic dominance" (Harris 2023) underscores that certain ways of knowing and interpreting the world wield greater influence and authority. It suggests that prevailing narratives are not merely the result of natural consensus but are influenced by power structures that prioritize specific perspectives (Mumford and Shires 2023; Cristiano et al. 2024). Moreover, visibility in history is closely linked to tangible power dynamics. Crucially, the history of cyber-security tends to focus on "successful" and hence visible incidents, rather than a comprehensive account that includes "non-incidents" (Smeets 2022). Those in control of material resources, such as access to technology, proprietary data, and media, play a pivotal role in shaping which histories are told and whose perspectives are deemed authoritative.

This book has a Western focus and with it comes an underlying normativity that permeates the choices for topics to spend time on and influences the arguments that are made. It also comes with a "traditional" understanding of security (a topic discussed further in Chapter 2). Therefore, this book is not free of judgments about a specific form of liberal/democratic politics that I, an academic from a small country with an old, direct democracy involved in the field of cyber-security for many years, consider a desirable and valuable form of social order. The choice of focus is primarily driven by research pragmatism, seeing how the dominant narrative is readily accessible and widely represented in academic literature that will be referenced throughout the pages that follow.

In saying "Western focus," we need to further acknowledge that the dominant history is most heavily influenced by the United States, its perceptions, practices, and epistemic dominance. It is where most of the cyber-security literature comes from and where most of the academic positions focusing on the intersection between politics and technology are. Even when considering that some IT-security research, practices, and companies emerged outside of the United States, the underlying ideas about digital technologies, power, and insecurity in the literature available to us originate from the United States. The very technology at the core of cyberspace is imbued with values that align strongly with American neoliberalism and the "Californian ideology" (cf. Bendrath 2001), characterized by a hopeful belief in technological determinism (Barbrook and Cameron 1995).

Simultaneously, the success story of cyberspace is inseparable from the US hegemony in international politics and economics. Digital technologies have played a fundamental role in shaping global economies, social interactions, and the dissemination of US perspectives on the connection between information and freedom worldwide (cf. Winseck 2019). The US position as a technological hegemon has been challenged recently, especially in the ongoing and escalating competition for technological superiority between the United States and China. Although this competition is not the primary focus of this book, it represents a struggle over the values embedded in digital technologies and will undoubtedly have a significant impact on our digitalized futures and how we research it.

Aim, Content, and Structure

This book offers a nuanced comprehension of the relationship between digital technologies and politics. Its aim is to resonate with a diverse audience, including undergraduate and postgraduate students, researchers, course instructors, policymakers, and other professionals. The eight chapters allow readers to navigate them in any order, with the historical narrative woven throughout large parts of the book mirroring the progressive accumulation of knowledge about cyber-security politics over the years. To enhance accessibility, key concepts and notable incidents are strategically highlighted within "boxes." Moreover, each chapter concludes with a summary, providing readers with a quick recap and reinforcing key takeaways.

Chapter 2, entitled **What Is Cyber-Security Politics?**, picks apart conceptions of "cyber-security," "cyberspace," and "cyber-security politics" to further clarify the book's scope by establishing a shared understanding of key concepts in the field. It also provides a cursory overview of the type of research that has been conducted in the past, and then addresses the sources of empirical material available for studying the intersection of cyber-security and politics. It is designed to help the reader to get a quick overview of the most important debates and research trends.

In Chapter 3, **Cyber-Security Becomes Political: Threat Frames and Countermeasures**, the examination of cyber-security politics and its evolution begins. The chapter explores the diverse and uneven securitization of cyber-threats, involving multiple threat representations by different stakeholders with different interests. This highlights the inherently political nature of cyber-security and explains ongoing debates about roles and responsibilities in countering cyber-threats. Though this chapter has a historical focus, roughly covering the period between the 1980s and the 2000s, the threat-politics of that time echo until today.

The period that Chapter 3 covers was defined by the expectation of the coming cyber-doom but a paradoxical absence of any truly serious attacks. Chapter 4, **A Problem Matures When States Become Active**, focuses on the fundamental changes in threat-levels when states began to invest into cyber-capabilities. A new reality emerged through a dialectic, interactive development between the aspirations of states and a growing market for cyber-security solutions. A focus on three famous incidents help to exemplify this change and its implications: Stuxnet (2010), the Snowden revelations (2013), and the hack-and-leak operation during the American elections (2015/16). In addition, the chapter engages with autocratic regimes and their specific take on cyber-security with implications for human security.

Chapter 5, **The Cyber-Threat Landscape**, looks at the development of cyber-threat categories such as cyber-terrorism and cyber-war. The construction and stabilization of these categories through the years serve cognitive and political purposes and, at the same time, reveal a lot about the knowledge that was gained about international cyber-security politics in the last 40 years. The ability to use precise language when talking about incidents is paramount for both scholarly undertakings and more policy-oriented work.

Chapter 6, **International Cyber-Security Norms, Practices, and Strategy**, looks at international efforts to establish norms of good behavior in cyberspace and at other reactions by states to counter the perceived threat. In the 1990s, diplomatic processes at the level of the United Nations (UN) began to address the threat of cyber-warfare and prevent catastrophic scenarios. However, it was soon apparent that cyberspace had become a space for strategic interactions below the threshold of traditional warfare, conducted covertly during peacetime. These activities lack regulation under international law. Because of such activities and the parallel rise of "strategic competition" as a signifier for great power rivalry, the United States shifted its cyber-strategy from resilience and deterrence to "persistent engagement," with a series of consequences for the global cyber-threat landscape.

A key "driver" for the evolution of cyber-security politics are cyber-incidents and what they reveal about the intentions and capabilities of political actors. In Chapter 7, **Cyber-Incidents: A Conceptualization**, the parameters of such incidents are discussed. Key aspects are explored, including "attribution" and its political implications, the portrayal of hackers and state capabilities, the underlying problem of (computer) vulnerabilities, and the methods used for hacking. An in-depth understanding of what an "incident" is and how it comes about is crucial if we want to understand some of the technical possibilities and restraints of international cyber-security.

After learning about the interactive evolution of cyber-operations as a tool in international politics and cyber-incidents and threat categories, Chapter 8, **Cyber-Operations: Use and Utility**, combines the knowledge gained in the previous chapters to give a frank assessment of the role of cyber-operations in current international politics. It focuses on showcasing existing data and empirical analyses of politically motivated cyber-incidents. The chapter explores factors influencing states' choices in using cyber-operations and examines the political utility of cyber-tools in various contexts, not the least drawing lessons from the war in Ukraine to challenge some of the long-standing assumptions about cyber-operations' utility in conflict.

In the conclusion, **The Politics of Cyber-Security Now and in the Future—Concluding Remarks,** eight key insights are identified as the main takeaways of the book. The impact of technologies is not autonomous; rather, it depends on how humans utilize them in specific contexts. This interdependence emphasizes the need to avoid overlooking technological path-dependencies and constraints that arise at the intersection of technology and human life.

References

Baliga, S., Bueno de Mesquita, E. and Wolitzky, A. (2020). Deterrence with Imperfect Attribution. *American Political Science Review* 114(4): 1155–1178.

Barbrook, R. and Cameron, A. (1995). The Californian Ideology. *Mute* 1(3). Available at: www.metamute.org/editorial/articles/californian-ideology

Bayuk, J., Healey, J., Rohmeyer, P., Sachs, M.H., Schmidt, J. and Weiss, J. (2012). *Cyber Security Policy Guidebook.* Wiley and Sons.

Bendrath, R. (2001). The Cyberwar Debate: Perception and Politics in US Critical Infrastructure Protection. *Information & Security: An International Journal* 7: 80–103.

Brunner, C. (2021). Conceptualizing Epistemic Violence: An Interdisciplinary Assemblage for IR. *International Political Review* 9(1): 193–212.

Buchanan, B. (2020). *The Hacker and the State: Cyber Attacks and the New Normal of Geopolitics.* Harvard University Press.

Buzan, B. and Hansen, L. (2009). *The Evolution of International Security Studies.* Cambridge University Press.

Clarke, R. (2016). Big Data, Big Risks. *Information Systems Journal* 26(1): 77–90.

Cristiano, F., Kurowska, X., Stevens, T., Hurel, L.M., Fouad, N.S., Dunn Cavelty, M., Broeders, D., Liebetrau, T. and Shires, J. (2024). Cybersecurity and the Politics of Knowledge Production: Towards a Reflexive Practice. *Journal of Cyber Policy.* https://doi.org/10.1080/23738871.2023.2287687

Dunn Cavelty, M. and Egloff, F. (2019). The Politics of Cyber-security: Balancing Different Roles of the State. *St Antony's International Review* 5(1): 37–57.

Dwyer, A., Stevens, C., Muller, L.P., Dunn Cavelty, M., Coles-Kemp, L. and Thornton, P. (2022). What Can a Critical Cybersecurity Do?. *International Political Sociology* 16(3): olac013.

Egloff, F.J. (2020). Public Attribution of Cyber Intrusions. *Journal of Cybersecurity* 6(1): tyaa012.

Fayi, S.Y.A. (2018). What Petya/NotPetya Ransomware Is and What Its Remidiations Are. In: Latifi, S. (ed.) *Information Technology—New Generations.* 15th International Conference on Information Technology. Springer, pp. 93–100.

Fritsch, S. (2014). Conceptualizing the Ambivalent Role of Technology in Inter-national Relations: Between Systemic Change and Continuity. In: Mayer, M., Carpes, M. and Knoblich, R. (eds.) *The Global Politics of Science and Tech-nology –Vol. 1: Concepts From International Relations and Other Disciplines.* Springer, pp. 115–138.

Gorwa, R. and Smeets, M. (2019, July 25). Cyber Conflict in Political Science: A Review Of Methods and Literature. *SocArXiv Papers.* Available at: https://doi.org/10.31235/osf.io/fc6sg

Greenberg, A. (2018). The Untold Story of NotPetya, the Most Devastating Cyber-attack in History. *Wired,* August 22. Available at: https://www.wired.com/story/notpetya-cyberattack-ukraine-russia-code-crashed-the-world/

Greenberg, A. (2019). *Sandworm: A New Era of Cyberwar and the Hunt for the Kremlin's Most Dangerous Hackers.* Doubleday.

Harris, K. (2023). Epistemic Domination. *Thought: A Journal of Philosophy.* https://doi.org/10.5840/tht202341317

Healey, J. (ed.) (2013). *A Fierce Domain: Conflict in Cyberspace, 1986 to 2012.* Cyber Conflict Studies Association.

Herr, T., Laudrain, A.P.B. and Smeets, M. (2020). Mapping the Known Unknowns of Cyber-Security Education: A Review of Syllabi on Cyber-Conflict and Secu-rity. *Journal of Political Science Education,* 17(Supp. 1): 503–519.

Herrera, G.L. (2003). Technology and International Systems. *Millennium –Journal of International Studies* 32(3): 559–593.

International Institute for Strategic Studies (2015). *Evolution of the Cyber-Domain: The Implications for National and Global Security.* Routledge.

International Institute for Strategic Studies (2021). Cyber Capabilities and National Power: A Net Assessment. Available at: www.iiss.org/research-paper//2021/06/cyber-capabilities-national-power

Jackson, P.T. and Nexon, D.H. (1999). Relations Before States: Substance, Process and the Study of World Politics. *European Journal of International Relations* 5(3): 291–332.

Jasanoff, S. (ed.) (2004). *States of Knowledge: The Co-production of Science and Social Order.* Routledge.

Krause, K. (2019). Technologies of Violence. Myriam Dunn Cavelty and Jonas Hagmann in Conversation With Keith Krause. In: Kaltofen, C., Carr, M. and Acuto, M. (eds.), *Technologies of International Relations: Continuity and Change.* Palgrave Macmillan, pp. 97–106.

Leese, M. and Hoijtink, M. (eds.) (2019). *Technology and Agency in International Relations.* Routledge.

Leiner, B.M., Cerf, V.G., Clark, D.D., Kahn, R.R., Kleinrock, L., Lynch, D.C., Pos-tel, J., Roberts, L.G. and Wolff, S. (2009). A Brief History of the Internet. *ACM SIGCOMM Computer Communication Review* 39(5): 22–31.

Libicki, M. (2000). *Who Runs What in the Global Information Grid: Ways to Share Local and Global Responsibility.* RAND Corporation.

Lindsay, J.R. (2015). Tipping the Scales: The Attribution Problem and the Feasibil-ity of Deterrence Against Cyberattack. *Journal of Cyber-Security* 1(1): 53–67.

Lupovici, A. (2016). The "Attribution Problem" and the Social Construction of "Violence": Taking Cyber-Deterrence Literature a Step Forward. *International Studies Perspectives* 17(3): 322–342.

Matthewman, S. (2011). *Technology and Social Theory*. Palgrave Macmillan.

Mayer, M., Carpes, M. and Knoblich, R. (2014). The Global Politics of Science and Technology: An Introduction. In: Mayer, M., Carpes, M. and Knoblich, R. (eds.) *The Global Politics of Science and Technology*. Springer, pp. 1–35.

McCarthy, D.R. (2018). Introduction: Technology in World Politics. In: McCarthy, D.R. (ed.) *Technology and World Politics: An Introduction*. Routledge, pp. 1–21.

Mumford, D. and Shires, J. (2023). Toward a Decolonial Cybersecurity: Interrogating the Racial-Epistemic Hierarchies That Constitute Cybersecurity Expertise. *Security Studies* 32(4–5): 622–652.

Nelkin, D. (1992). *Controversy: Politics of Technical Decisions* (3rd ed.). SAGE.

Powers, S.M. and Jablonski, M. (2015). *The Real Cyber War: The Political Economy of Internet Freedom*. University of Illinois Press.

Price, M. (2018). The Global Politics of Internet Governance: A Case Study in Closure and Technological Design. In: McCarthy, D.R. (ed.) *Technology and World Politics: An Introduction*. Routledge, pp. 126–145.

Rid, T. and Buchanan, B. (2015). Attributing Cyber Attacks. *Journal of Strategic Studies* 38(1–2): 4–37.

Sismondo, S. (2010). *An Introduction to Science and Technology Studies* (2nd ed.). Blackwell Publishing Ltd.

Smeets, M. (2022). A US History of Not Conducting Cyber Attacks. *Bulletin of the Atomic Scientists* 78(4): 208–213.

Stevens, T. (2023). *What Is Cybersecurity for?* Bristol University Press.

Tropina, T. and Callanan, C. (2015). *Self- and Co-regulation in Cybercrime, Cybersecurity and National Security*. Springer Briefs in Cybersecurity. Springer.

US DoJ (2020). *Six Russian GRU Officers Charged in Connection With Worldwide Deployment of Destructive Malware and Other Disruptive Actions in Cyberspace*. Press Release, October 19, 2020. Office of Public Affairs, U.S. Department of Justice. Available at: www.justice.gov/opa/pr/six-russian-gru-officers-charged-connection-worldwide-deployment-destructive-malware-and

Vial, G. (2019). Understanding Digital Transformation: A Review and a Research Agenda. *The Journal of Strategic Information Systems* 28(2): 118–144.

Winseck, D. (2019). Internet Infrastructure and the Persistent Myth of U.S. Hegemony. In: Haggart, B., Henne, K. and Tusikov, N. (eds.) *Information, Technology and Control in a Changing World*. Palgrave Macmillan, pp. 93–120.

Work, J.D. (2020). Evaluating Commercial Cyber-Intelligence Activity. *International Journal of Intelligence and Counter-Intelligence* 33(2): 278–308.

2

WHAT IS CYBER-SECURITY POLITICS?

The characterization of (international) politics of cyber-security in this book revolves around two closely intertwined factors. First, it centers on the utilization of *digital technologies* by human actors in specific economic, social, and political contexts. Second, it involves enduring and often conflicting *negotiation processes* occurring in both formal and informal settings between the state, its bureaucracies, society, and the private sector. These negotiations aim to define roles, responsibilities, legal boundaries, and acceptable rules of behavior.

This chapter aims to establish a shared understanding of fundamental concepts bridging the two realms of cyber-security and politics. By exploring diverse definitions and interpretations, the chapter contends that these variations offer insights into the perspectives and motivations of different actors. The first section deals with "cyber-security and cyberspace," highlighting the interplay between physical and virtual elements of digital technologies. The second section examines the subtle distinctions between normal, every-day politics and security politics, emphasizing what happens if cyber-security is framed as a national security issue. This discussion highlights the complexity of cyber-security, calling for an approach that spans the whole spectrum between tendencies for securitization and technological routines. The third subchapter focuses on the burgeoning academic discipline and field of study centered around cyber-security and politics. By the end of the chapter, readers are expected to have gained a comprehensive understanding of the dynamic relationship between the evolving meanings of concepts in socio-political processes and an awareness of their implications on the constantly changing landscape of cyber-security politics.

DOI: 10.4324/9781003497080-2

Cyber-Security and Cyberspace: A Fragmented, Divided, and Contested Multiplicity

The use of the "cyber"-prefix has become pervasive and ubiquitous. By adding "cyber" to other nouns, a conceptual link to cyberspace is established—a virtual, large-scale, dynamic domain of data exchange that operates through a series of physical objects like computers, cables, or mobile phones and the corresponding communication protocols (Kello 2013: 17). Often, the physical infrastructure and hardware that enables global connectivity is called "the Internet." Various security challenges arise due to cyberspace's inherent features such as interconnectedness, global accessibility, and rapid technological evolution (for some basics about the technology of the internet, cf. Choucri and Clark 2019; Van Puyvelde and Brantly 2019: 24–40; T. Stevens 2023: 14–35). The term "cyber-security" connotes multifaceted practices to address the inherent vulnerabilities.

That being said, cyberspace does not exist as a tangible object. Instead of being a stable construct with clear boundaries, cyberspace undergoes constant dynamic transformations. Furthermore, it lacks a fixed meaning; various actors contribute to its fluid definition, shaping it according to their specific preferences or the objectives they have in mind for utilizing cyberspace (Cohen 2007; Branch 2021). As Betz and Stevens noted over a decade ago (2011: 36): "What we decide to include or exclude from cyberspace has significant implications for the operations of power, as it determines the purview of cyberspace strategies and the operations of cyber-power." Considering the multifaceted nature of cyberspace, it is apt to characterize it as a "fragmented, divided, and contested multiplicity" (Graham 1998: 178), not a singular space but rather many different spaces (Bingham 1996: 652). As cyberspace materializes through a collective understanding, it assumes the form of a "consensual hallucination," as the science fiction writer William Gibson (who is credited for coining the word "cyberspace") described it (Gibson 1989: 128).

Importantly though, cyberspace and cyber-security also have a physical—or, as some scholars would say, "material"—reality: both exist because of networked digital technologies and physical infrastructures such as sea cables or satellites. Overall, the digital era is defined by the use of binary digits (bits: ones and zeros) to represent information. Bits are physical manifestations of electrical or magnetic states. Computations involve input, processing, memory usage, storage, and output, all controlled by software instructions executed by hardware components. As Lessig famously suggests, computer code (software) functions as a form of law because the architecture of the code dictates what actions are possible or restricted within a digital environment (Lessig 1999). Although it is feasible to delve into the study of cyber-security politics without holding a computer science degree or possessing programming skills, it becomes essential to familiarize oneself with certain technical specificities and concepts. This understanding is crucial for discerning the capabilities that digital technologies can facilitate and recognizing the limitations within which they operate. In instances where needed, this book will furnish additional technical details to support comprehension.

Over the years, many observers of the policy-discourse have bemoaned the conceptual unclarities around cyber-terms. Inversely, definitional quandaries are an integral, even axiomatic, part of cyber-security politics and present us with interesting research avenues. Routine discussions about the right use of words serve important political functions and even have performative effects. For example, an agreement on when a cyber-incident becomes a cyber-crisis has a political ordering function because it gives specific responsibilities to different units in a society, be it in terms of analytical capacities to "see" the crisis in time or concerning response capabilities to deal with it. Another key example from the international realm is the disagreements between the United States, Russia, and China over the very definition of cyber-security (Giles and Hagestad 2013; Broeders et al. 2019), which make diplomatic cooperation between the big powers difficult as they influence what a state considers legitimate practices with regard to the digital realm.

We can also observe that cyber-security itself means different things to different people and disciplines and that its overall meaning has changed over time. Foremost, cyber-security is a relatively new term for a set of much older practices around the security of computers and networks, though with nuances (Von Solms and Van Niekerk 2013). Because of its success in crowding out other labels, cyber-security is sometimes frowned upon and even resisted by practitioners in the IT-security field. They see it as a marketing term and not as a term that adds anything new and meaningful to the debate (Dwyer et al. 2022). What Powers and Jablonski have identified as a "silicon triangle" between policymakers, industry, and the public (2015: 50), is also causing unease among some cyber-security scholars and practitioners.

It can, however, be argued that only the relative flexibility of cyber-security as a concept can explain the ease with which it is at the same time moving upward in the political agenda and expanding sideways to a multitude of policy domains (Dunn Cavelty and Egloff 2019). Concerning the "upward" move, the political salience of the term has changed over time, as a result of cyber-incidents and how they shaped the threat perception. In the early 2000s, a small circle of experts discussed cyber-security primarily as a technical risk management issue in connection with critical infrastructure protection (CIP). Now the highest government circles deal with cyber-security as a key challenge to national security, with intelligence agencies and military branches involved. This development is what the literature calls "securitization," the political process through which regular political issues are transformed into matters of "security," thereby enabling extraordinary, rule-altering or rule-breaking means to be used (Buzan et al. 1998, cf. Dunn Cavelty 2008).

That said, cyber-security is not only moved "upward" in the political agenda but also expanding sideways as a problem area to a multitude of additional policy domains in parallel to the advancing digitalization of ever more aspects of the economy, society, and politics (Dunn Cavelty and Egloff 2019). From early on, the security dimension was closely interwoven with and amplified by an economic dimension. Some scholars suggest that "digital information is commodified through its securitization" in the first place and that "information that was primarily of use value, including phone call and internet-use metadata, was transformed into having exchange value through the lens of security" (Powers and Jablonski 2015: 73). Such developments once again point to the need to be sensitive toward interaction effects.

In sum, when we add "cyber" to "security," the meaning varies with the type of security one is referring to (Nissenbaum 2005). On the one hand, cyber-security is anchored in the realm of digital technologies and the practices developed by computer specialists to make computers and computer networks more secure (de Leeuw and Bergstra 2007). Seen from a technical viewpoint, cyber-security is about the so-called CIA triad, the protection of confidentiality, integrity, and availability (CIA) of information (Kissel 2013: 95). Information security or information assurance is the overall goal and signifies the condition when the risks to the CIA of information are adequately managed.

On the other hand, cyber-security is always more than information security: rather than just seeking to protect information assets, it also extends to humans and their interests. Beyond the technical realm, cyber-security has also become a type of security that refers to offensive and defensive activities of state and non-state actors in cyberspace, serving the pursuit of wider security and political goals through the exploitation of various related opportunities. This second type is much more important in this book, however, without looking at the interaction of different communities and understandings, we cannot comprehend the constantly changing policy field (Dunn Cavelty and Egloff 2019; Liebetrau and Christensen 2021).

Cyber-Security Politics Between Exceptionality and Routine

Cyber-security politics can be read in two ways, creating two different meanings: As cyber-security *politics*, as the politics engaging with questions of cyber-security in a broad sense, including routine, everyday risk management processes, or as cyber-*security politics*, which pertains to the security political aspects of the issue. This book is about both. Cyber-security politics is best understood as running on a continuum between securitization tendencies and technological routine depending on the context and sub-issue under scrutiny (Dunn Cavelty 2020).

Politics: Making Cyber-Security About Social Interactions in Specific Settings

Foregrounding "politics" serves to counteract two unhelpful tendencies we find in cyber-security debates. First, cyber-security is often portrayed as a completely novel issue that fundamentally departs from the past. Second, it is frequently framed as driven purely by technical innovation. While the cyber-realm possesses distinctive and, some might argue, unparalleled characteristics such as rapid technological advancements, short innovation cycles, and significant influence wielded by private actors in the tech sector (Matania and Sommer 2023), it is important to recognize that despite the changes in scale, scope, and speed of information flows and digital computations, there is a lot of continuity in how humans organize themselves. Fundamental principles of human societies, rooted in social, political, and cultural structures, persist even in the face of technological evolution.

For this reason, this book firmly positions the subject matter within the realm of politics. The aim is to show that enduring human dynamics influence how societies organize, govern, and interact within the evolving landscape of the cyber-era. It thus emphasizes that cyber-security is not solely and not primarily about technology but also about intentional social interactions. This perspective compels us to contextualize cyber-security politics within its appropriate historical frameworks and to comprehend technological advancements, including the nature of technological tools and their enabling and constraining characteristics, as interconnected with human deliberations and choices. Such a view also counteracts overly alarmist accounts of the disruptive nature of emerging technologies (Seifert and Fautz 2021).

In simple terms, politics is about decisions made by and for groups of people and it can be defined as "any persistent pattern of human relationships that involves, to a significant extent, power, rule or authority" (Dahl 1963: 3). In that sense, politics is to be found everywhere "where interactions between people are structured by (differences in) power, authority and control" (van der Eijk 2018: 10). Though such a definition can be applied to many, if not most, social interactions, most scholars in political science are principally interested in politics with "the state" at its center (Sharma and Gupta 2006). This is also the case for this book: The state and its various roles in cyber-security are a strong organizing principle for the content.[1]

In liberal democratic countries, the role of the state in cyber-security is a politically contested space. This means that cyber-security must be understood in its multiple facets and as a crosscutting policy field in which political trade-offs are necessary. Therefore, the word "politics" in cyber-security politics may serve as an indication that we are interested in how humans form social groups and that it is important to focus on direct and indirect, formal and informal interactions between social groups. In certain settings, states, the state and its bureaucracies, society, and the private sector should be geared toward defining roles, responsibilities, legal boundaries, and acceptable rules of behavior with regard to cyber-security matters. In addition to formal, direct interactions by different actors in a classical bargaining set-up, this definition also includes political deliberations of an indirect and informal nature. Whereby a formal-direct setting plays a role, for example, for the United Nations Group of Governmental Experts (UNGGE) on advancing responsible state behavior in cyberspace, an informal-indirect setting is at play when an organized hacker group writes a public position paper on government malware.

The (Non-)Essence of Security Politics

Security politics are a subset of politics. Volumes continue to be filled on the topic and how we should go about studying it (Buzan and Hansen 2009; Columba and Vaughan-William 2010; Dunn Cavelty and Balzacq 2017). The editor of a best-selling security studies textbook observes that "[t]he good news is that a consensus has emerged on what Security Studies entails—it is to do with threats—and the even better news is that hidden within that simple definition lies the complexity that you are about to delve into" (Collins 2019: 1). While such complexity is only natural given any major field of academic inquiry, security is particularly prone to definitional disagreements since it is a so-called essentially contested concept, for which no amount of debate can bring about scholarly consensus (Gallie 1956). One of the main reasons for this is the close interconnection between security and a set of values that vary depending on one's political position and viewpoint.

In the era of (European) state building, the notion of collective security and the establishment of states have ends and means for each other (Tilly 1985). Indeed, everyday politics is made hard without a certain level of security and stability, and the maintenance of stability and security requires functioning politics. Because of how fundamental security is to human civilization, many consider it a goal above others, as "high politics," taking a special place at the top of the political hierarchy, sanctioning the use of extraordinary, rule-breaking, even undemocratic measures (Buzan et al. 1998, following the political ideas of Carl Schmitt). However, security politics have changed considerably from being defined as exclusively being about "the threat, use and control of military force" in the last decades (Walt 1991: 212). Many of the top security issues today are not about armed conflict but about the risk of disruption of modern life in open, liberal, and digitalizing societies.

The expansion of security politics toward terrorism, pandemics, climate change, energy security, social inequality, and other issues such as cybersecurity has an impact on the conceptualization and practices of security politics. The 21st-century threat discourse looks inward and to society's vulnerabilities as much as outward toward enemy "Others." Prevention of security incidents, coupled with resilience strategies and crisis management, becomes as important as defense and protection measures. Security is no longer just about "exceptional measures" and the military as traditional security instrument but also about the technologies and strategies through which security is sought and produced on a continuous basis, such as risk management or surveillance (C.A.S.E. Collective 2006: 469). This brings into focus certain tools from normal politics like regulation that begin to serve a security function, less traditional security actors from the private sector that have a central role in the creation of knowledge about threats or even in the provision of security, or the work of normal, routine parliamentary politics dealing with security issues (Petersen 2012; Neal 2019; Dunn Cavelty and Hagmann 2021).

Furthermore, if we consider that security politics are about "interactions through which values are allocated authoritatively for a society" (Easton 1965: 21), it becomes clear that defining the parameters of any type of security is more than a simple scholarly undertaking. Security is inevitably linked to the identification of valuable objects in need of protection from threats (Baldwin 1997), assigning legitimate claims to protection to some security objects and political subjects, but not to others (Hagmann 2015).

Going beyond that, given that there is no inevitability attached to the threat-security logic or to how a state chooses to react to a particular issue, this opens a space for the advancement of better, more efficient, or more legitimate political alternatives—which is at the core of critical approaches to security. Some of them go as far as to reject the concept of "security" as it is used in mainstream IR scholarship altogether because it is imbued with the narrow notion of benign statehood. The term "security" itself is the result of a process of (in)securitization (Balzacq et al. 2010) and thus closely related to state violence. As a result, security for the "state" is not always security for "the people"—actions by the state can and very often do have negative consequences for parts of its population, directly or indirectly. This brings notions of "national security" into direct opposition to notions of "human security" (Dunn Cavelty 2014), which also biases the debate toward big impact events, such as the destruction of critical infrastructures through cyber-means, when arguably, national security-centric practices such as surveillance already have a huge impact on many individuals (Deibert 2018). Critical scholars seek to remedy this by focusing on practices of resistance that empower the individual and create positive environments of security (Hoogensen and Stuvøy 2006).

Given such fundamental differences, debates, and viewpoints, this book chooses to treat security as context-specific and contingent goal of politics, paying attention to its varied meanings that emerge in temporally and geographically contextual political processes. General observations about cyber-security politics are possible, but to understand details, we are compelled to look much more closely at how different polities are defining and handling the issue.

Researching Cyber-Security Politics

At the time of writing this book, the academic study of cyber-security politics is about two decades old—that is, young in comparison to other fields in security studies (such as conflict studies), but old enough to make statements about the shape of this emergent field. Scholarly works examining conflictual behavior in the realm of computer networks and information technology—where actors utilize these tools to disrupt, disable, control digital infrastructures, or engage in cyber-espionage for political, military, or economic advantages—have experienced a noticeable increase in volume in the last five years, coupled with a diversification of topics and a growing emphasis on pairing conceptual work with sound empirics (Dunn Cavelty et al. 2024). These are signs of a maturing field.

There are several contextual factors that explain the evolution of cyber-security research over the years (Whyte 2018; Dunn Cavelty and Wenger 2020). Most prominently, a change in focal points and research methodologies is often linked to empirical changes observable in the object studied, whereby these changes can go both ways. The study object influences directions of research through the puzzles and research questions, but research also illuminates aspects of the phenomenon that have gone unnoticed before. Indeed, the interplay between cyber-incidents that are considered politically relevant, political contexts, capabilities to see and study incidents, and so forth, is all closely connected. In more abstract terms, technological dynamics interact with social and political dynamics. Technological possibilities and constraints influence socio-economic processes. In turn, political preferences and contexts shape the evolution of digital technologies and create opportunities for new markets and solutions. This also applies fundamentally to the actors developing these technologies and to the dynamic interplay of cyber-security markets and politics.

Since technical innovation, but also relevant policy practices are determined not by scientific but by nonscientific stakeholder communities in the policy and the private sector, many existing and relevant publications on cyber-security politics are not academic per se but have an applied policy focus. This is a well-known pattern: When "new issues" arise in politics, there is always a high demand for problem-solving, actionable knowledge. Consequently, we often see that policy-relevant knowledge, produced mainly in think tanks, or in military academies, comes first and only then turns into an "academic specialty" (Waever 2010: 652) as is the case for cyber-security politics. This type of literature and the broader think tank community continue to play a very important role to this day, not least because of its quick reaction time when new topics arise in the policy discourse. Similarly, blogs such as "Lawfare"[2] or "War on the Rocks"[3] have been influential in providing an outlet for analysts and academics for disseminating their opinions, ideas, and research findings to a broader public, including the policy community.

In the initial phases of scholarly engagement with cyber-security, there was a pronounced emphasis on conceptual development. The field has dedicated considerable effort to delineating and refining fundamental terminologies and concepts. Scholarly endeavors were directed toward conceptualizing the core nature of terms such as "cyber-war," "cyber-coercion," "cyber-deterrence," and "cyber-weapon," accompanied by theoretical advancements, notably concerning the strategic value of cyber-capabilities. However, as the field progressed, a discernible shift in methodological preferences became evident. Contemporary research in cyber-security now reflects a heightened commitment to case study design and empirical data collection. Scholars have moved beyond the sole task of defining key concepts and establishing foundational theories, embracing a more rigorous phase focused on testing and validating these conceptual frameworks. This evolution is further accentuated by the increasing prevalence of quantitative studies that employ survey or experimental designs, marking a substantial transformation in the field's research methodologies (Dunn Cavelty et al. 2024).

Cyber-incidents with security political consequences are rare events, and our current knowledge about them relies heavily on data from commercial threat reporting and news reports that are already politicized and influenced by the demands of powerful buyers and the interests of capable providers or sensationalists in nature (Lindsay 2017). In addition, cyber is a domain characterized by covert operations and attribution challenges, which creates issues for those interested in interactions between states and larger conflict dynamics. There is data on threats that is not collected because the threat intelligence companies that could collect it have no business case (Maschmeyer et al. 2021). Other data is qualitatively poor because of high uncertainties with regard to perpetrators, motivations, and effects, yet other data is highly classified and cannot be accessed.

That said, the data issue is neither exclusive to cyber-research nor is it insurmountable; it just restricts the type of research questions that can be answered and the type of methodological approaches that can be used (Lilli 2023). As cyber-security politics research evolves, new data sources are tapped into. Early research focused its analysis on official statements by heads of state, high-ranking officials, or heads of international institutions. The use of elite interviews, surveys, or media analysis are popular ways to collect empirical data. However, it became clear with time that a focus on elite speech acts could not tell us enough about the everyday, formative practices of actors that are not so easily visible. Those state and non-state actors "under the radar"—that is, specialized bureaucratic units, consultants, or other experts—have the capacity to establish "the truth" about certain threats, thus prestructuring the discursive field in relevant ways (Huysmans 2006: 72).

The realization that a focus on visible policy made academia blind toward impactful practices by hidden security actors led cyber-security research to diversify. The interest of researchers shifted to the role of the creators (mostly private entities) and exploiters (sub-, semi-, and non-state actors) of digital technologies in shaping the behavioral standards that new regulation needs to consider (Hurel and Lobato 2018). Since part of the problem in understanding state behavior in cyberspace is the opaqueness of cyber-operations and the limited visibility and ambiguity of many of the involved actors, this cluster has also become interested in intelligence services and their operations (Georgieva 2020; Chesney and Smeets 2023). Not least, recent research recognizes that the political reading of cyber-security cannot be divorced from knowledge practices in different communities, hence also increasingly focusing on cyber-security companies (C. Stevens 2020; Dwyer 2023; Muller and Welfens 2023). Like in other areas of security studies, participant observations and ethnographical work became the go-to methods to get closer to state and non-state actors such as specialized bureaucratic units, consultants, private companies, or other experts (T. Stevens 2018).

Other researchers used methods of investigative journalism—finding informants or other secretive sources—to shine light on important, under-researched areas (Zetter 2015; Soesanto 2023). Such methods are necessary to gain access to information from people in the hacker or threat intelligence communities, which was very helpful for the field to develop an understanding of attack techniques and mindsets. Leaks about state practices and capabilities (Snowden or Shadow Brokers, see Chapter 4) or more recent leaks about cyber-criminal activities (prominent examples are the crime groups Conti or TrickBot (Cyjax 2022)) are another very interesting data source for cyber-security researchers, notwithstanding some of the ethical questions that emerge (Flynn 2006).

We also have datasets on state-attributed incidents that emerged, not least to test hypotheses in methodologically sound ways (cf. Valeriano and Maness 2014). Apart from the *Dyadic Cyber Incident and Campaign Data* (DCID)[4] as one of the earliest such efforts, there are other resources such as the Council on Foreign Relations' *Cyber-Operations Tracker* (COT),[5] the Cyber-Peace Institute's data collection focusing on cyber-attacks in the war against Ukraine,[6] or the *European Repository on Cyber-Incidents*,[7] all attempting to collect systematic data about cyber-threats. A threat intelligence community-based data collection on advance persistent threats (APT) Groups and Operations provides invaluable details about threat groups.[8] The *Cyber Vault Project of the National Security Archive*,[9] an online resource documenting the cyber-activities of the US and foreign governments as well as international organizations, is a highly valuable resource for scholars as well.

Another recent trend in the social sciences is data collection through experimental and pseudo-experimental designs, such as war games, focused on elites and non-elites. This type of research has also been taken up by researchers in the cyber-security field (Dean and McDermott 2017). The aim is to use micro-foundational reasoning to understand decision-making processes leading up to the use of cyber-operations (Gomez and Villar 2018; Gomez 2019) and to gain insights into how the public feels about cyber-issues (Snider et al. 2021; Shandler et al. 2022; Shandler and Gomez 2023). Public opinion research has also turned to questions of cyber-security, for example, to gauge how the US public evaluates the use of so-called zero-day vulnerabilities (Leal and Musgrave 2023).

In summary, as is the case in various other fields, researchers actively seek out compelling data sources or initiate data collection through well-established methods. It is worth noting that the accessibility of data often exerts a significant influence on the research process. Researchers craft their inquiries based on data that is readily accessible or obtainable. Moreover, data availability can dictate the viability of specific research queries. When data pertaining to a particular topic is scarce or challenging to acquire, researchers may find themselves adapting their research questions or methodologies to accommodate the data at hand. As a result, the interplay between available data and research is a dynamic force that both constrains and fuels the evolution of research inquiries. This symbiotic relationship underscores the importance of researchers maintaining a keen awareness of the data at their disposal and its inherent limitations when shaping research questions and designing studies.

Summary and Key Points

This chapter established the foundation for our exploration of the intersection between cyber-security and politics. By discussing "cyber-security," "cyberspace," and "cyber-security politics," the latter in two variations, it emphasized the contingent nature of politics and the role of contestation in shaping political realities. Indeed, a central debate in the evolving policy landscape revolves around determining the optimal balance between security-focused politics and conventional political approaches to address cyber-threats. This involves defining the roles and responsibilities of various bureaucratic units and establishing the applicable legal framework for them. The dynamics of cyber-security politics exist on a spectrum, ranging from tendencies toward securitization, which signifies the treatment of the issue as an (inter-)national security issue, to embracing technological routines and everyday practices. At all times, different perspectives coexist.

The pervasive influence of digital technologies on daily life, power dynamics, wealth distribution, and conflict has led to more demand for knowledge at the intersection between technology and politics over the years. The discernible surge in the volume of scholarly work dedicated to this topic, prominently featured in highly ranked journals, signifies the growing stature of cyber-security research in IR (Dunn Cavelty et al. 2024). The interplay between available data and research methodologies emphasizes the importance of researchers being cognizant of how to generate new data to tackle relevant questions. In the future, knowledge about the interactions between cyber-security and politics will become even more important, offering great opportunities for researchers. For those seeking to transition to the private or the public sector after their studies, knowledge about cyber-security at the intersection of policy and politics is also a huge asset. Too few experts exist who can speak with depth and authority about digital transformation, security, and social consequences.

Notes

1. The prevailing schools of thought in International Relations (IR) rely on an idealized model of a political order that emerged in Europe in the mid-17th century and established the principle of territorial state sovereignty, an undisputed monopoly of violence, and other stables (Ould Mohamedou 2020: 1341). This idealized model is only found within a limited geographical context and struggles to be universally applicable. It also introduces an inevitable Western bias into the debate that this book is aware of but chooses not to deal with.
2. www.lawfareblog.com/
3. https://warontherocks.com/
4. https://drryanmaness.wixsite.com/cyberconflict/cyber-conflict-dataset
5. www.cfr.org/cyber-operations/
6. https://cyberconflicts.cyberpeaceinstitute.org/
7. https://eurepoc.eu
8. https://apt.threattracking.com
9. https://nsarchive.gwu.edu/project/cyber-vault-project

References

Baldwin, D.A. (1997). The Concept of Security. *Review of International Studies* 23(1): 5–26.

Balzacq, T., Basaran, T., Bigo, D., Guittet, E. and Olsson, C. (2010). Security Practices. In: *Oxford Research Encyclopedia of International Studies*. Available at: https://oxfordre.com/internationalstudies/view/10.1093/acrefore/9780190846626.001.0001/acrefore-9780190846626-e-475

Betz, D. and Stevens, T. (2011). *Cyberspace and the State: Toward a Strategy for Cyber-Power*. Adelphi Papers, vol. 424. The International Institute for Strategic Studies.

Bingham, N. (1996). Objections: From Technological Determinism towards Geographies of Relations. *Environment and Planning D: Society and Space* 14(6): 635–657.

Branch, J. (2021). What's in a Name? Metaphors and Cybersecurity. *International Organization* 75(1): 39–70.

Broeders, D., Adamson, L. and Creemers, R. (2019). Coalition of the Unwilling? Chinese and Russian Perspectives on Cyberspace. In: *The Hague Program for Cyber Norms Policy Brief*, November. Available at: https://ssrn.com/abstract=3493600

Buzan, B. and Hansen, L. (2009). *The Evolution of International Security Studies*. Cambridge University Press.

Buzan, B., Waever, O. and De Wilde, J. (1998). *Security: A New Framework for Analysis*. Lynne Rienner.

C.A.S.E. Collective (2006). Critical Approaches to Security in Europe: A Networked Manifesto. *Security Dialogue* 37(4): 443–487.

Chesney, R. and Smeets, M. (eds.) (2023). *Deter, Disrupt, or Deceive: Assessing Cyber Conflict as an Intelligence Contest*. Georgetown University Press.

Choucri, N. and Clark, D.D. (2019). *International Relations in the Cyber Age: The Co-Evolution Dilemma*. MIT Press.

Cohen, J.E. (2007). Cyberspace as/and Space. *Columbia Law Review* 107(1): 210–256.

Collins, A. (2019). *Contemporary Security Studies*. Oxford University Press.

Columba, P. and Vaughan-William, N. (2010). *Critical Security Studies: An Introduction*. Routledge.

Cyjax (2022). *Who Is Trickbot? Analysis of the Trickbot Leaks*. Available at: www.cyjax.com/wp-content/uploads/2022/07/Who-is-Trickbot.pdf

Dahl, R.A. (1963). *Modern Political Analysis*. Prentice-Hall.

Dean, B. and McDermott, R. (2017). A Research Agenda to Improve Decision Making in Cyber Security Policy. *Penn State Journal of Law & International Affairs* 5(1): 29–164.

Deibert, R. (2018). Toward a Human-Centric Approach to Cyber-Security. *Ethics & International Affairs* 32(4): 411–424.

de Leeuw, K. and Bergstra, J. (2007). *The History of Information Security: A Comprehensive Handbook*. Elsevier Science.

Dunn Cavelty, M. (2008). *Cyber-Security and Threat Politics: US Efforts to Secure the Information Age*. Routledge.

Dunn Cavelty, M. (2014). Breaking the Cyber-Security Dilemma: Aligning Security Needs and Removing Vulnerabilities. *Science and Engineering Ethics* 20(3): 701–715.

Dunn Cavelty, M. (2020). Cyber-Security Between Hypersecuritization and Technological Routine. In: Tikk, E. and Kerttunen, M. (eds.) *Routledge Handbook of International Cyber-security*. Routledge, pp. 11–21.

Dunn Cavelty, M. and Balzacq, T. (2017). *The Routledge Handbook of Security Studies*. Routledge.

Dunn Cavelty, M. and Egloff, F.J. (2019). The Politics of Cyber-Security: Balancing Different Roles of the State. *St Antony's International Review* 15(1): 37–57.

Dunn Cavelty, M., Pulver, T. and Smeets, M. (2024). The Evolution of Cyber Conflict Studies. *International Affairs*.

Dunn Cavelty, M. and Hagmann, J. (2021). The Politics of Security and Technology in Switzerland. *Swiss Political Science Review* 27(1): 128–138.

Dunn Cavelty, M. and Wenger, A. (2020). Cyber Security Meets Security Politics: Complex Technology, Fragmented Politics, and Networked Science. *Contemporary Security Policy* 41(1): 5–32.

Dwyer, A. (2023). Cybersecurity's Grammars: A More-than-human Geopolitics of Computation. *Area* 55(1): 10–17.

Dwyer, A., Stevens, C., Muller, L.P., Dunn Cavelty, M., Coles-Kemp, L. and Thornton, P. (2022). What Can a Critical Cybersecurity Do?. *International Political Sociology* 16(3): olac013. https://doi.org/10.1093/ips/olac013

Easton, D. (1965). *A Framework for Political Analysis*. Prentice-Hall.

Flynn, K. (2006). Covert Disclosures: Unauthorized Leaking, Public Officials and the Public Sphere. *Journalism Studies* 7(2): 256–273.

Gallie, W.B. (1956). Essentially Contested Concepts. *Proceedings of the Aristotelian Society* 56(1): 167–198.

Georgieva, I. (2020). The Unexpected Norm-Setters: Intelligence Agencies in Cyberspace. *Contemporary Security Policy* 41(1): 33–54.

Gibson, W. (1989). *Neuromancer*. Berkley Publishing Group.

Giles, K. and Hagestad, W. (2013). Divided by a Common Language: Cyber-Definitions in Chinese, Russian and English. In: Podins, K, Stinissen, J. and

Maybaum, M. (eds.) *Proceedings of the 5th International Conference on Cyber-Conflict*. CCD COE Publications, pp. 1–17.

Gomez, M.A. (2019). Sound the Alarm! Updating Beliefs and Degradative Cyber-Operations. *European Journal of International Security* 4(2): 190–208.

Gomez, M.A. and Villar, E.B. (2018). Fear, Uncertainty, and Dread: Cognitive Heuristics and Cyber Threats. *Politics and Governance* 6(2): 61–72.

Graham, S. (1998). The End of Geography or the Explosion of Place? Conceptualizing Space, Place and Information Technology. *Progress in Human Geography* 22(2): 165–185.

Hagmann, J. (2015). *(In-)Security and the Production of International Relations*. Routledge.

Hoogensen, G. and Stuvøy, K. (2006). Gender, Resistance and Human Security. *Security Dialogue* 37(2): 207–228.

Hurel, L.M. and Lobato, L.C. (2018). Unpacking Cyber-Norms: Private Companies as Norm Entrepreneurs. *Journal of Cyber-Policy* 3(1): 61–67.

Huysmans, J. (2006). *The Politics of Insecurity. Fear, Migration and Asylum in the EU*. Routledge.

Kello, L. (2013). The Meaning of the Cyber Revolution: Perils to Theory and Statecraft. *International Security* 38(2): 7–40.

Kissel, R. (2013). Glossary of Key Information Security Terms. *NIST Interagency Reports NIST IR 7298*(3). https://doi.org/10.6028/NIST.IR.7298r3

Leal, M.M. and Musgrave, P. (2023). Backwards from Zero: How the U.S. Public Evaluates the Use of Zero-Day Vulnerabilities in Cybersecurity. *Contemporary Security Policy* 44(3): 437–461.

Lessig, L. (1999). *Code and Other Laws of Cyberspace*. Basic Books.

Liebetrau, T. and Christensen, K.K. (2021). The Ontological Politics of Cyber-Security: Emerging Agencies, Actors, Sites and Spaces. *European Journal of International Security* 6(1): 25–43.

Lilli, E. (2023). How Can We Know What We Think We Know About Cyber Operations? *Journal of Global Security Studies* 8(2): 1–18. https://doi.org/10.1093/jogss/ogad011

Lindsay, J.R. (2017). Restrained by Design: The Political Economy of Cyber-Security. *Digital Policy, Regulation and Governance* 19(6): 493–514.

Maschmeyer, L., Deibert, R.J. and Lindsay, J.R. (2021). A Tale of Two Cybers—How Threat Reporting by Cybersecurity Firms Systematically Underrepresents Threats to Civil Society. *Journal of Information Technology & Politics* 18(1): 1–20.

Matania, E. and Sommer, U. (2023). Tech Titans, Cyber Commons and the War in Ukraine: An Incipient Shift in International Relations. *International Relations*. https://doi.org/10.1177/00471178231211500

Muller, L.P. and Welfens, N. (2023). (Not) Accessing the Castle: Grappling With Secrecy in Research on Security Practices. *Secrecy and Society* 3(1). https://doi.org/10.55917/2377-6188.1073

Neal, A.W. (2019). *Security as Politics: Beyond the State of Exception*. Edinburgh University Press.

Nissenbaum, H. (2005). Where Computer Security Meets National Security. *Ethics and Information Technology* 7(2): 61–73.

Ould Mohamedou, M.M. (2020). In Search of the Non-Western State: Historicising and De-Westphalianising Statehood. In: Berg-Schlosser, D., Badie, B. and Morlino, L. (eds.) *The SAGE Handbook of Political Science*. SAGE, pp. 1335–1348.

Petersen, K.L. (2012). Risk Analysis—A Field Within Security Studies? *European Journal of International Relations* 18(4): 693–717.

Powers, S.M. and Jablonski, M. (2015). *The Real Cyber-War: The Political Economy of Internet Freedom*. University of Illinois Press.

Seifert, F. and Fautz, C. (2021). Hype after Hype: From Bio to Nano to AI. *Nanoethics* 15(2): 143–148.

Shandler, R. and Gomez, M.A. (2023). The Hidden Threat of Cyber-Attacks—Undermining Public Confidence in Government. *Journal of Information Technology & Politics* 20(4): 359–374.

Shandler, R., Gross, M.L., Backhaus, S. and Canetti, D. (2022). Cyber-Terrorism and Public Support for Retaliation–A Multi-Country Survey Experiment. *British Journal of Political Science* 52(2): 850–868.

Sharma, A. and Gupta, A. (eds.) (2006). *The Anthropology of the State: A Reader*. Blackwell Publishing.

Snider, K., Zandani, S., Shandler, R. and Canetti, D. (2021). Cyber-Terrorism, Cyber-Threats and Attitudes Toward Cyber-Security Policies. *Journal of Cybersecurity* 7(1): tyab019. https://doi.org/10.1093/cybsec/tyab019

Soesanto, S. (2023). Ukraine's IT Army. *Survival* 65(3): 93–106.

Stevens, C. (2020). Assembling Cyber-security: The Politics and Materiality of Technical Malware Reports and the Case of Stuxnet. *Contemporary Security Policy* 41(1): 129–152.

Stevens, T. (2018). Global Cybersecurity: New Directions in Theory and Methods. *Politics and Governance* 6(2). https://doi.org/10.17645/pag.v6i2.1569

Stevens, T. (2023). *What Is Cybersecurity for?* Bristol University Press.

Tilly, C. (1985). War Making and State Making as Organized Crime. In: Evans, P., Rueschemeyer, D. and Skocpol, T. (eds.) *Bringing the State Back in*. Cambridge University Press, pp. 169–191.

Valeriano, B. and Maness, R. (2014). The Dynamics of Conflicts Between Rival Antagonists, 2001–2011. *Journal of Peace Research* 51(3): 347–360.

van der Eijk, C. (2018). *The Essence of Politics*. Amsterdam University Press.

Van Puyvelde, D. and Brantly, A. (2019). *Cybersecurity: Politics, Governance and Conflict in Cyberspace*. Polity.

Von Solms, R. and Van Niekerk, J. (2013). From Information Security to Cyber-Security. *Computers & Security* 38(October): 97–102.

Waever, O. (2010). Towards a Political Sociology of Security Studies. *Security Dialogue* 41(6): 649–658.

Walt, S.M. (1991). The Renaissance of Security Studies. *International Studies Quarterly* 35(2): 211–239.

Whyte, C. (2018). Dissecting the Digital World: A Review of the Construction and Constitution of Cyber-Conflict Research. *International Studies Review* 20(3): 520–532.

Zetter, K. (2015). *Stuxnet and the Launch of the World's First Digital Weapon*. Crown.

3

CYBER-SECURITY BECOMES POLITICAL

Threat Frames and Countermeasures

This chapter delves into the early days of cyber-security politics and explores the reasons behind its emergence as a top priority in security politics. First, we delve into the cyber-threat narrative, tracing its origins back to the 1980s. This narrative demonstrates a diverse and uneven securitization process that follows various tracks, entailing multiple representations—we will call them "frames"—put forth by different interest groups or stakeholders with different claims to protection (Dunn Cavelty 2008). It is this interplay of competing threat frames, encompassing sub-issues such as cyber-crime, cyber-espionage, and cyber-warfare (see also Chapter 5 on threat categories), that underscores the deeply political nature of cyber-security. Second, we explore the accompanying set of protective concepts that emerged in tandem and continue to shape the landscape today: public-private partnerships and public and private self-help. Ongoing debates surrounding the roles and responsibilities of various societal actors in countering specific threats stem from the distinct threat representations that we look at in the first subchapter. These debates involve different stakeholders challenging and countering one another's threat frames, presenting alternative perspectives, or even attempting to de-securitize the issue altogether.

The (Political) Framing of Cyber-Threats

In political processes that elevate issues to the level of security politics, a persuasive discursive connection is established between something perceived as threatening, known as the "threat subject," and something of value that needs protection, referred to as the "referent object" (Buzan et al. 1998).

DOI: 10.4324/9781003497080-3

The essence of such processes lies in defining and addressing hostile factors politically and administratively (Huysmans 2006: 61). The objective reality of the threat becomes secondary. What matters is how successfully and convincingly threats are framed in social and political arenas, and what impact these representations have. That also means that the framing of an issue in political terms is not predetermined; it can vary depending on how a polity perceives and addresses a threat (Huysmans 2000).

The progression of an issue on the political agenda is also influenced by a combination of gradual, ongoing pressures and sudden, impactful events (Kingdon 1984). Statistics, studies, or budgetary implications often serve to demonstrate the existence of a problem that requires attention within the political system. Additionally, policy diffusion, whereby the policies and actions of other states influence the shaping of cyber-security politics, is another development to consider. Within this context, cyber-incidents play a significant role as "focusing events." These incidents, whose characteristics will be explored further in Chapter 7, act as shocks that bring attention to overlooked aspects of the threat or highlight the need for improved countermeasures. They shed light on the capabilities of adversaries and the vulnerability of the targets, sparking national or international discussions on the necessity for change in countermeasures. Cyber-incidents are commonly regarded as catalysts in historical accounts (Warner 2012; Naughton 2016) and frequently serve as essential elements in constructing narratives of cyber-security history (Middleton 2017).

This subchapter explores four interconnected but distinct framings that have emerged, each with its own defining characteristics. The first framing revolves around digital disruptions caused by malicious software. The second framing focuses on the theft of valuable, sensitive, or classified data. The third framing highlights the significance of "information" in redefining concepts of warfare. Last, the fourth framing centers on cyber-induced disruptions or destruction of critical infrastructures. These early years were crucial in establishing the essence of the threats discussed today, with subsequent changes primarily occurring in the increased intensity of the threat due to the emergence of more valuable targets, thereby amplifying the potential for economic or political damage.

Digital Crime: Viruses, Worms, and New Vulnerabilities

In the early 1980s, the easier availability of personal computers gave tech-savvy users access to the slowly emerging computer networks. Many of them dialed into bulletin board systems with a modem and exchanged information on how to tinker with technology. Together with the emergence of a "counterculture" in the form of individual hackers and the formation of hacker communities, which had a political and moral agenda mainly centered on the freedom of information, the vulnerability of the network toward disruptions came to the attention of decision-makers (Ross 1990).

Relatively early in the discourse, the popular conception of the hacker as an adolescent boy, hunched over his computer and posing a latent, but severe threat to national security, was both reflected in and popularized by movies such as *War Game*, and supported at the same time by real-world hacking incidents (Dunn Cavelty 2019). Computer hackers were increasingly branded as criminals in government circles, not least because computer break-ins seemed to become more widespread and received a lot of media attention, with numerous books appearing that addressed computer insecurity in the early 1980s (cf. Mungo and Clough 1992; Norman 1983; Parker 1983; Bequai 1986). The categorization of what was legal and what was illegal had stabilized at the latest with the passing of the Computer Fraud and Abuse Act (CFAA) in the United States in 1986 (Sieber 1986), which formed the basis for many other countries' conceptualization of illegal activities.

In these early days, malicious software (malware) in the form of viruses and worms represented a "visible"—as in countable—part of the cyber-threat. The new "authoritative voice" in the field, the antivirus industry, invested a great deal of resources into spreading public information about the danger from hackers (Skibell 2002), based on techniques to "count" malware infections that served as a basis for statistics. In contrast to today, however, the history of viruses and worms was defined mainly by single actors, often computer students, often with low criminal intent. Among the early disruptions, one stands out as part of the founding myth of cyber-security as a key national security threat. In 1988, ARPANET, the precursor of the internet, had its first major network incident unrelated to crime: the "Morris Worm" (see Box 3.1). Morris, a computer student at Cornell University at the time, intentionally released a piece of software to test whether it could self-replicate through the network. The worm ended up using so many system resources that the attacked computers could no longer function, and large parts of the internet went down. Morris was the first individual to be convicted for felony under the Computer Fraud and Abuse Act. The worm's technical effect prompted the Defense Advanced Research Projects Agency (DARPA) to set up a center to coordinate communication among computer experts during IT emergencies and to help prevent future incidents: a Computer Emergency Response Team (CERT) (now CISRTs, standing for Computer Security Incident Response Teams) (Scherlis et al. 1990). The blueprint of this center and its technical skill set served as a role model for many similar centers around the world to this day.

BOX 3.1   THE MORRIS WORM, 1988

The "Morris Worm," also known as the "Internet Worm" or the "Great Worm," is one of the most famous and influential events in the history of computer security. It was created by Robert Tappan Morris, a computer science graduate student at Cornell University, and it was unleashed on the internet on November 2, 1988. The Morris worm was not intended to be malicious but was designed as an experiment to gauge the size of the internet. However, due to a coding error, it ended up infecting systems multiple times and caused widespread disruption.

The worm infected thousands of computers and led to a significant slowdown of large portions of the internet. This rapid propagation and the resulting damage highlighted the vulnerability of interconnected computer systems. Morris became the first person to be prosecuted under the CFAA in the United States. He was convicted of unauthorized access to computer systems and was sentenced to probation, community service, and a fine. The legal case surrounding the Morris worm set an early precedent for prosecuting cyber-criminals.

The Morris worm served as a wake-up call for the emerging field of computer security and played a big role in shaping cyber-security policy and regulation. Governments and organizations started to take cyber-security more seriously, leading to the development of laws and regulations aimed at protecting computer systems and networks from unauthorized access and attacks.

The worm also had a substantial psychological impact, by making decision-makers aware of how insecure and unreliable the internet was (Parikka 2005). While it had been acceptable in the 1960s that pioneering computer professionals were investigating computer systems, the situation had changed by the 1980s. Society was becoming dependent on computing, not least in many businesses. Tampering with computers suddenly meant potentially endangering people's careers and property, and some even said their lives (Spafford 1989). These ideas may partially explain several repeated instances of digital mass hysteria, which signifies extreme media attention on certain incidents, connected to fears of grave consequences in the absence of them. Examples of this phenomenon are *Michelangelo* (discovered in 1991), a virus that overwrote the first hundred sectors of a hard disk with nulls; *Melissa* (1999), the first virus that used electronic mail to spread on a large scale and unprecedentedly fast; and *ILOVEYOU*

(2000), another fast-spreading virus that destroyed files including photographs, audio files, and documents. Apart from causing annoyance, minor disruptions, and some financial damage, the viruses brought questions of IT-security into the limelight and might even have a positive impact through raising awareness. However, what would become a recurring pattern of rampant threat inflation and future doom scenarios was already apparent from the outset.

At the core of the first framing are two important concepts that have influenced the debate until today and reappear in variations in other framings: vulnerability and dependency. They develop a particular mobilizing power, especially when they are involved in interaction. Computer networks are proven to be full of primary vulnerabilities that can be exploited by malicious actors, feeding into a secondary vulnerability brought on by the increasing dependency of society on computers. What emerged was a very broad and highly flexible, expansive framing. Within it, it is possible to read all the incidents as confirmation of this reinforcing dynamic, even if they do not trigger any substantial consequences.

Digital Spies: Classified National Security Information as New Object of Value

The first framing's attention to computer *crime* does not per se carry a national security connotation (apart from the fact that it shaped feelings of vulnerability). However, this dimension was emerging in parallel to other computer incidents because of successful computer intrusions that involved data theft by foreign individuals. Through this link to the old practice of espionage, cyber-security was elevated to the level of urgency/gravity required for an issue to move from a political to a security political status. Key documents at the time specifically addressed the problem with a focus on "classified national security information," designating a new object of value (cf. Reagan 1984: § 2). It was also stated that information security was a vital element of the operational effectiveness of the national security activities of the government and of military combat-readiness, thus making the national security connotation even more explicit.

An early famous case is "the Cuckoo's Egg" incident, which was documented by Clifford Stoll, a system administrator at Lawrence Berkeley National Laboratory in California, in his book with the same name (1989). Several points stand out: the way he and his colleagues tracked the perpetrators and documented their modus operandi over months; the issues this intrusion created for the American security agencies (FBI, CIA, NSA, among others) in terms of jurisdiction; and how the attribution to a German hacker recruited by the KGB was done (cf. Stoll 1989).

Another famous case during the discussed period are break-ins involving NASA, the Pentagon, and other government agencies starting in 1996. In 1999, the US government began to investigate what became known as "Moonlight Maze" (see Box 3.2). Despite limited proof at the time, the intrusions were attributed to the Russian government. Only very recently, a group of threat intelligence specialists and academics were able to show a likely connection between the activities in the 1990s and the Russian-language threat actor known as *Turla* (Guerrero-Saade et al. 2018).

BOX 3.2   MOONLIGHT MAZE, 1996–1998

"Moonlight Maze" refers to a series of cyber-attacks that occurred in the late 1990s and early 2000s, targeting various US government agencies, research institutions, and defense contractors. The attacks were significant for cyber-security politics due to their scale, sophistication, and the implications they had for national security. The attackers used advanced techniques to maintain access to compromised systems for an extended period, allowing them to exfiltrate large amounts of data over several years.

Moonlight Maze prompted a coordinated response from US government agencies, including the FBI and the NSA. It led to increased investments in cyber-security and the development of strategies to detect and defend against similar cyber-threats. The source of the Moonlight Maze attacks was never definitively confirmed, but there is strong evidence to suggest that it originated in Russia.

The acknowledged risk of being targeted by foreign intelligence services had an unintended consequence: it resulted in hasty and speculative attributions whenever computer intrusions against high-security targets came to light. An illustrative case is the "Rome Lab incident" in 1994, where the theft of names and passwords quickly led to assumptions of involvement by an enemy state (Federation of American Scientists 1996). However, the actual culprits turned out to be a 16-year-old British student and a 22-year-old Israeli technician with no connections to any foreign intelligence operation. The actions of the "414s," a group of teenage hackers from Milwaukee in 1982/83, evoked similar concerns. Their targeting of high-profile entities like the Los Alamos National Laboratory heightened sensitivities and garnered significant media attention (Middleton 2017: 11–13). Despite the limited number of espionage cases linked to foreign governments during that time, the prevailing sense of vulnerability was enough to fully securitize the threat. The prevailing sentiment was that if teenagers could easily penetrate computer networks, it was highly likely that better-organized entities, such as states, would possess even more advanced capabilities to do so.

Like the previous framing, technical vulnerabilities played a central role in shaping the perception of this threat. However, the referent object shifted to "data of value," which was simultaneously more specific yet allowed for a broad understanding of value connected to a market and national security logics. This encompassed the use of digital technologies for wealth generation, intellectual property, military research and development, as well as other data considered "secret" by national security entities. With a clearer association to national security, this framing focused more explicitly on state actors as threats, making it easier to establish connections between cyber-threats and existing strategic rivals. This created a debate surrounding the "attribution problem" and its central role in making cyberspace an intriguing domain of power projection for states, particularly weaker ones lacking conventional strength to challenge their adversaries, as most experts falsely believed at the time.

Digital War: Technology and Information Superiority

While the development of the internet originated in a military context, by the early 1990s, it had transitioned into a predominantly civilian-operated network. Nonetheless, the military had recognized centuries ago that gaining an informational advantage over adversaries ("information dominance") and the ability to disrupt or manipulate enemy forces' information flows were integral components of a successful military strategy (Edwards 1997). Consequently, the armed forces demonstrated interest in computing devices from the moment they emerged. For the narrative presented in this book, it was mainly the experiences made during the Persian Gulf War of 1991 that served as a pivotal moment in US military thinking about these matters. The war marked the beginning of a sustained debate within US military circles on information warfare and information operations (InfOps), accompanied by a surge of publications from think tanks and military academies that explored the "Revolution in Military Affairs" (RMA) that the information age seemed to usher in.

Among the thinkers kicking off the debate were Arquilla and Ronfeldt and their seminal text on cyber-war (1992, reprinted in Arquilla and Ronfeldt 1997). Like other strategists at the time, Ronfeldt and Arquilla attributed the success of the United States and its international allies in the Gulf War to the preservation of their own networks coupled with the disruption of the enemy's. Subsequently, Arquilla and Ronfeldt developed the concepts of cyber-war and netwar, which, in the words of the authors, are "comprehensive approaches to conflict based on the centrality of information [combining] organizational, doctrinal, strategic, tactical and techno-logical innovations for both offense and defense" (Arquilla and Ronfeldt 1997: 6). The two concepts revolve around information and communica-tion, are instances of war about knowledge, and are mainly network based. Both cyber-war and netwar as outlined here are important contributions that shaped what came afterward because their conceptualization greatly influenced the way in which the military and the larger national security apparatus came to understand conflict in the information age (and try to act on it). Importantly, however, the term "cyber-war" is not used by any official sources in the military domain.

In the following years, a variety of formal and informal doctrine docu-ments about conflict based on the centrality of information were published (Soesanto 2019). For a while, information warfare remained essentially limited to military measures in times of crisis or war. This began to change around the mid-1990s, when targeting the entire information infrastructure of an adversary—political, economic, and military—throughout the contin-uum of operations from peace to war was discussed. Acknowledging this, the DoD and the Joint Chiefs of Staff moved to adopt the term information operations instead of information warfare in 1997 (Dunn 2002: 118–119). The conceptualizations that arose during this period also gave rise to a distinction between "information operations" as a broad concept encom-passing psychological operations and influence operations, and "computer network operations" (CNOs) that specifically targeted an enemy's infra-structure, often involving activities commonly referred to as "hacking." This differentiation was crucial for the development of capabilities and sub-sequent strategy formation in the field—not least the tasks envisaged for the US Cyber Command (USCYBERCOM), which started operating in 2010.

This third framing of cyber-security, within the context of military affairs and warfighting, differs from previous framings in that it is predom-inantly optimistic rather than threat based. It establishes a connection to a new source of power that the United States perceives itself as being well-positioned to harness. This perspective, outlined by, Kramer et al. (2009), emphasizes the benefits and opportunities presented by cyber-capabilities or "cyber-power." This framing aligns with the historical trend of pur-suing technological superiority in military affairs, like the arms develop-ment that followed World War II. Importantly, as is discussed in the next chapter, the aspiration to become a cyber-power had tangible effects on the establishment of bureaucratic units, the development of doctrines, and the acquisition of capabilities that really positioned the United States as a cyber-superpower in years to come.

Observers at the time were convinced that victory was no longer dependent on physical force but would be based on the ability to achieve information superiority and secure "information dominance" over the adversary. This thinking was marked by strong technological determinism and sweeping claims of revolutionary change due to information and communication technologies (ICTs). Visions of clean, high-tech wars conducted from a remote distance were considered a future reality because of these developments (Virilio and Lotringer 1998; der Derian 2000). Furthermore, the recognition that conflict in the 21st century and beyond would undergo fundamental change, prompted important questions about how, when, and under what circumstances military action would intersect with civilian infrastructures, both digital and non-digital. These considerations encompassed legal debates regarding the applicability of international law governing armed conflict to the realm of cyberspace (see Chapter 6), but it also led strategic thinkers to turn their attention to the potential negative aspects and implications of information warfare.

Digital Doom: Civilian Public Infrastructure as Main Focal Point

While military strategists recognized the tremendous opportunities afforded by technology-enabled "information dominance" for achieving victory in warfare, they were also keenly aware of the increasing security vulnerabilities stemming from society's growing reliance on computer systems (Rattray 2001). Several notable instances of computer intrusions, such as the Moonlight Maze incident, served as stark reminders of these new vulnerabilities. Additionally, exercises like "The Day After" in 1996 and "Eligible Receiver" in 1997 played a significant role in assessing the plausibility of information warfare scenarios and identifying key issues to be addressed in this domain (Anderson and Hearn 1996; Molander et al. 1996). These exercises helped shed light on the challenges faced by bureaucracies in coordinating their response to this emerging problem area, revealing the complexities of developing effective strategies and coordinating efforts in the face of evolving cyber-threats (Martelle 2018).

The perception of vulnerability quickly extended beyond military and defense networks to encompass civilian critical infrastructures. The advancements in information processing and communication technologies, coupled with their global proliferation, particularly the rise of the internet, led to a transformative impact on various aspects of society through the pervasive presence of information and communication. In the late 1980s, documents emerged linking cyber-threats to civilian critical infrastructures (cf. Computer Science and Telecommunications Board 1989). This linkage played a crucial role in elevating the perceived threat to one that posed a challenge to the entire society (Dunn and Kristensen 2008). While CIP encompasses more than just cyber-security, the digitalization of these infrastructures has become a key driver in shaping the perception of the threat landscape.

In the aftermath of the Oklahoma City Bombing, President Bill Clinton established the President's Commission on Critical Infrastructure Protection (PCCIP) to examine the security of vital systems, including transportation, water, telecommunications, gas, oil, and more. Comprising members from both the public and private sectors, the PCCIP published its report in the autumn of 1997 (Presidential Commission on Critical Infrastructure Protection 1997). The report highlighted the interdependence of electrical energy, communications, and computers, emphasizing that the security, economy, way of life, and even the survival of industrialized nations relied heavily on these interconnected elements. It underscored the vulnerability of critical infrastructures to both physical disruptions and emerging virtual threats. While the study evaluated various critical infrastructures or "sectors" such as finance, energy, transportation, and emergency services, the primary focus was on cyber-risks. This choice stemmed from the relative novelty of cyber-threats at the time and the recognition that many other infrastructures were reliant on data and communication networks.

The PCCIP report played a pivotal role in raising awareness about the importance of protecting critical infrastructures from cyber-attacks. It highlighted the need for enhanced cyber-security measures and prompted further discussions and initiatives aimed at safeguarding the essential systems that underpin modern society. The PCCIP also linked the cyber-security discourse firmly to the topic of critical infrastructures, thereby combining old and new elements of a security conception based on vulnerabilities and dependencies. The idea of critical infrastructures as vulnerable nodes goes back to aerial bombing, vulnerability mapping, and civil defense (Collier and Lakoff 2008). The new way of thinking about vulnerabilities focused more on complex networks, and the possibility of cascading effects, but also on economic factors because of the ownership of critical infrastructure by private actors. The new type of actors and the economic rationale that had to be considered changed the security conceptions and the debate about countermeasures.

The discourse surrounding the information revolution and its political implications must be examined within the broader strategic landscape that emerged after the Cold War, wherein the concept of asymmetric vulnerabilities gained significant prominence, not least as we entered the "age of terrorism." Concerns about the vulnerabilities of "sprawling, open country knitted together by transportation, power and communications systems designed for efficiency not security" (K. Brown 2006: 51) intertwined with fears of intangible adversaries capable of exploiting these vulnerabilities through the anonymity provided by information networks. The information revolution was perceived to provide newfound capabilities to malicious actors, including small states and non-state actors. These actors were believed to possess inexpensive, increasingly sophisticated, rapidly proliferating, and user-friendly tools, which empowered them to cause harm from remote locations.

Furthermore, cyberspace eliminated the geographical barriers that traditionally provided some level of protection. Consequently, strategic circles extensively discussed the possibility of an "Electronic Pearl Harbor" (Schwartau 1994), alluding to a sudden and devastating cyber-attack that could thrust the United States into conflict or cripple the nation in an instant. Rogue states and terrorist organizations were regarded as the primary sources of this threat, viewed as entities willing to resort to extreme measures to achieve their objectives. As a result, the potential impact of a destructive cyber-attack, executed unexpectedly and with destructive consequences, has dominated discussions and policy considerations in relation to national security for years.

Countering Cyber-Threats: A Focus on Protective Measures

By the turn of the millennium, the threat perceptions along the four framings had stabilized sufficiently for them to be visible as distinguishable ways of thinking about the threat-landscape. As a result, a diverse threat-image was established, with malicious actors ranging from individual hackers, to organized crime, to terrorist groups, to states, with no consensus about what the biggest or most urgent threat was. In parallel, the same threat-imaginary and similar political answers were spreading to other countries. Central to the salient "protection philosophy" was the publication of the PCCIP in 1997 and the subsequent policy diffusion with regard to the threat perception and the type of defensive countermeasures. Given that the private sector owned most of the critical infrastructure and assets, cyber-security was described as a shared responsibility that cannot be accomplished by the government alone but must be tackled in a partnership (Presidential Commission on Critical Infrastructure Protection 1997: 19–20). This is the focus of the first subchapter.

The idea of "shared threats" somewhere between local threats (hackers and petty criminals that the government did not feel responsible for) and "national security threats" (intelligence and military activities of foreign states) makes sense theoretically, but in practice, agreeing on who has what role and responsibility in the protection of digital assets remains a highly contested issue. The so-called referent object of security (Buzan et al. 1998: 36)—that which is of value and is deemed in need of protection in the security discourse—often differs for individuals, civil society organizations, different businesses, and governments because they follow different logics, tied to different responsibilities and goals. Little surprising, there was not always consensus about which of those threat aspects needed to be tackled by whom, in what ways. The arising tensions between the different stakeholders are the focus of the second subchapter.

Policy Diffusion of a Three-Pronged Defensive Approach

When "new" threats are included on the security political agenda, appropriate policy measures need to be negotiated and adopted. Some of the key questions arising with regard to cyber-threats at the end of the 1990s were: What are the most urgent cyber-threats we need to counter? What are the main assets under threat? Who is responsible for protecting them? Do we need new legislation? Do we need additional resources, and who should get them? Such political processes are not typically studied by IR scholars because they concern domestic politics. However, the domestic debates about how to protect against cyber-threats at the end of the 1990s shed an important light on ideas of security and insecurity that have a direct link to how states began to act internationally in the decades after.

In this subchapter, the focus is not on the differences between countries' policy approaches regarding cyber-security, such as the establishment of separate ministries or the involvement of existing programs (but see Sabillon et al. 2016; Bossong and Wagner 2017; Weiss and Jankauskas 2019; Solar 2020; Romaniuk and Manjikian 2021). Instead, the aim is to describe the general "protection philosophy" that emerged after the publication of the PCCIP in 1997. The ideas presented in that document resonated with states following a neoliberal democratic model, leading to the adoption of similar concepts regarding critical infrastructure sectors and the need for shared responsibility through public-private partnerships (Shafqat and Masood 2016). Kostyuk (2020: 11) refers to this phenomenon as "strategy adoption as an example of policy diffusion, in which one government's decision to adopt a strategy influences other governments' decisions to adopt similar strategies." However, it was already evident by the turn of the millennium that the "regime type" played a crucial role in shaping the framing and approach to cyber-security (Giles and Hagestad 2013). Western democratic states prioritized the protection of critical infrastructures and, by extension, their society and economy, while states with autocratic tendencies focused on strategies aimed at safeguarding regime security through information control.

The policies implemented at the end of the 1990s in the United States and subsequently adopted by other democratic countries aimed at protection through a threefold approach: law enforcement efforts against cyber-crime, public-private partnerships for safeguarding critical infrastructure, and a combination of private and public initiatives for securing other networked infrastructures (Bendrath 2001; Dunn Cavelty and Suter 2009). A key principle that emerged was the assignment of primary responsibility for network protection to the respective owners: governments protecting government networks, militaries focusing on military networks, companies securing their own infrastructures, and individuals taking charge of their personal computer security. This approach reflects a neoliberal market-oriented logic that seeks to minimize state intervention through regulations (Srinivas et al. 2019), emphasizing the pursuit of mutual benefits.

However, it quickly became evident that certain assets controlled by the private sector were deemed so vital for societal functioning that they required specific attention from the government. This was prompted by the growing number of cyber-incidents, highlighting insufficient investment in cyber-security. Referred to as critical (information) infrastructure protection, the strategy initially focused on preparation through preventive measures, such as information assurance practices (May et al. 2018). The concept of resilience was later introduced as a complement to this strategy. Resilience acknowledges the inevitability of disruptions and refers to a system's ability to recover from shocks, either returning to its original state or adapting to a new state. It offers an additional safety net against large-scale, unforeseen events, regardless of the perpetrator (Perelman 2007; Dunn Cavelty et al. 2015, 2023). While the government positioned itself as a key player in ensuring security, most arrangements with the private sector remained voluntary, leading critics to argue that they lack teeth. The most recent US national cyber-security strategy is the first to depart from this by hinting at more regulation (The White House 2023).

Remarkable about this policy solution is the limited involvement of the state, despite the strong national security implications associated with the threat perceptions (Kruck and Weiss 2023), rendering the protection of critical infrastructures from cyber-attacks neither an unambiguous public nor solely a private challenge. While military sources and strategists played a significant role in shaping the overall threat perceptions and raising awareness about cyber-threats, the reality that most critical infrastructures were privately owned and operated hindered the traditional national security entities, particularly the military, from assuming a broader role in safeguarding the entire nation against cyber-threats. On the domestic front, the military's responsibility was limited to protecting their own networks. Thus, the task of establishing security within the domestic sphere primarily fell on nongovernmental actors. Interestingly, although cyber-security concerns "security," it deviates from conventional defense approaches and aligns more with a risk management framework, which involves weighing security investments against acceptable risks (Kristensen 2008).

The second notable aspect is that this protection philosophy, influenced by neoliberal principles, aims to minimize disruptions in critical assets and services, benefiting both business and public actors. Consequently, it did not attempt to definitively identify the most dangerous cyber-threat. As a result, a range of faceless threats took root. Although discussions in policy-oriented literature touched on different forms of threats, such as cyber-terrorism or cyber-warfare, most assessments were speculative due to a lack of data on adversary capabilities and the likelihood of severe cyber-attacks. This uncertainty led to a tendency to lean toward the notion of "when, not if" regarding cyber-threats. Additionally, the "all-hazard" defensive approach, complemented by the concept of resilience, addressed the pre- and post-attack phases without specific clarity on threat forms. However, this approach presented challenges down the line: How can we determine the required level of security when a risk-free environment is unattainable? In other words, how many cyber-incidents are deemed acceptable? This question remains unanswered and subject to ongoing debate.

What Threat, What Countermeasure? Areas of Tension

Not least because of such uncertainties about the nature and level of the threat, the establishment and consolidation of this three-pronged approach were not without challenges and complexities. As the second aspect of cyber-security politics, it involves ongoing and often contentious negotiation processes, taking place in formal and informal settings, between the state, its bureaucracies, society, and the private sector. These negotiations aim to define roles, responsibilities, legal boundaries, and acceptable rules of behavior.[1] This subchapter will shed light on some of the conflicts that arise among different stakeholders at the domestic level, giving rise to these contentious negotiations.

One area of contention lies within bureaucracies. Within governments, there are struggles to determine leadership, resource allocation, and other factors, given the diverse nature of the threat landscape (Wilson 1989). The second area of conflict revolves around defining the role of the state and its relationship with actors from the private sector and civil society. In both these areas, tensions arise from disagreements about the fundamental concept of "security," as outlined in Baldwin's influential article (1997: 12–17): Whose security is at stake? What values are prioritized in the pursuit of security? How much security is deemed necessary? What are the specific threats that need to be addressed? What means should be employed to achieve security? And what are the costs associated with ensuring security?

The contested nature of these questions becomes particularly evident in the realm of cyber-security, where the term "security" holds distinct meanings for different communities (see Chapter 2 for further insights). At a fundamental level, the objective of securing digital technologies is rooted in risk management practices developed by computer specialists to enhance the security of computer systems and networks. However, cyber-security encompasses more than just information security—it also encompasses the well-being and interests of individuals (Von Solms and Van Niekerk 2013). As highlighted by critical security literature for decades, there is an inherent tension between the abstract notion of "national security" and the concept of "human security" (Deibert 2018).

National security tends to perceive threats as primarily external challenges to a nation's sovereignty, which is largely predicated on the integrity of its geographical territory. However, this perspective fails to address the actual nature and scale of threats faced by the diverse range of individuals residing within a state's borders. From a human security standpoint, the primary focus shifts to the well-being and protection of individuals rather than the interests of the state. Significantly, actions undertaken in the name of national security can directly contradict the needs and security concerns of individuals. A prime example of this incongruity is observed in autocratic states that employ spyware to target and suppress dissidents, illustrating how national security measures can run counter to human security imperatives.

Not least because of such conflicting ideas about what type of security cyber-security should be, the role of the state in cyber-security remains politically contested. The question is not whether there *is* a role for the state, but who should have what kind of role and responsibility in different governance arrangements that aim to enhance national and international security (Dunn Cavelty and Egloff 2019). It is not surprising, therefore, that the state represents a wide array of interests across different policy issues in this domain. As a result, thematic alliances emerge, involving various government departments, interest groups from the economy, and segments of society.

To analyze these dynamics, the three-sector model of society is useful, which distinguishes between the government, private sector, and civil society, also known as the nonprofit sector (Galbraith 1985). These three sectors can be seen to form a triangle, characterized by specific areas of tension or strongly divergent expectations between all the poles. First, tensions arise between the state and the private sector concerning the degree of state involvement in business affairs. Second, tensions surface between the state and civil society, often revolving around the delicate balance between security and civil liberties. Last, tensions manifest between the private sector and civil society, particularly with regard to consumer protection.

In the realm of tension between the state and the economy, a policy approach that addresses the adverse ramifications of liberalization, privatization, and globalization in terms of security, while preserving their positive outcomes is the optimal outcome. The challenge lies in cultivating trust between the government and businesses and determining the necessary state intervention to mitigate risk aggregations and contagion effects that jeopardize society. To tackle these issues, public-private partnerships emerged as multifaceted voluntary arrangements that aim to establish mechanisms for information sharing and address various aspects (Carr 2016). However, their performance is rather mixed, not least because of their voluntary nature (Petersen and Tjalve 2013; Bossong and Wagner 2017; Christensen and Petersen 2017). In recent years, there has been a growing trend toward increased regulation in the field of cyber-security, and this trajectory is expected to persist in the foreseeable future.

A related concern revolves around data access and encryption. The Snowden revelations in 2013 exposed the cooperation between technology companies, telecoms, and the NSA in providing backdoors for user surveillance. While many companies denied knowledge of these practices, the aftermath led to increased transparency efforts, with companies like Yahoo, Apple, and Facebook releasing their first transparency reports, disclosing the frequency of requests for user information by government agencies and law enforcement (Hill 2013). In 2016, Apple took a firm public stance against the FBI's request to create software for decrypting an iPhone 5C recovered from a terrorist shooter. Although the FBI eventually managed to bypass the phone without Apple's assistance, this incident reignited the long-standing debate on encryption, which law enforcement and intelligence agencies perceive as a threat. The infamous Crypto Wars, dating back to the invention of public-key encryption in 1976, witnessed recurrent clashes over government attempts to gain access to encryption through hardware or key escrow (Diffie and Hellman 1976; Schulze 2017). Companies, on the other hand, tend to argue that encryption is needed for trust in electronic transactions (Murphy 2020; Macnish 2021). However, this dispute remains largely unsolvable as proponents on each side emphasize fundamentally different objectives and perceive distinct threats.

In the realm of the state-citizen tension, striking a politically desired balance between security and freedom in the digital domain becomes imperative. The quest for enhanced security often clashes with civil rights, specifically the fundamental right to informational self-determination and online anonymity. Amidst in-depth discussions on cyber-threats, it is crucial to recognize that cyber-security is just one of the numerous intricate, cross-sectoral challenges that the state confronts today. The perceived harm caused by past cyber-incidents may not be significant enough or may not be experienced directly, thereby impeding the acceptance of substantially higher costs and infringements on civil liberties. Instead, the harm associated with other issues, such as terrorism, is leveraged to legitimize limitations in the realm of cyber-security discourse, such as the encryption policy debate. The privacy versus liberty debate unveils a clash of divergent perspectives on security values. National security objectives, entwined with the war on terrorism, prompt intelligence and law enforcement agencies to strive for extensive data collection. However, this conflicts with the notion that privacy is an inherent human right, as detailed, for instance, in the International Covenant on Civil and Political Rights (ICCPR). Alternatively, as many hackers argue, privacy itself serves as a pillar of security, as ensuring privacy guarantees the information security goal of confidentiality.

Within the realm of conflict between citizens and businesses, the establishment of a conducive framework for a thriving security ecosystem becomes crucial. How can the market, grappling with quasi-monopolies, be effectively regulated to strike an optimal balance between functionality and safety? What measures can be implemented to incentivize service providers to undertake greater safety obligations? How can users be educated to prioritize safety over functionality? Moreover, how can (global) legal frameworks be harmonized to mitigate the risks of loopholes and the prevalence of inexpensive but inadequate solutions? Consumers exert limited control over the fate of their data collected by companies through applications and services. Furthermore, the comprehensive compilation of disparate data sources can unveil aspects of our personalities that we may not willingly disclose to these companies. A prominent case highlighting these concerns is the Cambridge Analytica scandal (A.J. Brown 2020) (Box 3.3).

BOX 3.3   CAMBRIDGE ANALYTICA, 2018

The Cambridge Analytica scandal was a significant data privacy controversy that came to light in 2018. Cambridge Analytica, a British political consulting firm, was accused of harvesting the personal data of millions of Facebook users without their consent. The firm allegedly obtained the data through a third-party app called "This Is Your Digital Life," which was developed by a researcher named Aleksandr Kogan.

The app, ostensibly a personality quiz, not only collected data from users who participated but also accessed information about their Facebook friends without explicit permission. This resulted in the unauthorized collection of data from tens of millions of users, which Cambridge Analytica then used to create psychological profiles for targeted political advertising during the 2016 United States presidential election.

The scandal raised serious concerns about data privacy, user consent, and the ethical use of personal information for political purposes. It led to increased scrutiny of tech companies, including Facebook, and sparked discussions about the need for stronger regulations to protect user data and privacy in the digital age.

Summary and Key Points

This chapter has provided an overview of the evolution of cyber-security into a security political issue and a first set of policy reactions by states. Its shape and form at the time were an outcome of the interplay between digital technologies, political processes, and the interpretation of incidents. The basis for this development lies in the increased accessibility of personal home computers and the proliferation of the internet as a commercially operated network. As the number of users and applications grew, the value of the internet expanded in parallel. This expansion facilitated the connection of computer networks to conventional security concerns. The interactions between humans and technologies manifest in the increasing use of the network, the subsequent growth of the network, and the increasing value of the network due to increased usage.

By understanding the dynamics that have shaped the field in the past, we gain valuable insights that can inform our vision of possible futures while mitigating the likelihood of unwanted consequences due to mismatched policy reactions. First, we examined the diverse and often uneven securitization process of the cyber-threat narrative, starting in the 1980s. This narrative consists of four threat frames presented by different interest groups: digital crime, digital espionage, digital warfighting, and digital doom. Second, we explored the concurrent emergence and enduring influence of protective concepts, such as public-private partnerships, public and private self-help, and resilience. These concepts are deeply entwined with threat perceptions. Because different societal actors have divergent interests based on different threat perceptions and value preferences, there are ongoing debates about their roles and responsibilities in addressing the evolving threat. Exploring these dynamic spaces presents exciting avenues for future research and deepens our understanding of cyber-security challenges.

Two elements are noteworthy: First, the addition of the "cyber"-prefix to established threat categories like "terrorism," "war," and "espionage" was used to signal the seriousness of the (new) threat. The interlinkage of computer networks with conventional security concerns involving political adversaries and strategic rivals marked a critical turning point in the topic's securitization. Second, and paradoxically, the notion of a new and pressing threat requiring urgent political attention was built entirely on the interpretation of minor disruptions as harbingers of future doom. In other words, the potential, imagined consequences in the future played a more substantial role than the actual effects. This, as we will explore next, had real, material consequences that changed the threat-landscape fundamentally.

Note

1. Part of this section is drawn from Dunn Cavelty and Egloff (2019).

References

Anderson, R.H. and Hearn, A.C. (1996). *An Exploration of Cyberspace Security R&D Investment Strategies for DARPA: "The Day After . . . in Cyberspace II."* RAND Corporation.

Arquilla, J. and Ronfeldt, D. (eds.) (1997). *In Athena's Camp: Preparing for Conflict in the Information Age.* RAND Corporation.

Baldwin, D.A. (1997). The Concept of Security. *Review of International Studies* 23(1): 5–26.

Bendrath, R. (2001). The Cyberwar Debate: Perception and Politics in US Critical Infrastructure Protection. *Information & Security: An International Journal* 7: 80–103.

Bequai, A. (1986). *Technocrimes: The Computerization of Crime and Terrorism.* Lexington Books.

Bossong, R. and Wagner, B. (2017). A Typology of Cyber-Security and Public-Private Partnerships in the Context of the EU. *Crime, Law and Social Change. An International Journal* 67(3): 265–288.

Brown, A.J. (2020). "Should I Stay or Should I Leave?": Exploring (Dis)continued Facebook Use After the Cambridge Analytica Scandal. *Social Media + Society* 6(1). https://doi.org/10.1177/2056305120913884

Brown, K.A. (2006). *Critical Path: A Brief History of Critical Infrastructure Protection in the United States.* George Mason University Press.

Buzan, B., Wæver, O. and de Wilde, J. (1998). *Security: A New Framework for Analysis.* Lynne Rienner.

Carr, M. (2016). Public-Private Partnerships in National Cyber-Security Strategies. *International Affairs* 92(1): 43–62.

Christensen, K.K. and Petersen, K.L. (2017). Public–Private Partnerships on Cyber Security: A Practice of Loyalty. *International Affairs* 93(6): 1435–1452.

Collier, S.J. and Lakoff, A. (2008). How Infrastructure Became a Security Problem. In: Dunn, M. and Kristensen, K.S. (eds.) *The Politics of Securing the Homeland: Critical Infrastructure, Risk, and Securitisation.* Routledge, pp. 17–39.

Computer Science and Telecommunications Board (1989). *Growing Vulnerability of the Public Switched Network: Implications for National Security Emergency Preparedness*. National Academy Press.

Deibert, R. (2018). Toward a Human-Centric Approach to Cyber-Security. *Ethics & International Affairs* 32(4): 411–424.

Derian, J.D. (2000). Virtuous War/Virtual Theory. *International Affairs* 76(4): 771–788.

Diffie, W. and Hellman, M.E. (1976). New Directions in Cryptography. *IEEE Transactions on Information Theory* 22(6): 644–654.

Dunn Cavelty, M. (2008). *Cyber-Security and Threat Politics: US Efforts to Secure the Information Age*. Routledge.

Dunn Cavelty, M. (2019). The Materiality of Cyberthreats: Securitization Logics in Popular Visual Culture. *Critical Studies on Security* 7(2): 138–151.

Dunn Cavelty, M. and Egloff, F. (2019). The Politics of Cyber-security: Balancing Different Roles of the State. *St Antony's International Review* 5(1): 37–57.

Dunn Cavelty, M., Eriksen, C. and Scharte, B. (2023). Making Cyber Security More Resilient: Adding Social Considerations to Technological Fixes. *Journal of Risk Research* 26(7): 801–814.

Dunn Cavelty, M., Kaufmann, M. and Kristensen, S.K. (2015). Resilience and (In) security: Practices, Subjects, Temporalities. *Security Dialogue* 46(1): 3–14.

Dunn Cavelty, M. and Suter, M. (2009). Public-Private Partnerships Are No Silver Bullet: An Expanded Governance Model for Critical Infrastructure Protection. *International Journal of Critical Infrastructure Protection* 4(2): 179–187.

Dunn, M. (2002). *Information Age Conflicts: A Study on the Information Revolution and a Changing Operating Environment*. Zürcher Beiträge zur Sicherheitspolitik und Konfliktforschung, No. 64. Center for Security Studies.

Dunn, M. and Kristensen, S.K. (eds.) (2008). *The Politics of Securing the Homeland: Critical Infrastructure, Risk, and Securitisation*. Routledge.

Edwards, P.N. (1997). *The Closed World Computers and the Politics of Discourse in Cold War America*. MIT Press.

Federation of American Scientists (1996, June 5). *Security in Cyberspace: U.S. Senate Permanent Subcommittee on Investigations (Minority Staff Statement)*. Appendix B. The Case Study: Rome Laboratory, Griffiss Air Force Base, NY Intrusion. Available at: https://irp.fas.org/congress/1996_hr/s960605b.htm

Galbraith, J.K. (1985). *The New Industrial State*. Princeton University Press.

Giles, K. and Hagestad, W. (2013). Divided by a Common Language: Cyber-Definitions in Chinese, Russian and English. In: Podins, K., Stinissen, J. and Maybaum, M. (eds.) *Proceedings of the 5th International Conference on Cyber-Conflict*. CCD COE Publications, pp. 1–17.

Guerrero-Saade, J.A., Raiu, C., Moore, D. and Rid, T. (2018). *Penquin's Moonlit Maze: The Dawn of Nation-State Digital Espionage*. Available at: https://media. kasperskycontenthub.com/wp-content/uploads/sites/43/2018/03/07180251/ Penquins_Moonlit_Maze_PDF_eng.pdf

Hill, K. (2013). Thanks, Snowden! Now All the Major Tech Companies Reveal How Often They Give Data to Government. *Forbes*, November 14. Available at: www.forbes.com/sites/kashmirhill/2013/11/14/silicon-valley-data-handover-infographic/?sh=7f6a67945365

Huysmans, J. (2000). The European Union and the Securitization of Migration. *Journal of Common Market Studies* 38(5): 751–777.

Huysmans, J. (2006). *The Politics of Insecurity: Fear, Migration and Asylum in the EU*. Routledge.

Kingdon, J.W. (1984). *Agendas, Alternatives, and Public Policies*. Harper Collins College Publishers.

Kostyuk, N. (2020). *Public Cyberinstitutions: Signaling State Cybercapacity*, PhD Thesis University of Michigan. Available at: https://deepblue.lib.umich.edu/bitstream/handle/2027.42/163168/nadiya_1.pdf?sequence=1

Kramer, F.D., Starr, S.H. and Wentz, L. (eds.) (2009). *Cyberpower and National Security*. Center for Technology and National Security Policy, NDU Press.

Kristensen, K.S. (2008). "The Absolute Protection of our Citizens": Critical Infrastructure Protection and the Practice of Security. In: Dunn, M. and Kristensen, K.S. (eds.) *The Politics of Securing the Homeland: Critical Infrastructure, Risk and Securitisation*. Routledge, pp. 63–83.

Kruck, A. and Weiss, M. (2023). The Regulatory Security State in Europe. *Journal of European Public Policy* 30(7): 1205–1229.

Macnish, K. (2021). An End to Encryption? Surveillance and Proportionality in the Crypto-Wars. In: Henschke, A., Reed, A., Robbins, S. and Miller, S. (eds.) *Counter-Terrorism, Ethics and Technology: Advanced Sciences and Technologies for Security Applications*. Springer.

Martelle, M. (ed.) (2018). *Eligible Receiver 97: Seminal DOD Cyber Exercise Included Mock Terror Strikes and Hostage Simulations*. The Cyber Vault Project, Briefing Book #634. Available at: https://nsarchive.gwu.edu/briefing-book/cyber-vault/2018-08-01/eligible-receiver-97-seminal-dod-cyber-exercise-included-mock-terror-strikes-hostage-simulations

May, C., Baker, M., Gabbard, D., Good, T., Grimes, G., Holmgren, M., et al. (2018). *Advanced Information Assurance Handbook*. Report. Carnegie Mellon University. https://doi.org/10.1184/R1/6571844.v1

Middleton, B. (2017). *A History of Cyber Security Attacks: 1980 to Present*. Auerbach Publications.

Molander, R.C., Riddle, A.S. and Wilson, P.A. (1996). *Strategic Information Warfare: A New Face of War*. RAND Corporation.

Mungo, P. and Clough, B. (1992). *Approaching Zero: The Extraordinary Underworld of Hackers, Phreakers, Virus Writers, and Keyboard Criminals*. Random House.

Murphy, C.C. (2020). The Crypto-Wars Myth: The Reality of State Access to Encrypted Communications. *Common Law World Review* 49(3–4): 245–261.

Naughton, J. (2016). The Evolution of the Internet: From Military Experiment to General Purpose Technology. *Journal of Cyber Policy* 1(1): 5–28.

Norman, A.R.D. (1983). *Computer Insecurity*. Chapman and Hall.

Parikka, J. (2005). *Digital Contagions: A Media Archaeology of Computer Viruses*. Peter Lang.

Parker, D.B. (1983). *Fighting Computer Crime*. Charles Scribner's Sons.

Perelman, L.J. (2007). Shifting Security Paradigms: Toward Resilience. In: McCarthy, J.A. (ed.) *Critical Thinking: Moving from Infrastructure Protection to Infrastructure Resilience*. CIP Program Discussion Paper Series. George Mason University, pp. 23–48.

Petersen, K.L. and Tjalve, V.S. (2013). (Neo)Republican Security Governance? US Homeland Security and the Politics of "Shared Responsibility." *International Political Sociology* 7(1): 1–18.

President's Commission on Critical Infrastructure Protection (1997). *Critical Foundations: Protecting America's Infrastructures*. US Government Printing Office.

Rattray, G. (2001). *Strategic Warfare in Cyberspace*. The MIT Press.

Reagan, R. (1984). *National Policy on Telecommunications and Automated Information Systems Security*. National Security Decision Directive NSDD 145, September 17. The White House.

Romaniuk, S.N. and Manjikian, M. (eds.) (2021). *Routledge Companion to Global Cyber-Security Strategy*. Routledge.

Ross, A. (1990). Hacking Away at the Counterculture. *Postmodern Culture* 1(1). https://doi.org/10.1353/pmc.1990.0011

Sabillon, R., Cavaller, V. and Cano, J. (2016). National Cyber-Security Strategies: Global Trends in Cyberspace. *International Journal of Computer Science and Software Engineering* 5(5): 67–81.

Scherlis, W.L., Squires, S.L. and Pethia, R.D. (1990). Computer Emergency Response. In: Denning, P. (ed.) *Computers Under Attack: Intruders, Worms, and Viruses*. Addison-Wesley, pp. 495–504.

Schulze, M. (2017). Clipper Meets Apple vs. FBI—a Comparison of the Cryptography Discourses from 1993 and 2016. *Media and Communication* 5(1): 54–62.

Schwartau, W. (1994). *Information Warfare: Chaos on the Electronic Super Highway*. Thunder's Mouth Press.

Shafqat, N. and Masood, A. (2016). Comparative Analysis of Various National Cyber Security Strategies. *International Journal of Computer Science and Information Security* 14(1): 129–136.

Sieber, U. (1986). *The International Handbook on Computer Crime: Computer-Related Economic Crime and the Infringements of Privacy*. John Wiley and Sons.

Skibell, R. (2002). The Myth of the Computer Hacker. *Information, Communication & Society* 5(3): 336–356.

Soesanto, S. (2019). *The Evolution of US Defense Strategy in Cyberspace (1988–2019)*. CSS Cyber Defense Trend Analysis. Available at: https://css.ethz.ch/content/dam/ethz/special-interest/gess/cis/center-for-securities-studies/pdfs/Cyber-Reports-2019-08-The-Evolution-of-US-defense-strategy-in-cyberspace.pdf

Solar, C. (2020). Cyber-Security and Cyber Defence in the Emerging Democracies. *Journal of Cyber Policy* 5(3): 392–412.

Spafford, E.H. (1989). The Internet Worm: Crisis and Aftermath. *Communications of the ACM* 32(6): 678–687.

Srinivas, J., Kumar Das, A. and Kumar, N. (2019). Government Regulations in Cyber-Security: Framework, Standards and Recommendations. *Future Generation Computer Systems* 92: 178–188.

Stoll, C. (1989). *The Cuckoo's Egg: Tracking a Spy through the Maze of Computer Espionage*. Doubleday.

The White House (2023). National Cybersecurity Strategy. *The White House*. Available at: www.whitehouse.gov/wp-content/uploads/2023/03/National-Cybersecurity-Strategy-2023.pdf

Virilio, P. and Lotringer, S. (1998). *Pure War*. Semiotext.

Von Solms, R. and Van Niekerk, J. (2013). From Information Security to Cyber Security. *Computers & Security* 38: 97–102.

Warner, M. (2012). Cyber-security: A Pre-history. *Intelligence and National Security* 27(5): 781–799.

Weiss, M. and Jankauskas, V. (2019). Securing Cyberspace: How States Design Governance Arrangements. *Governance* 32(2): 259–275.

Wilson, J.Q. (1989). *Bureaucracy: What Government Agencies Do and Why They Do It.* Basic Books.

4

A PROBLEM MATURES WHEN STATES BECOME ACTIVE

During the latter half of the 2000s, a fundamental transformation occurred in the landscape of cyber-security politics, ultimately giving rise to a "new" reality. This transformation unfolded through an interactive process involving the aspirations of states, the development of infrastructures, the evolution of capabilities, and the adoption of practices. Before, cyber-security primarily revolved around concerns related to criminal activities, resulting in minor inconveniences and occasional disruptions such as service outages, data breaches, increased security expenses, and financial losses. While the overall number of cyber-incidents increased during this period, state-sponsored cyber-incidents remained exceedingly rare (the distributed denial of service (DDoS)-attacks in Estonia in 2007, with suspected Russian state involvement (Box 5.2), and disruptive operations at the beginning of the Russian military campaign against Georgia in 2008 (Box 5.5) are notable exceptions). However, widespread anxieties regarding potential catastrophic scenarios loomed large in the collective consciousness. These concerns centered on the possibility of large-scale cyber-attacks with far-reaching consequences.

In hindsight, the significance of such "multi-dimensional cyber-disaster scenarios" (Hansen and Nissenbaum 2009: 1164) can be acknowledged to be even greater than previously recognized, particularly due to their material effects. The perception that adversaries would exploit cyberspace for political and strategic advantages led countries like the United States, Russia, and China to systematically invest in cyber-capabilities[1] for conducting operations against their political rivals and adversaries. While doctrinal advancements had already commenced earlier, it was during the 2000s that

DOI: 10.4324/9781003497080-4

the future-oriented concept of "cyber-war" turned into a somewhat self-fulfilling prophecy. Unlike conventional and nuclear weapons, where arms race dynamics are often driven by intelligence-based evidence of adversaries' capabilities, the development of cyber-capabilities was primarily motivated by the belief that others were acquiring such capabilities. From the 2010s onward, a notable portion of cyber-attacks became more sophisticated, targeted, and clearly linked to political and strategic objectives, prompting other states to enhance their own capabilities (Smeets 2022a).

This change highlights four crucial points. First, it illustrates how states, despite contrary beliefs in their powerlessness vis-à-vis cyberspace (Barlow 1996), influence the technological landscape by making strategic investments. Second, shaping any environment requires significant resources across different areas, which means that mainly big actors are in advantageous positions. Third, cyber-security became intricately entwined with broader strategic and political contexts and a major component of what is now called "strategic competition" between the great powers. This strategic competition encompassed not only traditional military dimensions but also economic, technological, and information domains, all of which intersect within the cyber-security landscape (Winkler 2023). Fourth, with the emergence of state-backed targeted hacking operations, a specialized industry emerged to address these high-level threats, commonly known as "advanced persistent threats" (APTs). The ability to attribute attacks to specific political actors thanks to these special capabilities fundamentally changed cyber-security politics, allowing for the application of traditional state-on-state security logics.

After 2010, the buildup of capabilities by state actors was revealed through prominent cyber-incidents. Three of them serve as examples for this change and its consequences, each discussed below in one subchapter: Stuxnet (2010), the Snowden revelations (2013), and the hack-and-leak operation during the American elections (2015/16). These examples—selected here for their impact and ability to change the debate—reveal how the actions of powerful states changed the actual threat by heightening the potential for graver attacks, and how these incidents revealed specific aspects of state actions that had a tremendous influence on what and how we study cyber-security today. Through these incidents, which are moments of disruption of what is the "normal" performance of computers and networks, we get glimpses into a world that is normally hidden from our view due to the levels of secrecy involved in cyber-operations (Best and Walters 2013; Balzacq and Dunn Cavelty 2016). In addition, the chapter discusses the role authoritarian regimes and their surveillance and control apparatus play in a fourth subchapter, which has a direct link to many of their activities internationally.

Stuxnet: The Technical Blockbuster

Stuxnet is the name given to a computer worm that was discovered in June 2010 and is without a doubt still "one of the great technical blockbusters in malware history" (Gross 2011). Here is what happened: After Stuxnet was discovered on Windows machines due to mysterious reboots and blue screens of death in the summer of 2010, it became clear very quickly that this multipart worm was out of the ordinary. It looked and behaved differently from the typical criminal malware known to date: it did not steal information; it did not herd infected computers into so-called botnets to launch criminal attacks; and it seemed to be far more targeted, not designed to spread indiscriminately. Reverse engineering was able to show that it was written to specifically attack Siemens Supervisory Control and Data Acquisition (SCADA) systems that are used to control and monitor industrial processes. The analysis further revealed that beyond four zero-day exploits—a cyber-attack vector or technique that takes advantage of an unknown or unaddressed security flaw in computer software, hardware or firmware—there were other advanced features, including a Windows rootkit, a distributed command and control network, the ability to peer-to-peer update, legitimate signed digital certificates, and various antivirus evasion techniques (Falliere et al. 2011). In short, Stuxnet was a complex piece of software in malware terms, and it was clear that whoever had written it had acquired insider knowledge about industrial processes. Based on reverse engineering, Symantec estimated at the time that it may have taken a team of eight to ten people six months to complete (Farwell and Rohozinski 2011; Stevens 2020).

Following its discovery, a detective-like investigation unfolded within the technical community as various individuals and companies worked to piece together information, leading to an unofficial attribution. In August 2010, Symantec reported that nearly 60% of the infected computers worldwide were in Iran. It was also revealed that Stuxnet was likely to have caused damage to several centrifuges in Iran's nuclear program, marking one of the first instances where malware had bridged the cyber-physical gap. Given the malware's behavior and manifestation, and the systems that were targeted, the involvement of one or multiple state actors, primarily the United States and Israel, seemed likely (Langner 2013).

In June 2012, two years after its discovery, a *New York Times* article suggested that the development of Stuxnet was part of a joint intelligence operation between the United States and Israel called "Operation Olympic Games." According to the article by Sanger (2012a), it was asserted that Stuxnet had been deliberately programmed and released to sabotage the Iranian nuclear program. The objective behind this operation was to cripple or, at the very least, impede Iran's progress in nuclear develop-ment. Some sources suggest that the intention was to prevent Israel from resorting to another potentially risky and escalatory air strike. Despite the absence of official admissions from either state, it is widely accepted today that Stuxnet was indeed a collaborative effort between the United States and Israel (Sanger 2012b).

The significance of Stuxnet lies not only in its technical complexity but also in its strategic implications. Stuxnet remains one of the few documented instances of a cyber-operation led by Western powers targeting an adver-sary's industrial control systems to cause an effect, giving it a special status (Smeets 2022b). For many observers at the time, Stuxnet was believed to mark the beginning of the unchecked use of cyber-weapons now that the "digital first strike" had occurred (Gross 2011). The rampant speculations about the future of cyber-aggression were once again guided by an alarm-ist atmosphere, starting with the (wrong) assumption that now all restraint was gone (Lindsay 2013). To the contrary, however, Stuxnet should serve as a profound lesson in the formidable challenges associated with executing a precise and targeted cyber-attack while maintaining sufficient control over its impact, as well as the extensive planning and execution timeframes involved.

The preparations for Stuxnet's deployment trace back to the George W. Bush presidency in 2006, emphasizing the long-term nature of this under-taking. A noteworthy component of the overall cost estimate—Smeets mentions US\$50–US\$100 million or more (Smeets 2022a: 46; cf. Slayton 2017)[2]—encompasses substantial investments in meticulously testing the malware to attain the requisite precision, ensuring that it exclusively deliv-ers the intended effect on the designated system while avoiding unintended consequences. Additionally, the imperative of sustaining covert operations after breaching the adversary's network emerges as paramount for mission success, recognizing that the initial point of infection seldom represents the attacker's ultimate objective.

In addition to shedding light on the essential requirements for conduct-ing sophisticated, targeted cyber-attacks with manageable consequences, Stuxnet provides valuable insights into the challenging realm of attribu-tion. Three key aspects merit attention: First, the attribution of Stuxnet was not primarily accomplished by specialized threat intelligence companies or state agencies. Instead, it was pieced together independently by infor-mation security professionals and investigative journalists such as Brian Krebs, Ralph Langner, David E. Sanger, Kim Zetter, and antivirus compa-nies like Kaspersky and Symantec, along with their teams of researchers. This highlights that attribution involves a combination of comprehensive technical knowledge of artifacts and modus operandi, as well as the inclu-sion of nontechnical evidence, often circumstantial in nature.

Second, despite the absence of explicit clarifications from the accused states at the time, the attribution process conducted by different experts, based on available evidence, proved remarkably accurate. Several of the identified points were later confirmed by insider sources. That way, Stuxnet underscores that a broader strategic context surrounding a cyber-operation, coupled with the "qui bono" logic ("to whose benefit"), can yield crucial evidence for attribution. Third, unless a perpetrator publicly and credibly assumes responsibility for an attack, providing comprehensive details about decision-making processes, targeting strategies, and more, uncertainties about specific aspects are likely to persist unless persistent investigation occurs. In the case of Stuxnet, new information emerged as late as 2019 when Zetter and Modderkolk (2019) published a story revealing the involvement of an inside mole allegedly recruited by Dutch intelligence. This individual, an engineer, reportedly introduced the malware to the nuclear facility using a USB stick. A more recent report suggests that the Dutch government, including the intelligence services, did not know that this operation involved malware (NL Times 2024).

Stuxnet also highlights an additional point that often goes unacknowledged in discussions surrounding cyber-operations. While Stuxnet itself was groundbreaking and rightfully garnered significant attention, assessing its ultimate success, which includes an honest appreciation of its overall impact, proves much more challenging (see also Chapter 8). Although we have evidence of the effects of Stuxnet on the Iranian nuclear program, determining the extent of the delay and its overall significance remains uncertain. Estimates vary, with some suggesting a few months of setback while others propose a delay of up to two years (Katz 2010). However, these estimations lack data to support their claims. More reliable information indicates that Iran's enrichment capacity may even have increased following the attack, potentially as a response to the sabotage (Vaez and Ferguson 2011).

Another effect of Stuxnet is believed to have been the prevention of an Israeli air strike, which was considered too escalatory. By disrupting Iran's nuclear infrastructure, the release of Stuxnet potentially mitigated the need for a direct military intervention (Sanger 2012b: 190–191). However, it is important to note that the operation failed to fundamentally altering Iran's position or intentions concerning its atomic program, pointing to the limited coercive value of cyber-operations. Despite the disruptive nature of Stuxnet, Iran remained committed to its nuclear ambitions. A series of car bomb attacks targeted Iranian nuclear scientists later in 2010. Though it is unclear who was behind the assassinations, Kim Zetter (2010) plausibly speculates that "the assassinations . . . could indicate that whoever targeted Iran felt the malware was insufficient to halt Iran's nuclear program."

What are other adverse or unintended effects of Stuxnet that can be identified? One notable consequence is the acceleration of investment into Iran's offensive cyber-capabilities, with the emergence of Iranian APT actors around 2013 (Baezner 2019), turning Iran from an actor mainly concerned with domestic surveillance and control into a cyber-rival that the United States takes seriously (Lewis 2019). While it seems likely that Iran would have invested into such cyber-capabilities eventually, even without experiencing the impact of Stuxnet, the malware had a profound and alarming effect on several political adversaries of the United States and accelerated their capability build-up.

The ripple effects of Stuxnet were also felt among US allies, albeit with mixed consequences. First, numerous governments began releasing or updating their cyber-security strategies and establishing new cyber-defense units, some of which had a partially military focus. While these measures were likely intended primarily for defensive purposes, they contributed to what observers have described as an "arms race dynamic" (Beckerman 2022). Second, and on a more positive note, the discovery of the worm prompted increasingly serious attempts to reach agreements among states regarding the nonaggressive use of cyberspace (see Chapter 6). These efforts reflect a growing recognition of the need for international cooperation in addressing cyber-threats (Dunn Cavelty 2015).

Indeed, Stuxnet had a highly impactful secondary impact by triggering significant political reactions globally, which had long-term and lasting consequences. One of the most significant outcomes was the foregrounding of state actors in the cyber-security narrative. Stuxnet validated the long-standing expectation that states would leverage cyberspace for political and strategic purposes, even incorporating destructive effects, as depicted in the cyber-doom scenarios. However, it is important to note that Stuxnet also challenged and corrected several assumptions that had shaped early threat perceptions. Upon closer examination, the malware revealed discrepancies with the anticipated doom-scenarios, thereby highlighting the need for a nuanced understanding of cyber-threats.

In sum, Stuxnet marked a significant turning point in the realm of cyber-threats. However, perceiving Stuxnet as a singular rupture fails to capture the complete picture. It is important to recognize that the development and impact of Stuxnet spanned several years, from its initial infection around 2007 to the eventual realization of its intended effect. Furthermore, to understand the underlying dynamics, we must situate cyber-security politics within a broader geopolitical context. Rather than viewing cyberspace as a domain with its own isolated logic, the shaping of cyberspace as a strategic domain happened as an extension of real-world dynamics, resulting from the convergence of technological, social, and political developments over the past decade (Deibert 2022). The next major incident, the Snowden Leaks, made that very clear.

The Snowden Leaks and the Role of Intelligence

The Snowden revelations represent the second major "incident" that played a pivotal role in shaping our understanding of cyber-security today. In June 2013, *The Guardian*, a British newspaper, broke the story by reporting the first leak of highly classified documents from the NSA. Subsequently, additional articles were published in the following years, shedding light on the extent of the disclosures.[3] Edward Snowden, a 29-year-old intelligence contractor working for Booz Allen Hamilton at the time, was responsible for pilfering an estimated 1.5 million files,[4] a fraction of which were later made public and analyzed by journalists. Snowden claimed that he released the documents exposing widespread global surveillance programs conducted by the NSA and its Five Eyes alliance partners with the intention of initiating a significant dialogue about the necessary limits on government surveillance authority (Greenwald et al. 2013)

The repercussions of the Snowden revelations extended beyond their intended purpose, fundamentally reshaping our understanding of state practices in cyberspace in at least two crucial ways. First, it exposed the extensive capabilities of American and British intelligence agencies in collecting massive amounts of data from internet traffic through various programs and tactical tools, including TEMPORA, TURMOIL, and TURBINE. These disclosures also revealed their long-term plans to undermine existing encryption standards (Larson 2013). This sparked a global political outrage and debate about mass surveillance and the end of privacy in the digital age, though without changing the larger public's behavior. It did also reveal how closely some of the American tech companies were collaborating with the NSA under the PRISM program, "the number one source of raw intelligence used for NSA analytic reports" (Washington Post 2013) and emphasized how political the relationship between public and private actors was. Snowden specifically named Microsoft, Yahoo!, Google, Facebook, Paltalk, YouTube, Skype, and Apple as willing participants to enable the NSA to gather browsing data as an "upstream collection" strategy (Snowden 2019: 347).

To comprehend the power the intelligence agencies had accumulated in secret, it is crucial to first understand the existential crisis they faced after the end of the Cold War and the opportunities afforded by the digital infrastructure to change that. The intelligence community, particularly in the United States, experienced a significant blow to their credibility following the failure to connect the dots and prevent the 9/11 terrorist attacks, considered one of the worst intelligence failures in American history. This event expedited the transformation of intelligence practices from the analog world to the more open, interconnected, and intrusive digital realm (Steed 2022).

The internet, with its early protocols that prioritized functionality over security and privacy, created a perfect environment for data collectors to thrive (DeNardis 2014: 73). This was further amplified by the emergence of "surveillance capitalism," a term coined by Shoshana Zuboff (2015, 2019), which refers to the collection of vast volumes of personal data by tech giants like Google and Facebook for targeted advertisements based on predictive algorithms (van Aalst 2022). The combination of lax security protocols and the rise of surveillance capitalism turned the digital landscape into an intelligence Eldorado. Substantial investments by powerful intelligence agencies like the NSA and the British equivalent, the Government Communications Headquarters (GCHQ), allowed them to leverage the inseparable connection between computers and espionage to their advantage (Kaplan 2017; Buchanan 2020). These investments provided them with an edge in conducting cyber-operations.

Second, in addition to revealing passive surveillance and analytical capabilities, the Snowden files shed light on active exploitation and manipulation of cyberspace. The documents unveiled that the Five Eyes, an international alliance of intelligence agencies, systematically compromised private networks, technologies, and standards, intentionally keeping them insecure to exploit (Zajko 2018: 39). Intelligence agencies also engage in the acquisition of zero-day exploits, as exposed after the Snowden Leaks (Osborne 2013), although some have since established their own bug hunting teams to reduce dependence on external market players. When government agencies "stockpile" such exploits, they choose to withhold knowledge of critical cyber-security vulnerabilities to exploit them instead of making them public for patching. Furthermore, the NSA and GCHQ discussed deceptive tactics, propaganda use, mass messaging, and the dissemination of stories on social media platforms (Greenwald 2014). An 18-page presidential memo revealed that Obama ordered intelligence officials to compile a list of targets for cyber-attacks (The Guardian 2013). According to the leaked information, the United States conducted 231 offensive cyber-attacks in 2011 (Gellmann and Nakashima 2013).

Active exploitation is one of the four functions of US intelligence. Apart from collection, analysis, and counterintelligence, the intelligence community is also involved in covert action, the responsibility of which traditionally lies with the Central Intelligence Agency (CIA). Covert action, as an official definition states, is "used to *influence* political, military, or economic conditions or situations abroad, where it is intended that the role of the U.S. Government will not be apparent or acknowledged publicly" (Brown and Rudman 1996: 17). Offensive cyberspace operations—in turn, defined as operations "intended to project power by the application of force in and through cyberspace" (Joint Chiefs of Staff 2013)—can be classified as covert action under certain conditions (DeVine 2022: 6). In the context of a shift away from global terrorism as the key focus of American strategy toward "strategic competition" with a handful of political adversaries "waged with adversaries below the threshold of armed conflict" (West 2021: 274), clandestine activity even became a principal means of action, moving cyberspace operations from the fringes to the center of strategic options.

Unlike the clear-cut destructive nature of military cyber-attacks depicted in doomsday scenarios, intelligence activities encompass a more nuanced and ambiguous realm. This ambiguity arises from the fact that the line between offensive and defensive actions is blurry and challenging to discern in theoretical terms. As highlighted in Ben Buchanan's book, the act of infiltrating the networks of other nations holds significant defensive advantages as well (Buchanan 2017). Simultaneously, intelligence operations are subject to various constraints dictated by the imperative of maintaining operational secrecy, which incurs substantial costs. Operating in a contested environment, intelligence actors face increased risks that can compromise their ability to maintain secrecy in two significant ways: intrusion detection and method leaks (Steed 2022: 209). If an infiltrating actor is discovered within a network and the network owner possesses robust forensic capabilities, it becomes highly likely that a threat actor's capabilities, which may include their command-and-control infrastructure, will be exposed (for more on this, see Chapter 8). Consequently, the spy must invest in developing new tools for subsequent attacks. Notably, there have been prominent leaks of intelligence tools, such as the Vault7 revelations concerning CIA capabilities and the Shadow Brokers leaks (Box 4.1).

BOX 4.1 SHADOW BROKERS AND VAULT7 LEAKS, 2016–2017

Between 2016 and 2017, a hacker group known as "Shadow Brokers" publicly disclosed a vast collection of hacking tools and exploits originating from the "Equation Group," an entity likely associated with the NSA. Among these capabilities was an exploit named "EternalBlue," which targeted a vulnerability in unpatched Windows systems. Exploiting this vulnerability, two major global cyber-attacks, WannaCry and NotPetya, took place in 2017.

The Vault7 leaks exposed a range of cyber-tools and hacking capabilities allegedly used by the CIA of the United States in March 2017 via WikiLeaks. It compromised 91 malware tools out of the more than 500 tools believed to be in use in 2016 (United States of America v. Joshua Adam Schulte 2020). These tools targeted a wide range of devices and platforms, including smartphones, computers, routers, and smart TVs. The leaks raised significant privacy and surveillance concerns. They revealed that intelligence agencies had the capability to compromise and exploit consumer devices, potentially undermining individuals' privacy, and security. The leaks fueled debates about the balance between national security and individual privacy.

Before the Snowden leaks, the role of the intelligence community in shaping the cyber-threat landscape was overlooked by researchers. This can be attributed to the secretive nature of intelligence operations and the predominant attention given to the *military* dimension of cyber-operations. In many ways, it was the only information that was publicly available. For example, the Pentagon officially recognized cyberspace as the "fifth" domain of warfare, alongside land, sea, air, and space in 2011 after establishing the US Cyber Command (CYBERCOM) in 2010 (Lynn 2010). However, while the military openly published its doctrinal papers and military institutions contemplated the implications of information warfare, it was the signals intelligence community that exerted significant influence over the practical use of the network through daily operations spanning many years. This had profound consequences for various aspects of the cyber-domain, including practices, threat landscapes, norms, and more.

Upon reflection, the prominence of intelligence activities in the field of cyber-security is no major surprise. First, practical and active operations carry greater weight in building capabilities and training skilled personnel compared to purely theoretical approaches. This is particularly true considering the limited and specific use cases for military cyber-operations. Developing capabilities that can be employed daily proves to be more effective in practice (Smeets 2022a). Second, the United States had a vested interest in upholding the norms it actively promoted in cyberspace. These norms included refraining from engaging in destructive cyber-operations targeting critical infrastructures and affirming the applicability of existing international law to cyberspace, opposing Russia's differing perspective (see Chapter 6). In addition, cyber-operations align well with the intricacies of strategic competition, existing within the gray area between war and peace (Kello 2017). This is the zone we turn to next.

Inside the Gray Zone: Of Systems and Semantics

In that "gray zone," there is a third significant event that profoundly shaped our understanding of cyber-threats. It unfolded in 2015 when multiple US institutions, including the US Democratic National Committee (DNC), fell victim to network intrusions (see Box 4.2). The responsible parties were Russian hacker groups known as "APT28" and "APT29," also referred to as Fancy Bear and Cozy Bear by others. These groups employed spear-phishing emails to deliver Remote Administration Tools (RAT) malware, enabling them to gain unauthorized access to sensitive data. The stolen information was released during the US presidential elections, meeting an already highly polarized society. In October 2016, the US government officially accused the Russian government of orchestrating these network intrusions. In 2018, a grand jury in the District of Columbia indicted 12 Russian nationals for hacking offenses related to the 2016 US presidential election. All 12 defendants are members of the GRU, a Russian Federation intelligence agency within the Main Intelligence Directorate of the Russian military.

This so-called hack-and-leak operation, which connotes the combination of data theft with data dumping to exert an influence (Shires 2019), brought to light the significant threat posed by strategic manipulation, commonly referred to as influence operations, to democratic processes (Whyte 2020). It is possible that this interference benefited the Republican candidate, Donald Trump, in his victory over Hillary Clinton, even though it is scientifically impossible to provide evidence for or against this. The incident and its discussion in the media may also have contributed to a loss of trust in the legitimacy and integrity of the democratic process, although establishing precise causal pathways remains challenging (Jamieson 2018; Jensen et al. 2019).

It is important to recognize that the incident mentioned earlier should not be viewed in isolation, but rather as a convergence of various underlying trends. These trends include the increasing capabilities and activities of intelligence agencies in conducting cyber-operations below the threshold of war, the deteriorating relations between major global powers, and the adaptation of traditional information manipulation tactics to the new landscape of social media. The manipulation of public opinion by political actors is not a novel concept. As early as the 1990s, the US military began developing doctrines for information warfare in the information age, which encompassed strategies for influencing the content within the information environment to establish "information dominance" (Arquilla and Ronfeldt 1997). However, their focus remained primarily on measures focused on a theater of crisis or war, in contrast to the covert operations conducted by agencies like the CIA. Moreover, in Western countries, influencing one's own population is legally prohibited, as exemplified by the controversies surrounding Rumsfeld's Office for Strategic Influence (Brunner and Dunn Cavelty 2009).

In autocratic states, this is not the case. Autocratic regimes employ crucial activities such as banning opposition activists from mobilizing online, restricting the dissemination of critical information about the regime, and conducting surveillance to identify potential dissenters. These measures are employed to maintain their hold on power (Keremoğlu and Weidmann 2020). The rise of the internet, starting with its expansion in the United States and subsequently worldwide, was considered a significant threat to nondemocratic regimes. This threat became more pronounced when the United States, under Secretary of State Hillary Clinton, officially declared the promotion and facilitation of internet freedom as a human right in its foreign policy after 2010 (Hanson 2012). The Arab uprisings that began in late 2010 played a crucial role in shaping threat perception and reactions in autocratic states. As a result, authoritarian regimes became more aware that while digital technologies posed a threat to their control, they could also be utilized for the purpose of monitoring and controlling their population (Giles 2016). This heightened awareness prompted autocratic governments to further explore the use of digital technologies as a means of both oppression and surveillance. These uprisings also shed light on the involvement of Western companies in providing surveillance equipment to authoritarian governments (Timm and York 2012).

During the time of the Arab uprisings, Russia had already been refining its targeted manipulation of internet-based content for several years. Their propaganda approach drew on techniques employed during the Soviet Cold War era, focusing on obfuscation and influencing targets to act in the propagandist's interests. This approach was adapted to suit the new media environment (Paul and Matthews 2016). The concept of Russian "web brigades" was mentioned as early as 2003, but it gained attention in the West following the 2014 annexation of the Crimean Peninsula, which witnessed an increase in Russian troll activity in the comment sections of online newspapers (Gunitsky 2015). It took Western observers some time to connect the dots, but what was spreading across their information spaces was an extension of the "Gerasimov Doctrine" of nonlinear or hybrid warfare. This doctrine outlines Russia's strategy to achieve strategic advantage without provoking an armed response from NATO by operating below the threshold of armed conflict.

General Valery Gerasimov, Chief of the General Staff of the Russian Federation, was not the sole architect of this line of action, but it was he who famously published an article in the *Military-Industrial Kurier* in February 2013. In it, he invokes the lessons of the "Arab Spring" and states that "[t]he role of nonmilitary means of achieving political and strategic goals has grown, and, in many cases, they have exceeded the power of force of weapons in their effectiveness." Furthermore, "[a]ll this is supplemented by military means of a concealed character, including carrying out actions of informational conflict and the actions of special-operations forces" (translation and commentary by Galeotti 2014). Clearly, "hack-and-leak" operations are in line with this idea.

BOX 4.2 DNC HACK, 2016

This cyber-intrusion occurred in 2016, targeting the computer systems of the DNC, the primary organization of the Democratic Party in the United States. The hack gained significant attention due to its potential impact on the US presidential election. A forensic analysis concluded that the intrusion was carried out by two Russian state-sponsored hacking groups, Fancy Bear (associated with the Russian military intelligence agency, GRU) and Cozy Bear (associated with the Russian Federal Security Service, FSB). The hackers gained access to sensitive information, including emails, documents, and other internal communications of the DNC.

In July 2016, WikiLeaks began releasing thousands of emails from the DNC, which contained discussions, strategies, and internal party dynamics. The leaked emails caused significant controversy during the presidential campaign, particularly those revealing internal discussions within the DNC that led to the resignation of some party officials. US intelligence agencies, including the CIA, FBI, and NSA, concluded with high confidence that the Russian government directed the hacking operation and sought to influence the U.S. presidential election in favor of then candidate Donald Trump. These allegations have been the subject of ongoing investigations and public discourse.

The DNC hack represented a significant escalation, marking the first direct provocation and, in some respects, humiliation of the United States by Russia. It exposed the involvement of Russian foreign intelligence in a major cyber-operation, though raising questions about Russian President Vladimir Putin's exact objectives. However, it is highly probable that the DNC hack and similar attacks on other targets aimed to sow doubt and confusion, with the intention of eroding trust and confidence in the governments of targeted nations, in line with the strategy of subversion employed during the Cold War (Carson 2018). These cyber-attacks, employed as part of broader influence operations, align with a strategic approach, particularly when coupled with the use of social media by government officials within targeted countries to undermine trust in political processes and the media.

However, the perceived success of Russia's actions may have been short-lived, considering the responses from the United States and its allies. These responses included imposing sanctions, conducting covert counterstrikes, issuing indictments, and bolstering their systems and capabilities. Russia may have miscalculated the attribution capabilities of the United States or underestimated their willingness to publicly attribute cyber-attacks, despite the precedent set by the public attribution of the Sony Hack to North Korea in 2014 (St. James and Lee 2015) (see Box 4.3), which could have signaled a policy shift. In the long run, the costs of these actions may prove to be significantly higher than initially anticipated by Russia.

BOX 4.3   SONY PICTURE HACK, 2014

The Sony Hack of 2014 was a significant "hack-and-leak" cyber-attack targeting the entertainment company Sony Pictures Entertainment. The attack resulted in the theft of a vast amount of sensitive data, including employee information, confidential emails, unreleased films, and other intellectual property. The perpetrators, widely believed to be affiliated with North Korea, breached Sony's network, and distributed the stolen data online. The attack was allegedly motivated by Sony's production of the film "The Interview," a comedy centered around a fictional plot to assassinate North Korean leader Kim Jong-un. The incident caused damage to Sony, in terms of both financial losses and reputational harm. It also raised concerns about cyber-security vulnerabilities and the potential impact of state-sponsored cyber-attacks on private companies. The attribution to North Korea as the perpetrator also started a new chapter in the debate around "attribution" and the capabilities and willingness of the United States to attribute to political adversaries.

Russia's use of the internet and the media environment for broad destabilizing operations in the West became an evident dimension in hindsight, as already exemplified by the Estonia cyber-incident in 2007 (see Box 5.2). First, the tools employed in such contexts are widely accessible at relatively low costs. Patriotic hackers or opaque criminal groups associated with domestic or foreign elites opportunistically utilize these technologies for disruption and mild sabotage rather than outright destruction. Second, cyber-influence operations are increasingly leveraged to manipulate the information environment of conflicts, providing an asymmetric advantage (though with somewhat unclear gains). Third, the legal ambiguity surrounding intelligence operations enables state actors to evade formal condemnation and maintain plausible deniability. The opacity of actors and operations makes it unlikely that an attribution verdict would be sufficiently transparent and credible to warrant a military response (Wenger and Dunn Cavelty 2022).

The increase in murky influence operations has led some observers to claim that what we are seeing in cyberspace is in fact an intelligence contest (Chesney and Smeets 2020, 2023). Joshua Rovner defines an intelligence contest via five elements (Rovner 2023): First, as an effort to collect more and better information relevant to a long-term political competition; second to exploit that information for practical gain; third, a reciprocal effort to undermine adversary morale, institutions, and alliances; fourth, an effort to disable adversary intelligence capabilities through sabotage; and fifth, it is a campaign to preposition assets for future collection in the event of a conflict. Even if we are not willing to see all cyberspace activity as part of this logic (like Warner 2023; Fischerkeller and Harknett 2023) the mass of activity that matches these five elements is a clear indication of considerable role that intelligence activities and practices play in the field of cyber-conflict. Their strong position would also explain the rise of covert activities (or subversion, see Maschmeyer 2023), a task historically given to the intelligence community (Lindsay 2023: 62).

This overall development has introduced a complex new aspect to the cyber-security discourse, raising concerns about content and content control that democracies find uncomfortable. In democratic systems, it is problematic for "the state" to consider defining what constitutes "the truth" (Vivian 2018). The pursuit of visions of digital control, which involve monitoring and censorship of online content, can inadvertently play into the hands of autocratic forces by undermining the principles of openness and individual rights that are fundamental to democracy. Furthermore, the development underscored the significant role played by private companies, particularly social media platform owners, in shaping the environment that facilitates certain cyber-threats. The manipulation of algorithms, such as those employed by Twitter, is crucial for the effectiveness of these strategies. With the emergence of the "new right" as a political force in many countries, the clear distinction between external influence and internal disintegration becomes blurred. The interconnected nature of cyberspace highlights its integration into various aspects of society, raising questions about the boundaries and scope of the concept of "cyber." It is increasingly obvious that cyber-security cannot be viewed in isolation, but rather as part of a broader landscape that encompasses political, social, economic, and cultural dimensions.

Authoritarian Muscle Flexing

In the context of the changing threat landscape, it is crucial to acknowledge the increasing surveillance power wielded by autocratic governments, both within their own populations and internationally. This happens as both a cause and a consequence of the erosion of the post-Cold War international order due to the global reinforcement of authoritarian visions of governance. As China's influence in economics and military affairs has grown and Russia has sought to resist its post-imperial decline, cyberspace has played a pivotal role in highlighting the fundamental and irreconcilable differences that have emerged. Autocratic regimes have made significant investments to control the content produced and consumed by their populations (Deibert et al. 2008, 2010, 2011; Deibert 2013, 2020). Rather than suppressing digital cultures, some regimes have realized over time that a connected population can be effectively monitored, leading to the problematic use of spyware (Stafford and Urbaczewski 2004) and other surveillance tools.

This issue extends beyond the absence of laws governing such surveillance practices. Autocratic states engage in espionage against dissidents residing in other countries, as evidenced by cases like GhostNet (Deibert and Rohozinski 2009) and the utilization of Pegasus spyware (Marczak et al. 2018). One notable instance that drew significant attention to the use of spyware for the surveillance of anti-regime activists was the murder of Saudi dissident Jamal Khashoggi in 2018. The Saudi government employed the NSO Group's Pegasus spyware to spy on Khashoggi. This highlights the nontrivial connection between private companies and the provision of surveillance services, even evading regulatory measures in democratic states. Many Western states are also willing to curtail human rights directly or tolerate practices that undermine them under the guise of public safety and national security (Kaye 2021; Deibert 2023).

The convergence of surveillance capabilities, state-sponsored espionage, and the erosion of human rights gives rise to a distinct cyber-threat that arises for individuals from states (Deibert 2022). This threat has often been overlooked or perhaps ignored in the cyber-security literature in international relations, exposing a bias on (abstract) "national security" consequences. However, the exportation of these practices beyond autocratic state borders, the widespread use of digital tools for surveillance, and the severe implications on individual lives extend beyond mere privacy infringements and pose significant consequences for some individuals. In fact, the impact of this threat on human lives is among the most significant and far-reaching in the realm of cyber-security.

Taking a harm-oriented view brings another topic into the limelight that is equally ignored by cyber-security scholars: Internet shutdowns. An internet shutdown occurs when a government or other authorities intentionally disrupt or restrict access to the internet, either partially or entirely, within a specific geographic area or across an entire country. These shutdowns have become an increasingly common tactic employed by governments during periods of political unrest, protests, elections, or to suppress dissenting voices (Gohdes 2015, 2023; De Gregorio and Stremlau 2020; Keremoğlu and Weidmann 2020). In contrast to cyber-threats such as espionage at the government level or DDoS-attacks on government websites, internet shutdowns have a direct impact with economic and social consequences. Businesses that rely on the internet for their operations suffer financial losses, while access to essential services such as health care, education, and emergency assistance is disrupted. Marginalized communities that heavily depend on digital platforms for their livelihoods or for accessing critical information are disproportionately affected.

BOX 4.4   PEGASUS SPYWARE

Pegasus is a powerful spyware developed by the Israeli company NSO Group. It is designed to be covertly and remotely installed on mobile phones running both iOS and Android operating systems. Pegasus allows its operators to gain unauthorized access to the target device, enabling them to monitor calls, messages, emails, and collect various forms of data. Notable characteristics of Pegasus include its ability to exploit vulnerabilities in the target device's operating system to gain access, making it highly sophisticated and difficult to detect.

Pegasus has raised significant concerns about government surveillance and privacy violations. The software has been used by various (also democratic) governments and intelligence agencies around the world to target journalists, activists, dissidents, and political opponents. Its use has prompted debates about the balance between national security and individual privacy. The use of Pegasus has triggered legal and regulatory challenges in multiple countries. Governments have faced legal actions and demands for accountability regarding the use of such spyware.

In March 2023, the United States and over 20 other countries adopted a Code of Conduct "to counter state and non-state actors' misuse of goods and technology that violate human rights" (US Department of State 2023) and committed to work toward the development of a new multilateral approach to the regulation of spyware (Lubin 2023).

Summary and Key Points

The landscape of cyber-security underwent a significant transformation during the latter half of the 2000s, driven by factors such as evolving threat perceptions, emerging opportunities, and broader geopolitical and domestic issues. Motivated by the belief that adversaries were acquiring similar capabilities, states began to invest in developing cyber-capabilities and began conducting cyber-operations. Consequently, cyber-security became intricately linked with broader strategic and political contexts, shaping major power politics, and giving rise to a new form of competition.

The takeaway lessons for the study of international cyber-security politics are threefold. First, considering cyber-incidents as mere technical events divorced from broader socio-political and socio-technical trends obscures the underlying motives for their utilization as instruments of foreign and security policy. Political entities engineer and wield these tools within specific contexts to attain specific objectives. Furthermore, it is crucial to recognize that cyber-incidents are not isolated events. Instead, cyber-attacks constitute one facet out of the multifaceted political and strategic toolkit available to states, synergistically employed alongside other instruments to achieve overarching aims. It is therefore crucial to strive for better ways to understand them in interactive ways, as shapers of and shaped by larger political forces.

Second, we should endeavor to glean insights from some of the obvious blind spots in our study of cyber-security politics that were revealed by the incidents discussed in this chapter. Whereas Stuxnet seemed to confirm some of the fears previously held about "cyber-war," the new dimensions brought forth by Snowden and the DNC Hack caught researchers off-guard. This should prompt us to engage in reflective practice, probing the origins of our knowledge and the curation of cumulative wisdom over time. Across research paradigms, we should discuss the things we know and are certain about and what we believe to be the things we know and do not know (see also Lilli 2023).

Third, the incidents and what we learned from them not only birthed new, invigorating, and productive avenues of inquiry but also created new challenges for researchers in terms of necessary theoretical knowledge and empirical material. For example, the declassification of sensitive information in the Snowden revelations exposed intelligence practices to public scrutiny, granting researchers unparalleled access to formerly inaccessible data. However, this also introduced distinct challenges as scholars wrestled with analyzing phenomena deliberately shrouded in secrecy. Consequently, research methodologies evolved to resemble investigative journalism more than conventional scholarly methods as researchers began conducting interviews with firsthand witnesses and soliciting insights from insiders to gather primary data (Maurer 2018; Buchanan 2017). More recently, approaches to comprehending cyber-security dynamics have taken on the semblance of digital ethnography and, with it, new ethical questions (Pink et al. 2016). It is highly likely that the field will continue to evolve because of new revelations, which will in turn generate new research questions of value.

Notes

1. In the context of cyber-operations, a capability refers to the resources, skills, knowledge, operational concepts, and procedures to be able to have an effect in cyberspace (Uren et al. 2018).
2. Some newer sources claim over a billion dollars (NL Times 2024).
3. For a timeline of the leaks, see: www.businessinsider.com/snowden-leaks-timeline-2016-9?r=US&IR=T // for access to the documents that were released to/by journalists, see: https://github.com/iamcryptoki/snowden-archive // For a collection of all published stories, see: https://theintercept.com/collections/snowden-archive/ // For a critical article asking where the entire batch of documents is, see: www.electrospaces.net/2019/04/the-snowden-files-where-are-they-and.html
4. The actual number of documents that Snowden took away from the NSA is still unclear and disputed. The number in the text (1.5 million files) is taken from a review by the U.S. House of Representatives (2016: i).

References

Arquilla, J. and Ronfeldt, D. (eds.) (1997). *In Athena's Camp: Preparing for Conflict in the Information Age*. RAND Corporation.

Baezner, M. (2019). *Iranian Cyber-Activities in Context of Regional Rivalries and International Tensions*. CSS Cyberdefense Hotspot Analyses, May. Center for Security Studies (CSS).

Balzacq, T. and Dunn Cavelty, M. (2016). A Theory of Actor-Network for Cyber-Security. *European Journal of International Security* 1(2): 176–198.

Barlow, J.P. (1996). *A Declaration of the Independence of Cyberspace*. Available at: www.eff.org/cyberspace-independence

Beckerman, C.E. (2022). Is There a Cyber-Security Dilemma? *Journal of Cybersecurity* 8(1): tyac012.

Best, J. and Walters, W. (2013). Translating the Sociology of Translation. *International Political Sociology* 7(3): 345–349.

Brown, H. and Rudman, W.B. (1996). *Prepare for the 21st Century: An Appraisal of U.S. Intelligence*. Report of the Commission on the Roles and Capabilities of the United States Intelligence Community, March 1. Available at: www.govinfo.gov/app/details/GPO-INTELLIGENCE

Brunner, E. and Dunn Cavelty, M. (2009). The Formation of In-Formation by the US Military: Articulation and Enactment of Infomanic Threat Imaginaries on the Immaterial Battlefield of Perception. *Cambridge Review of International Affairs* 22(4): 625–642.

Buchanan, B. (2017). *The Cyber-Security Dilemma: Hacking, Trust and Fear Between Nations*. Oxford University Press.

Buchanan, B. (2020). *The Hacker and the State: Cyber Attacks and the New Normal of Geopolitics*. Harvard University Press.

Carson, A. (2018). *Secret Wars: Covert Conflict in International Politics*. Princeton University Press.

Chesney, R. and Smeets, M. (eds.) (2020). Roundtable: The Dynamics of Cyber Conflict and Competition. *Texas National Security Review* 3(4). Available at: https://tnsr.org/category/special-issue-cyber-competition/

Chesney, R. and Smeets, M. (eds.) (2023). *Deter, Disrupt, or Deceive: Assessing Cyber Conflict as an Intelligence Contest*. Georgetown University Press.

De Gregorio, G. and Stremlau, N. (2020). Internet Shutdowns and the Limits of Law. *International Journal of Communication* 14: 1–19.

Deibert, R.J. (2013). *Black Code: Inside the Battle for Cyberspace*. Signal.

Deibert, R.J. (2020). *Reset: Reclaiming the Internet for Civil Society*. House of Anansi Press.

Deibert, R.J. (2022). Subversion Inc: The Age of Private Espionage. *Journal of Democracy* 33(2): 28–44.

Deibert, R.J. (2023). The Autocrat in Your iPhone: How Mercenary Spyware Threatens Democracy. *Foreign Affairs* 102(1): 72–88.

Deibert, R.J., Palfrey, J.G., Jr., Rohozinski, R. and Zittrain, J. (2008). *Access Denied: The Practice and Policy of Global Internet Filtering*. MIT Press

Deibert, R.J., Palfrey, J.G., Jr., Rohozinski, R. and Zittrain, J. (2010). *Access Controlled: The Shaping of Power, Rights, and Rule in Cyberspace*. MIT Press.

Deibert, R.J., Palfrey, J.G., Jr., Rohozinski, R. and Zittrain, J. (2011). *Access Contested: Security, Identity, and Resistance in Asian Cyberspace*. MIT Press.

Deibert, R.J. and Rohozinski, R. (2009). Tracking GhostNet: Investigating a Cyber Espionage Network. *Information Warfare Monitor*, March 29. Available at: https://citizenlab.ca/wp-content/uploads/2017/05/ghostnet.pdf

DeNardis, L. (2014). *The Global War for Internet Governance*. Yale University Press.

DeVine, M.E. (2022). *Covert Action and Clandestine Activities of the Intelligence Community: Selected Definitions*. Congressional Research Service, Updated November 29. Available at: https://sgp.fas.org/crs/intel/R45175.pdf

Dunn Cavelty, M. (2015). The Normalization of Cyber-International Relations. In: Thränert, O. and Zapfe, M. (eds.) *Strategic Trends 2015: Key Developments in Global Affairs*. Center for Security Studies, pp. 81–98.

Falliere, N., O Murchu, L. and Chien, E. (2011). *W32.Stuxnet Dossier. Symantec Security Response*, Version 1.4, Last modified February 2011. Available at: https://docs.broadcom.com/doc/security-response-w32-stuxnet-dossier-11-en

Farwell, J.P. and Rohozinski, R. (2011). Stuxnet and the Future of Cyber War. *Survival* 53(1): 23–40.

Fischerkeller, M. and Harknett, R. (2023). Cyber Persistence, Intelligence Contests, and Strategic Competition. In: Chesney, R. and Smeets, M. (eds.) *Deter, Disrupt, or Deceive: Assessing Cyber Conflict as an Intelligence Contest*. Georgetown University Press, pp. 109–133.

Galeotti, M. (2014). The 'Gerasimov Doctrine' and Russian Non-Linear War. Blogpost on "In Moscow's Shadows." Available at: https://inmoscowsshadows.wordpress.

com/2014/07/06/the-gerasimov-doctrine-and-russian-non-linear-war/#more-2291

Gellmann, B. and Nakashima, E. (2013). U.S. Spy Agencies Mounted 231 Offensive Cyber-Operations in 2011, Documents Show. *The Washington Post*, August 30. Available at: https://www.washingtonpost.com/world/national-security/us-spy-agencies-mounted-231-offensive-cyber-operations-in-2011-documents-show/2013/08/30/d090a6ae-119e-11e3-b4cb-fd7ce041d814_story.html

Giles, K. (2016). *Handbook of Russian Information Warfare*. NATO Defense College.

Gohdes, A.R. (2015). Pulling the Plug: Network Disruptions and Violence in Civil Conflict. *Journal of Peace Research* 52(3): 352–367.

Gohdes, A.R. (2023). *Repression in the Digital Age: Surveillance, Censorship, and the Dynamics of State Violence*. Oxford University Press.

Greenwald, G. (2014). The "Cuban Twitter" Scam is a Drop in the Internet Propaganda Bucket. *The Intercept*, April 4. Available at: https://theintercept.com/2014/04/04/cuban-twitter-scam-social-media-tool-disseminating-government-propaganda/

Greenwald, G., MacAskill, E. and Poitras, L. (2013). Edward Snowden: The Whistleblower behind the NSA Surveillance Revelations. *The Guardian*, June 11. Available at: www.theguardian.com/world/2013/jun/09/edward-snowden-nsa-whistleblower-surveillance

Gross, M.J. (2011). A Declaration of Cyber-War. *Vanity Fair*, March 2. Available at: www.vanityfair.com/news/2011/03/stuxnet-201104

The Guardian (2013). Obama Tells Intelligence Chiefs to Draw Up Cyber Target List. *The Guardian*, June 7. Available at: https://www.theguardian.com/world/interactive/2013/jun/07/obama-cyber-directive-full-text

Gunitsky, S. (2015). Corrupting the Cyber-Commons: Social Media as a Tool of Autocratic Stability. *Perspectives and Politics* 13(1): 42–54.

Hansen, L. and Nissenbaum, H. (2009). Digital Disaster, Cyber-Security, and the Copenhagen School. *International Studies Quarterly* 53(4): 1155–1175.

Hanson, F. (2012). Baked in and Wired: eDiplomacy @ State. *Brooking Report*, October 25. Available at: www.brookings.edu/research/baked-in-and-wired-ediplomacy-state/

Jamieson, K.H. (2018). *Cyberwar: How Russian Hackers and Trolls Helped Elect a President—What We Don't, Can't, and Do Know*. Oxford University Press.

Jensen, B., Valeriano, B. and Maness, R. (2019). Fancy Bears and Digital Trolls: Cyber Strategy with a Russian Twist. *Journal of Strategic Studies* 42(2): 212–234.

Joint Chiefs of Staff (2013). JP 3–12, Cyberspace Operations, Joint Publication 3–12 (R), 5 February 2013. Available at: https://irp.fas.org/doddir/dod/jp3_12r.pdf

Kaplan, F. (2017). *Dark Territory: The Secret History of Cyber-War*. Simon & Schuster.

Katz, Y. (2010). Stuxnet Virus Set Back Iran's Nuclear Program by 2 Years. *Jerusalem Post*, December 15.

Kaye, D. (2021). The Spyware State and the Prospects for Accountability. *Global Governance: A Review of Multilateralism and International Organizations* 27(4): 483–492.

Kello, L. (2017). *The Virtual Weapon and International Order*. Yale University Press.

Keremoğlu, E. and Weidmann, N.B. (2020). How Dictators Control the Internet: A Review Essay. *Comparative Political Studies* 53(10–11): 1690–1703.

Langner, R. (2013). To Kill a Centrifuge: A Technical Analysis of What Stuxnet's Creators Tried to Achieve. *The Langner Group*, November. Available at: www.langner.com/en/wp-content/uploads/2013/11/To-kill-a-centrifuge.pdf

Larson, J. (2013). Revealed: The NSA's Secret Campaign to Crack, Undermine Internet Security. *ProPublica*, September 5. Available at: https://www.propublica.org/article/the-nsas-secret-campaign-to-crack-undermine-internet-encryption

Lewis, J.A. (2019). *Iran and Cyber Power*. Center for Strategic and International Studies Commentary. Available at: www.csis.org/analysis/iran-and-cyber-power

Lilli, E. (2023). How Can We Know What We Think We Know about Cyber Operations? *Journal of Global Security Studies* 8(2): ogad011. https://doi.org/10.1093/jogss/ogad011

Lindsay, J.R. (2013). Stuxnet and the Limits of Cyber Warfare. *Security Studies* 22(3): 365–404.

Lindsay, J.R. (2023). Hidden Dangers in the US Military Solution to a Large-Scale Intelligence problem. In: Chesney, R. and Smeets, M. (eds.) *Deter, Disrupt, or Deceive: Assessing Cyber Conflict as an Intelligence Contest*. Georgetown University Press, pp. 60–85.

Lubin, A. (2023). Regulating Commercial Spyware. *Lawfare*, August 9. Available at: www.lawfaremedia.org/article/regulating-commercial-spyware

Lynn, W.J. (2010). Defending a New Domain: The Pentagon's Cyberstrategy. *Foreign Affairs* 89(5): 97–108.

Marczak, B., Scott-Railton, J., McKune, S., Razzak, B.A. and Deibert, R.J. (2018). *Hide and Seek: Tracking NSO Group's Pegasus Spyware to Operations in 45 Countries*. Citizen Lab Research Report No. 113, September. University of Toronto.

Maschmeyer, L. (2023). Subversion, Cyber Operations, and Reverse Structural Power in World Politics. *European Journal of International Relations* 29(1): 79–103.

Maurer, T. (2018). *Cyber Mercenaries: The State, Hackers, and Power*. Cambridge University Press.

NL Times (2024). Dutch Man Sabotaged Iranian Nuclear Program Without Dutch Government's Knowledge: Report. *NL Times*, January 8. Available at: https://nltimes.nl/2024/01/08/dutch-man-sabotaged-iranian-nuclear-program-without-dutch-governments-knowledge-report

Osborne, C. (2013). NSA Purchased Zero-Day Exploits from French Security Firm Vupen. *ZDNet*, September 18. Available at: https://www.zdnet.com/article/nsa-purchased-zero-day-exploits-from-french-security-firm-vupen/

Paul, C. and Matthews, M. (2016). *The Russian "Firehose of Falsehood" Propaganda Model: Why It Might Work and Options to Counter It*. RAND Corporation.

Pink, S., Horst, H., Postill, J., Hjorth, L., Lewis, T. and Tacchi, J. (2016). *Digital Ethnography: Principles and Practice*. SAGE.

Rovner, J. (2023). The Elements of an Intelligence Contest. In: Chesney, R. and Smeets, M. (eds.) *Deter, Disrupt, or Deceive: Assessing Cyber Conflict as an Intelligence Contest*. Georgetown University Press, pp. 17–42.

Sanger, D.E. (2012a). Obama Order Sped Up Wave of Cyberattacks Against Iran. *New York Times*, June 1. Available at: https://www.nytimes.com/2012/06/01/world/middleeast/obama-ordered-wave-of-cyberattacks-against-iran.html

Sanger, D.E. (2012b). *Confront and Conceal: Obama's Secret Wars and Surprising Use of American Power*. Broadway Books.

Shires, J. (2019). Hack-and-Leak Operations: Intrusion and Influence in the Gulf. *Journal of Cyber Policy* 4(2): 235–256.

Slayton, R. (2017). What Is the Cyber Offense-Defense Balance? Conceptions, Causes and Assessment. *International Security* 41(3): 72–109.

Smeets, M. (2022a). *No Shortcuts: Why States Struggle to Develop a Military Cyber-Force*. Oxford University Press.

Smeets, M. (2022b). A US History of Not Conducting Cyber Attacks. *Bulletin of the Atomic Scientists* 78(4): 208–213.

Snowden, E. (2019). *Permanent Record*. Metropolitan Books.

Stafford, T.F. and Urbaczewski, A. (2004). Spyware: The Ghost in the Machine. *The Communications of the Association for Information Systems* 14(1): Article 49. Available at: http://aisel.aisnet.org/cais/vol14/iss1/49

Steed, D. (2022). Disrupting the Second Oldest Profession: The Impact of Cyber on Intelligence. In: Dunn Cavelty, M. and Wenger, A. (eds.) *Cyber Security Politics: Socio-Technological Transformations and Political Fragmentation*. Routledge, pp. 205–219.

Stevens, C. (2020). Assembling Cybersecurity: The Politics and Materiality of Technical Malware Reports and the Case of Stuxnet. *Contemporary Security Policy* 41(1): 129–152.

St. James, E. and Lee, T.B. (2015). The 2014 Sony Hacks, Explained. *Vox*, June 3. Available at: www.vox.com/2015/1/20/18089084/sony-hack-north-korea

Timm, T. and York, J.C. (2012). Surveillance Inc: How Western Tech Firms Are Helping Arab Dictators. *The Atlantic*, March 6. Available at: https://www.theatlantic.com/international/archive/2012/03/surveillance-inc-how-western-tech-firms-are-helping-arab-dictators/254008/

United States of America v. Joshua Adam Schulte (2020). *US v. Joshua Schulte Trial Transcript 2020-0206*. United States District Court Southern District of New York. Available at: www.documentcloud.org/documents/6771808-20200206-REDACTED.html

Uren, T., Hogeveen, B. and Hanson, F. (2018). *Defining Offensive Cyber Capabilities*. Australian Strategic Policy Institute Report. Available at: www.aspi.org.au/report/defining-offensive-cyber-capabilities

US Department of State (2023). Export Controls and Human Rights Initiative Code of Conduct Released at the Summit for Democracy. *Media Note*, March 30. Available at: www.state.gov/export-controls-and-human-rights-initiative-code-of-conduct-released-at-the-summit-for-democracy/

US House of Representatives (2016). *Review of the Unauthorized Disclosures of Former National Security Agency Contractor Edward Snowden*, September 5. Available at: https://irp.fas.org/congress/2016_rpt/hpsci-snowden.pdf

Vaez, A. and Ferguson, C.D. (2011). Towards Enhanced Safeguards for Iran's Nuclear Program Federation of American Scientists. *FAS Special Report No. 2*, October. Available at: https://pubs.fas.org/_docs/specialreport2_iran_nuclear_program.pdf

van Aalst, J. (2022). Understanding Big Other: Self-recognition in the Web of Eyes. *Diggit Magazine*, March 30. Available at: www.diggitmagazine.com/academic-papers/Big-Other-surveillance

Vivian, B. (2018). On the Erosion of Democracy by Truth. *Philosophy & Rhetoric* 51(4): 416–440.

Warner, M. (2023). The Character of Strategic Cyberspace Competition and the Role of Ideology. In: Chesney, R. and Smeets, M. (eds.) *Deter, Disrupt, or Deceive: Assessing Cyber Conflict as an Intelligence Contest*. Georgetown University Press, pp. 43–59.

The Washington Post (2013). NSA Slides Explain the PRISM Data-Collection Program. *The Washington Post*, June 6. Available at: https://www.washingtonpost.com/wp-srv/special/politics/prism-collection-documents/

Wenger, A. and Dunn Cavelty, M. (2022). Conclusion: The Ambiguity of Cyber Security Politics in the Context of Multidimensional Uncertainty. In: Dunn Cavelty, M. and Wenger, A. (eds.) *Cyber Security Politics: Socio-Technological Transformations and Political Fragmentation*. Routledge, pp. 239–266.

West, L.B. (2021). The Rise of the "Fifth Fight" in Cyberspace: A New Legal Framework and Implications for Great Power Competition. *Military Law Review* 229(3): 273–327.

Whyte, C. (2020). Cyber-Conflict or Democracy "Hacked"? How Cyber-Operations Enhance Information Warfare. *Journal of Cyber-security* 6(1): tyaa013.

Winkler, S.C. (2023). Strategic Competition and US–China Relations: A Conceptual Analysis. *The Chinese Journal of International Politics* 16(3): 333–356.

Zajko, M. (2018). Security against Surveillance: IT Security as Resistance to Pervasive Surveillance. *Surveillance & Society* 16(1): 39–52.

Zetter, K. (2010). Iran: Computer Malware Sabotaged Uranium Centrifuges. *Wired*, November 29. Available at: www.wired.com/2010/11/stuxnet-sabotage-centrifuges/

Zetter, K. and Modderkolk, H. (2019). Revealed: How a Secret Dutch Mole Aided the U.S.-Israeli Stuxnet Cyberattack on Iran. *Yahoo! News*, September 2. Available at: https://news.yahoo.com/revealed-how-a-secret-dutch-mole-aided-the-us-israeli-stuxnet-cyber-attack-on-iran-160026018.html

Zuboff, S. (2015). Big Other: Surveillance Capitalism and the Prospects of an Information Civilization. *Journal of Information Technology* 30(1): 75–89.

Zuboff, S. (2019). *The Age of Surveillance Capitalism: The Fight for a Human Future at the New Frontier of Power*. Public Affairs.

5

THE CYBER-THREAT LANDSCAPE

After looking at the evolution of cyber-security as a political and security issue, this chapter turns toward the emergence and ongoing development of different cyber-threat categories over time. The construction and stabilization of these categories serve cognitive and political purposes, although they are not centrally guided by any particular entity but evolve naturally as part of the political process.

One of the rationales behind the discursive and emergent practices of "threat-making" is to establish stable ontological categories that facilitate focused political discussions on what poses a threat and how to address it. In the absence of severe incidents in the first half of the cyber-security story, these categories also served as a link between the present and the anticipated future. Furthermore, threat categories enable data collection practices, such as risk analysis, and may play a role in funding allocation. Bureaucratic logics strongly contribute to the stabilization of threat categories by associating "cyber" with established bureaucratic structures and responsibilities, drawing connections to familiar categories like crime, terrorism, and war (albeit with varying degrees of stability).

In the early 2000s, cyber-incidents gained significant media attention, often accompanied by sensationalist narratives that portrayed a sense of imminent cyber-doom (Conway 2003). Especially the two terms "cyber-terrorism" and "cyber-war" were frequently used to describe harmless incidents, a hugely exaggerated portrayal of the threat emanating from cyberspace (Lawson 2013). This had consequences. First, the utilization of political violence categories like terrorism and war implies that such extreme forms of violence can be reached through cyber-means alone,

DOI: 10.4324/9781003497080-5

which is not the case. Second, relying on such threat-categories as mental shortcuts often leads policymakers to flawed conclusions regarding the level of threats and the necessary countermeasures.

As a result, some observers felt compelled to introduce a more nuanced estimate of the threat into the debate. While some questioned the simplistic assumptions about vulnerability that would automatically translate into grave attacks (Lewis 2002), others introduced qualitative differentiations between different types of online activities by focusing on the *actors* behind it, the *objectives* of the attack, and sometimes the potential *effects* of the cyber-activity (Denning 2001, first published in 1999; Schneier 2007).[1] To some degree, these attempts mirror strategic thought about escalation à la Kahn, whose famous *On Escalation* (1965) discussed numerous levels of confrontation between nuclear powers. Clarity around different levels of aggression is inevitable and invites discussions about appropriate responses (Morgan et al. 2008).

To counter the rampant securitization tendencies, this type of literature attempted to establish that only computer attacks whose effects are sufficiently destructive or disruptive should be regarded as a national security issue, whereas attacks that disrupt nonessential services, or that are mainly a costly nuisance, should not be (Wilson 2003). The most important threat categories that emerged over time are discussed in the subsequent chapters (see Table 5.1 for a summary).

How did the lessons learned after 2010 (refer to Chapter 4) impact the threat landscape and our understanding of various threat categories? On the one hand, all the concepts from cyber-crime to cyber-war remain relevant and define the scope of the cyber-threats discourse until today. Cyber-crime has maintained a consistent definition, but the phenomena we encounter are more diverse, indicating significant innovation occurring in the criminal market. Hacktivism continues to be attributed with more impact than it truly possesses, mainly due to media coverage. Additionally, cyber-terrorism and cyber-war are still copiously used terms in public debates, despite not accurately representing the phenomena they are associated with. This suggests a frustrating propensity to sensationalize the threat for bureaucratic and economic motives. It may also indicate a general lack of knowledge about cyber-security among individuals operating at the intersection of IT-security and international politics.

Cyber-Crime

Cyber-crime encompasses a wide range of illicit practices in two categories: the use of computers as tools for crime and computers being the targets themselves. This chapter primarily focuses on unlawful hacking and

TABLE 5.1 Cyber-Threat Categories

Threat-Form	Perpetrators	Intent	Types of Targets	Frequency
Cyber-crime	Mostly: Non-state actors with criminal intent (But some state actors use criminal methods as well)	Use of computers to conduct crime, computer as target	Any target through which money can be made (individuals, companies, etc.)	Very frequent
Hacktivism Patriotic Hackers	Non-state actors with political or activist aims Can be state-supported or state-instigated	Creating attention, disrupting services, sending a political message, being an annoyance	Targets whose (visible) disruption sends a message (often through media) Data with the potential to ridicule/blackmail people or organizations	Frequent, always related to political strife, conflict, grievances (attribution difficult)
Cyber-espionage	Mostly state actors or semi-state actors, often affiliated with intelligence agencies	Gain access to secret information (economic and political)	Targets that contain secret, valuable information—also infiltration of strategically relevant targets in computer networks	Several known (high-level) cases, hard to establish quantity (underreporting likely high)
Cyber-influence operations	Non-state actors with political or activist aims State actors (intelligence)	To shape or manipulate the beliefs, attitudes, behaviors, and perceptions of individuals or groups to achieve specific strategic or political objectives	Social media, traditional media, online forums, and interpersonal communication	Frequent (attribution difficult)

(Continued)

TABLE 5.1 (Continued)

Threat-Form	Perpetrators	Intent	Types of Targets	Frequency
Cyber-terrorism (Not terrorist use of the internet!)	Non-state actors or state actors with political, religious, or ideological aims	Terrorist intent and method: create fear, influence politics, communication strategy	Targets through which to instill fear, to endanger life, or cause significant economic or environmental damage	No known incidents that created terrorist-like effect
Cyber-war (operational) Also: cyber-in-war	State actors: military, intelligence, cyber-commands	Aid warfare activities through cyber-operations	Military communication infrastructure of enemy forces Command and control infrastructure	Auxiliary cyber-activities during military operations
Cyber-war (strategic)	State actors: military, intelligence, cyber-commands	Wage war primarily through cyberspace	Critical infrastructures of enemy society	No known incidents

the utilization of malware for criminal intents, which mainly falls within the latter category (Wall 2007).[2] While the nature of most cyber-crimes is not new, computers introduce a novel dimension by amplifying the scale, extent, and pace of criminal activities. The internet provides a near-ideal playground for semi- and organized crime due to its capacity to simultaneously reach numerous potential victims at scale (Grabosky 2001, 2013).

Crime itself is not inherently a security political issue. However, when discussing security politics, cyber-crime activity becomes part of the conversation if one or more of the following characteristics are present: a connection to a state or non-state actor with political motivations or significant damage caused by a single or cumulative incidents. In the early stages of cyber-security politics, the sheer volume of incidents was enough to generate a growing sense of alarm. The escalating economic losses were seen as a collective problem requiring additional measures from the government. Moreover, experts began to worry that the capabilities, tools, and services developed by organized crime could become accessible to state actors. The existence of high-quality and specialized criminal services was seen as lowering the barrier for non-state actors or terrorist organizations to engage in cyber-operations, especially since many of these services could be purchased. Additionally, concerns arose about potential collaboration between criminals and terrorist organizations, reflecting similar apprehensions in the offline world (Tabansky 2012; Makarenko 2004).

Like other IT-related jobs, cyber-crime has become increasingly professionalized over time. Some actors in the illicit "cyber-crime black market" operate globally within business ecosystems that resemble large IT-companies or at least start-ups, featuring hierarchical networks with strategic and operational vision, logistics, and deployment (McCusker 2006: 265). Others follow a more fluid "swarming model" (Brenner 2002: 50). The "Darknet," which refers to the illegal marketplace beyond the indexed and openly accessible internet, offers significant advantages to criminals due to readily available anonymization techniques and the ability to regroup flexibly (Lavorgna and Antonomoulos 2022). The development of criminal markets is driven by opportunities as well as supply and demand dynamics and cost-benefit considerations, much like legitimate markets (Koops 2010; Ablon et al. 2014).

Cyber-crime undergoes cycles of innovation in response to new security solutions, which, in turn, are reactions to cyber-crime schemes (Kraemer-Mbula et al. 2013). In addition to international cooperation and crackdowns on cyber-criminals, implementing technical solutions that make it harder for criminals to achieve their objectives is a crucial element in combating cyber-crime, considering the strong cost-benefit dynamics that drive criminal activities. The global cyber-security market has experienced significant growth in recent years, with revenue increasing from US$83 billion in 2016 to US$173.50 billion in 2023, reflecting an annual growth rate of over 10%. Concurrently, some sources estimate that the annual damages caused by cyber-crime will reach US$10.5–US$17.5 trillion by 2025.[3] However, accurately measuring aggregate global losses incurred through cyber-crime remains challenging due to measurement issues (Anderson et al. 2013).

Among all the threat categories, cyber-crime is the one cyber-threat that most clearly manifests as having an impact on people's lives due to its frequency. In an ever shifting and evolving market, one particularly nasty plague is ransomware. Ransomware is a type of malware that encrypts a victim's files or locks their computer systems, rendering them inaccessible. The attackers behind the ransomware then demand a ransom payment, typically in cryptocurrency, in exchange for providing the decryption key or restoring access to the compromised systems. Though its origins date back to the 1980s, ransomware gained widespread attention as a significant cyber-security threat around 2013 with the emergence of the CryptoLocker ransomware. CryptoLocker utilized strong, sophisticated encryption algorithms, demanded payment in cryptocurrency (Bitcoin), and employed robust command-and-control infrastructure, resulting in significant financial losses and widespread disruption (Ryan 2021: 65–69).

Given the success of ransomware, these attacks continued to evolve, with threat actors developing new techniques and tactics to evade detection and enhance their capabilities. The proliferation of ransomware-as-a-service (RaaS) models and the availability of ransomware tools on the dark web have made it easier for less sophisticated actors to carry out attacks, increasing the overall threat. Overall, the rise of ransomware as a prominent cyber-security issue is driven by various factors, including the increasing connectivity of devices, the anonymity provided by cryptocurrencies, the profitability of extortion schemes, and the evolving tactics and techniques employed by cybercriminals.

Ransomware clearly becomes a national security issue when we consider attacks against critical infrastructures, as was the case with Colonial Pipeline in 2021 (see Box 5.4) or the ransomware that hit a hospital in Düsseldorf in 2020 (Shandler and Gomez 2022). When essential services are disrupted or disabled, it can have severe consequences for public safety, economic stability, and national security. However, these targets are also attractive from a criminal's perspective because the pressing and time-sensitive need to keep these services up and running makes it more likely that a ransom is paid.

Even though criminal actors tend not to be politically motivated and their connections to a state are often murky at best, their activities can help states that are interested in destabilizing their adversaries. Given the current geopolitical tensions, the nationality of crime groups is therefore highly suspicious. For several reasons—among them technical expertise and tolerance of criminal activities—some of the most notorious cyber-crime groups are of Russian origins or have some affiliation with Russian hackers.

Not least, criminal methods also began to be used by state-sponsored groups, most famously by North Korea (and their Lazarus Group). The Lazarus Group gained global attention for its involvement in high-profile cyber-attacks, including the 2016 Bangladesh Bank cyber-heist and the 2017 WannaCry ransomware attack (Volz and Finkle 2017; Guerrero-Saade and Moriuchi 2018) (see Box 5.1). It is estimated that North Korea's government earned approximately US$2 billion through cyber-crime activities (Baezner and Cordey 2022). Some scholars have suggested that North Korea has managed to mitigate the impact of international economic sanctions this way (Fischerkeller and Harknett 2019: 276). In September 2023, the group stole approximately US$41 million in virtual currency from Stake.com, an online casino and betting platform (FBI 2023).

BOX 5.1 WANNACRY, 2017

The WannaCry ransomware attack was a global cyber-attack that occurred in May 2017. It targeted computers running the Microsoft Windows operating system, affecting hundreds of thousands of systems in more than 150 countries. WannaCry ransomware exploited a vulnerability in the Windows operating system called EternalBlue, which was allegedly developed by the United States' NSA but leaked to the public by a group called Shadow Brokers. This vulnerability allowed the ransomware to spread rapidly across networks without user interaction. The attack caused widespread disruption, affecting various organizations, including government agencies, health-care institutions, educational institutions, and businesses of all sizes. It is worth noting that a kill switch was discovered by a cyber-security researcher during the attack, which helped slow down the spread of WannaCry. Additionally, patches and security updates were released by Microsoft to address the EternalBlue vulnerability and protect against future attacks. According to various reports and analyses, it is estimated that the total amount of ransom payments received by the WannaCry attackers was relatively low compared to the scale of the attack. Some estimates put the total earnings at around US$130,000, although this figure may vary.

Hacktivism

Hacktivism, a term combining hacking and activism, refers to a form of political protest primarily conducted online. According to Karagiannopoulos, hacktivism is "the use of computer and network access and reconfiguration techniques that transgress or challenge cybercrime laws in order to produce or facilitate symbolic effects that confer a political message or protest a particular policy" (Karagiannopoulos 2018: 48). The tactics employed by hacktivists and their impact on the cyber-threat discourse are best understood within the context of the merging of hacking ethics with "informational societies and modern social protest and resistance" (Jordan and Taylor 2004: 2). While democratic countries generally recognize the right to protest, most hacktivist activities are considered illegal under existing computer laws.

Most frequently, hacktivists use DDoS-attacks to make a statement (DDoS stands for distributed denial of service). A DDoS-attack is a type of cyber-attack in which multiple compromised computers or devices, often forming a botnet, are used to flood a target system or network with a massive amount of traffic or requests. The aim of a DDoS-attack is to overwhelm the targeted system's resources, such as bandwidth, processing power, or memory, making it difficult or impossible for legitimate users to access the system or service. DDoS-attacks can cause severe disruption to businesses, organizations, and online services, resulting in financial losses, reputational damage, and inconvenience to users. However, DDoS-attacks do not cause lasting damage, and several security solutions are available. The public impact of DDoS-attacks is high; however, this form of attack is one of the few that is "visible" as it happens.

Unlike cyber-crime, hacktivism is inherently political, as it is driven by the intentions and motives of people who use the internet to express themselves politically. However, the term "political" encompasses a wide range of meanings and expressions in this context. The early history of hacktivism is closely intertwined with the emergence of hacker collectives like the Chaos Computer Club (CCC) in Germany or the Legion of Doom in the United States. These hacker groups are considered political due to their strong emphasis on freedom of speech and their resistance against government forces that sought to exert control over the "new" space of the internet (Mihalache 2002; Yen 2003). Today, one does not necessarily have to be closely associated with the hacker community to be a hacktivist, nor is extensive technological knowledge a prerequisite. Tools for conducting DDoS-attacks, for example, are readily available on the internet, making them accessible to individuals with varying levels of technical expertise.

In the 2000s, Anonymous emerged as the most renowned and arguably influential hacktivist collective (Coleman 2012). They successfully transformed digital activism from a "countercultural politics of resistance to a counterhegemonic politics of popular mobilisation" (Gerbaudo 2017). However, it is crucial to approach the discussion of such a diverse phenomenon with caution. The motivations of individuals participating in hacktivist activities vary widely. Some engage in these activities for the sake of a deliberately offensive and crude form of humor known as trolling, often found on platforms like 4chan, which has gained notoriety as a breeding ground for movements like Qanon (Sharevski and Kessel 2023). Others are driven by a deep sense of outrage and an activist conviction to bring about change in the world. Additionally, groups like LulzSec appeared in 2011 to be primarily motivated by the desire to expose and ridicule targets for their lack of IT-security (Dunn Cavelty and Jaeger 2015).

Although hacktivism has political causes, it is not automatically or inherently a security political issue. The link arises only under certain conditions. First, if the media labels a hacktivist activity as "cyber-war" and officials adopt this perspective, it can heighten the perception of a security threat despite the negligible consequences. Second, when hacktivists target entities that a state considers "critical," especially if it involves the potential exposure of classified information, the security implications may be taken more seriously. Third, suspicions of involvement by foreign hackers, possibly backed by state actors, can further elevate the security concerns surrounding hacktivist activities. Last, if hacktivist actions coincide with an ongoing conflict, it can contribute to the framing of hacktivism as a security concern.

"Cyber-War": There exists a symbiotic relationship between hacktivists and the media. Hacktivists actively seek media attention because their tactics, described as "semiotic guerrilla warfare" by Hebdige (2002), rely on public visibility and attention. As a result, they tend to target high-profile entities or engage in activities that are newsworthy. The disruptions caused by hacktivists are typically short-lived and have limited direct effects. However, due to their symbolic nature, they generate secondary effects through media coverage. The way in which the targeted entities handle these disruptions or respond to being targeted can often lead to further exposure and ridicule (Milan 2015). This cycle of media attention, symbolic impact, and public reaction can amplify the perceived significance of hacktivist activities beyond their immediate material consequences.

Targets: There have been hacktivist campaigns that targeted "critical infrastructures" or highly sensitive information, with notable examples including WikiLeaks and LulzSec. One prominent case is Anonymous' Operation Payback in 2010 (Coleman 2012). Initially, Operation Payback involved a series of attacks on major pro-copyright and anti-piracy organizations, law firms, and individuals. However, the situation escalated when it became entangled with a larger conflict surrounding freedom of information, particularly related to WikiLeaks' publication of classified US diplomatic cables. This led to intense pressure on WikiLeaks, with several companies freezing or discontinuing donations to the website. As a response, Operation Payback evolved into Operation Avenge Assange, which focused on launching DDoS campaigns against the targeted companies. Some of the notable targets included Visa, MasterCard, PayPal, and Swiss PostFinance. The financial sector and payment companies are defined as critical infrastructures by most countries. The campaign continued well into 2011, but eventually, arrests were made in multiple countries, including the Netherlands, the United Kingdom, Australia, Spain, Turkey, and the United States, signaling the legal consequences that hacktivists could face for their actions.

Patriotic Hackers: The security political implications are more readily established when hackers from one country target entities in another country, creating a link to an "enemy" even if the actors involved are primarily normal citizens. These groups are often referred to as "patriotic hackers" rather than "hacktivists." One significant case in this subcategory is the series of DDoS-attacks against Estonia in 2007 (Box 5.2), which had a profound impact on the cyber-security discourse despite its negligible effects on the population at the time. When groups of hackers target entities in another country, there is considerable uncertainty regarding their affiliation with their government. Often, there is no provable, direct link. However, some governments may accept or even sponsor hacktivist-type activities directed at rival countries as a cost-effective means of causing annoyance. The relatively low level of destructive effects resulting from hacktivism or trolling minimizes the risk of escalation, while maintaining plausible deniability, which allows states to officially distance themselves from such attacks.

Sideshow in Conflicts: Hacktivism is a to-be expected sideshow of any conflict, but there tends to be no measurable impact on the actual conflict dynamics. However, the context of ongoing conflicts or political tensions provides another avenue for establishing a clear link between online activities and security politics. This is particularly evident in cases such as the hostilities between India and Pakistan (Baezner 2018) or the long-standing conflict between Israel and Palestine (Cristiano 2019; Handler 2022). In these situations, the presence of a volatile and contentious context makes it even more tempting to label the online activities as "cyber-war." The war in Ukraine also shows multiple hacktivist activities with targets in the West, in Russia, and in Ukraine—with currently unclear consequences for international norms (Soesanto 2022). Even though they have little to no impact on the strategic dimension of the conflict and no impact on political actions and decisions, the high visibility of hacktivist activities gives the impression that the cyber-dimension of armed conflicts is much more influential than it is (see Chapter 8).

BOX 5.2   ESTONIA, 2007

When the Estonian authorities began removing a World War II Memorial—a bronze statue of a Soviet soldier—from the center of Tallinn to a military cemetery on the outskirts of the city, Tallinn erupted into two nights of riots and looting. One person died, 156 people were injured, and 1,000 people were detained. In parallel, Estonia was also hit by DDoS-attacks, which in some cases lasted weeks, disrupting the online services of Estonian banks, media outlets, and government bodies. As a result, cash machines and online banking services were sporadically out of action; government employees were unable to communicate with each other on email; and newspapers and broadcasters suddenly found they could not deliver the news. In contrast to the violence on the streets, these effects can be called minimal, and the effects were all reversible.

However, the DDoS-attacks in Estonia hold a very prominent and important position in the cyber-security discourse. The Estonian-Russian online squabble made global headlines, and various officials pounced on the cyber-war theme. One NATO official reportedly said: "I won't point fingers. But these were not things done by a few individuals. This clearly bore the hallmarks of something concerted. The Estonians are not alone with this problem. It really is a serious issue for the alliance as a whole" (Traynor 2007).

The official involvement of the Russian government remains unclear and unproven (Ottis 2008). However, some evidence points to government support. One of the key indicators of Russian involvement was the timing of the attacks. They began shortly after Estonia announced its decision to relocate a Soviet-era war memorial from central Tallinn, a move that was criticized by Russian officials and sparked protests in Russia. Additionally, the methods and targets of the attacks were consistent with the tactics used by Russian state-sponsored hackers in other cyber-campaigns.

Cyber-Espionage

Cyber-espionage refers to the illicit use of computers and malware to covertly collect information without the owner's consent, with the intention of gaining an advantage. It plays a significant role in the early history of cyber-security politics, as it establishes a clear and undisputed link between computers and national security. Unlike other threat categories, there is relatively little ambiguity when identifying incidents as cases of cyber-espionage. The identification of a data breach, where unauthorized copying of data from a target network occurs, is a key indicator. Even in cases where it is uncertain whether any data has been copied, the discovery of threat actor activity within a computer network raises immediate suspicions of espionage. The nature of cyber-espionage necessitates stealth, as attackers strive to remain undetected for as long as possible. This requires a certain level of skill, planning, and sophisticated techniques to bypass security measures and maintain covert access to target systems (Alperovitch 2011). It is also important to note that in most cases of cyber-espionage, attacks are targeted, as not all systems hold equal value. Therefore, the practice of cyber-espionage does not lend itself to mass infiltrations on a large scale (Buchan 2019).

Traditionally, espionage primarily involved state actors targeting other state actors, with a focus on critical governmental organs such as defense and foreign affairs departments (Buchan 2019: 172). However, in the cyber-age, the landscape of espionage has expanded to encompass a broader range of targets and actors. States now frequently target non-state actors, including international organizations, nongovernmental organizations, companies, and even individuals. This diversification of targets creates a connection to surveillance practices, particularly when state actors target dissident groups (see Box 5.3). Additionally, non-state actors have also engaged in cyber-espionage by illicitly accessing and copying confidential information from both state and non-state actors. One notable example is WikiLeaks, which, although often categorized as hacktivism, aimed to expose information rather than utilize it for gaining an advantage. Also, the scale of cyber-espionage—and hence the threat—has expanded due to the vast amount of data that can be exfiltrated remotely and at relatively low costs. For instance, the 2014 Sony hack resulted in approximately 100 terabytes of data being stolen, which, if stored on CD-ROMs, would require a stack of them reaching a height of 3,900 feet (Zetter 2014). This highlights the magnitude of the potential impact and the challenges posed by large-scale data breaches (Devanny et al. 2021).

Most scholars in the field of IR and international law consider espionage as "business as usual" because it is widely understood that all states conduct espionage and expect others to do the same (Brown 2016: 621). Some scholars have even put forth theories suggesting that espionage contributes to the stability of IR and creates a more balanced playing field (Bitton 2014). While states often have domestic legislation to restrict intelligence agencies from collecting information on their own citizens, international law remains largely silent on the matter (Fleck 2007). This means that cyber-activities constituting espionage are neither explicitly lawful nor unlawful under international law. However, a few scholars have examined this legal gap and have reached different conclusions regarding the legality of cyber-espionage (Buchan 2018; Pun 2018; Lubin 2020).

These debates point to the emergence of "norms" around cyber-espionage, even though they are not stable. The struggle between the United States and China to come to an agreement is an illustrative example (Segal 2013; Skinner 2014; Libicki 2017). The process began in 2009, but it took several years for tentative (bilateral) agreements to emerge in 2015. A major point of contention in these discussions was the distinction between political and economic espionage. Libicki argues that while cyber-espionage was considered acceptable state behavior when conducted to protect national security, it was deemed unacceptable if it was economically motivated, particularly if the stolen information was used to provide unfair trade advantages to corporations (Libicki 2017: 3).

BOX 5.3 FAMOUS CYBER-ESPIONAGE CASES

Moonlight Maze (1996–1998): Refers to a large-scale cyber-espionage campaign that took place in the latter half of the 1990s. It is considered as one of the earliest known instances of state-sponsored cyber-espionage targeting the United States. The campaign involved a series of coordinated cyber-attacks against various US government and military organizations, defense contractors, research institutions, and other entities, with the goal of stealing sensitive information. The attackers behind Moonlight Maze are believed to be a group of state-sponsored hackers originating from Russia (that later became known as Turla).

Titan Rain (2003–2007): Chinese military hackers infiltrated the US and UK government computers. Using various techniques, the hackers broke into the network computers and attempted to grab as much data as possible. Although the Chinese government's involvement in this operation was not confirmed, nations started to be warier about cyber-espionage attempts (Gülen 2023).

GhostNet (Discovered in 2009): This sizable surveillance network that organized an incursion into more than a thousand computers in 103 countries, was discovered by Canadian researchers in 2009. The network of the offices of the Dalai Lama was breached by perpetrators, who then utilized it to compromise other machines. The foreign ministers and embassies of Germany, Pakistan, India, Iran, South Korea, and Thailand were also attacked.

German Bundestag (2014–2015): This significant cyber-attack on the computer network of the German federal parliament, the Bundestag, was discovered in late April 2015 but was believed to have begun as early as May 2014. The attack resulted in a serious data breach, with access to a significant amount of sensitive information, including emails and documents. German authorities attributed the attack to the Russian state-sponsored hacking group known as APT28 or Fancy Bear.

SolarWinds (2020): The SolarWinds cyber-attack was a sophisticated supply chain attack in 2020. It involved malicious actors compromising the software build and update process of SolarWinds' Orion Platform, a widely used network management and monitoring tool. The cyber-attack had far-reaching consequences, as it compromised thousands of SolarWinds' customers, including major government agencies, corporations, and technology firms. Notable victims included several US government agencies, such as the Department of Homeland Security, the Department of State, and the Department of Defense, among others. While the initial focus was on the compromise of SolarWinds' software supply chain, the goal of the attackers appears to have been data exfiltration and espionage. The cyber-attack was attributed to an APT group believed to have ties to Russia, often referred to as APT29 or Cozy Bear. These threat actors are associated with Russian intelligence agencies.

Cyber-Influence Operations

The cyber-incidents during the 2016 US elections, attributed to the Russian government and its threat actors, marked a significant turning point in the cyber-security discourse. The hack-and-leak operations brought attention to the issue of strategic manipulation, also known as cyber-influence operations, as a threat to democratic processes (Whyte 2020). Indeed, some view the slow poison effects of influence operations as the most significant threats in the present era (Maschmeyer 2023). However, it is challenging to quantify the impact of cyber-influence operations beyond a general sense of unease.

The 2016 DNC hack shocked the community of cyber-security scholars not only due to its boldness but also because it exposed a substantial blind spot in the threat-debate. In hindsight, why did we not see the coming of cyber-influence operations as a key challenge? There are at least three factors that contributed to the lack of awareness. First, the rapid development of social media platforms with their algorithms and their role in shaping public opinion, which predestined them to be used in cyber-influence operations, caught many off guard (Karagiannopoulos 2021: 63). Second, the focus of cyber-security efforts has traditionally been on protecting against technical exploits, such as malware and hacking, rather

than on understanding the potential influence and psychological manipulation of public opinion. The rise of cyber-influence operations as a key
concern represented a shift in the threat landscape that required a broader
understanding of social engineering, information warfare, and manipulation techniques. Third, the issue of cyber-influence operations spans across
domains such as cyber-security, information warfare, and intelligence. Historically, these domains have operated in separate silos, with limited cross-
collaboration and sharing of information.

That said, the attempt by political actors to manipulate public opinion, both domestically and internationally, is not a recent phenomenon. As
early as the 1990s, when the US military began formulating its doctrine for
warfare in the information age, considerations on influencing the content
in the information environment to achieve "information dominance" were
prominent (Arquilla and Ronfeldt 1993). Initially, however, the concept
of information warfare was primarily associated with military measures
during times of crisis or war. Understanding the link to the world of intelligence is crucial, however; many intelligence organizations have responsibilities beyond espionage. These so-called covert operations can involve
a range of activities, including disinformation campaigns, propaganda
dissemination, and efforts to shape public opinion both domestically and
internationally (Rid 2020).

Liberal democracy operates on the principle that freedom of expression enables the dissemination of knowledge, the power of persuasion,
and the exercise of voluntary choice. However, cyber-influence operations
introduce the notion that information exchanges orchestrated by different
actors can be coercive and manipulative. This raises the tricky question of
how to maintain freedom while also effectively managing and countering
disinformation. This issue is particularly significant due to its implications
for fundamental values, trust, societal stability and, more broadly, our way
of life. We should not forget that a political response to a foreign influence
campaign can have very significant effects, like the concept of amplification
discussed in relation to terrorism debates (Schünemann 2022).

Cyber-Terrorism

Cyber-terrorism is a threat category that made an early appearance in the
history of cyber-security politics (Collin 1997). The US National Academy
of Sciences famously warned in 1991 that "tomorrow's terrorist may be
able to do more damage with a keyboard than with a bomb" (National
Academy of Sciences 1991: 1), with similar types of warnings in abundance afterward. It was estimated in 2012 that over 30,000 articles in the
press, magazines, and academic journals had been written on the subject

(Singer 2012). That said, the word is used in nonexpert contexts to refer to any kind of conflictual online exchange in a political context, without reflection on what should or should not be called cyber-terrorism.

Cyber-terrorism is not only an often-misused threat category but also one of the most contested. Part of the reason is the highly politicized debate around the definition of "terrorism" that carries over to the definition of cyber-terrorism. There is a consensus in terrorism studies that it is the intent or the purpose behind a terrorist act of violence that differentiates it from ordinary violence (Schmid 2011). Terrorism, then, "consists in the calculated production of a state of extreme fear of injury and death and, secondarily, the exploitation of this emotional reaction to manipulate behaviour" (Schmid and Jongman 2008: 20–21).

A definition distilled from a large number of legal texts reads as follows (Hardy and Williams 2014: 21): "Cyberterrorism means conduct involving computer or Internet technology that (1) is carried out for the purpose of advancing a political, religious or ideological cause; (2) is intended to intimidate a section of the public, or compel a government to do or abstain from doing any act; and (3) intentionally causes serious interference with an essential service, facility or system, if such interference is likely to endanger life or cause significant economic or environmental damage." While there are variations to be found in many definitions, there is some consensus that an act of cyber-terrorism only refers to a cyber-attack that causes sufficient destruction or disruption to generate fear or intimidate a society into an ideological goal. There is no consensus among scholars whether states can also be called terrorists, however, if terrorism is considered a method with fear as its intended effect (Crenshaw 2011), then the identity or ideology of the user of this methodology is secondary. That said, some scholars have insisted on linking cyber-terrorism to terrorist actors, to keep the definition as narrow and as concise as possible (Denning 2001; Jarvis et al. 2014; Gill et al. 2017).

According to these definitions, it is hard to find cyber-incidents that should be called cases of cyber-terrorism,[4] though most terrorist groups actively use cyberspace for propaganda, recruitment, fundraising, money-laundering, and for spreading misinformation. These activities are better subsumed under "terrorist use of the internet" (Box 5.4). Nonetheless, the perception of cyber-terrorism as a looming threat remains pervasive, and the question arises as to why terrorists have not fully embraced cyber-means to unleash havoc and destruction. Prior to a deeper understanding of how difficult destructive cyber-attacks are, there was a widespread belief that it was not a matter of if, but when such attacks would occur. Some circles believed that cyber-attacks would be attractive to terrorist groups due to lower financial costs compared to other types of attacks, the potential for anonymity, a wider range of available targets, and the ability to carry out attacks remotely (Weimann 2004).

It has since become evident that cyber-attacks are less well suited for terrorist goals than using low-tech means such as vehicles that are directed into crowds or attacks with a knife. While there may be low entry barriers for patriotic and activist hackers, the complexity and controlled impact of cyber-attacks require significant expertise and resources. Additionally, anonymity may not be desirable for terrorist actors as acts of terrorism are a "communication strategy." Cyber-attacks lack the theatricality of more conventional attacks unless it generates visible destruction, which is very hard to achieve unless we consider DDoS-attacks (which are visible but have no real impact; Conway 2014). In sum, creating malware that would generate severe effects is not simple, fast, and easy—which does not mean terrorist organizations could never do it, but means that the cost of creating them is higher than commonly assumed while their utility for terrorist purposes is low (Giacomello 2004).

BOX 5.4   OPERATION GLOWING SYMPHONY, 2016

Terrorist use of the internet was considered serious enough in the case of ISIS (the Islamic State of Iraq and Syria) for the USCYBERCOM to disrupt and counter ISIS's online presence and propaganda efforts, as well as to target their digital infrastructure and communications. According to released documents, the operations were considered the "most complex offensive cyberspace operation USCYBERCOM has conducted to date" (National Security Archives 2020). The materials that are available as a result of an FOIA request regarding the operation has increased our knowledge of how complex and challenging cyber-operations are (see also Temple-Raston 2019; Work 2019).

Cyber-War

Cyber-war is the second term that is heavily misused. Any major hacker intrusion with a political connotation is certain to be labeled as an instance of cyber-war by the media and some government officials alike, only exposing either a sensationalist intent or ignorance. There are at least three reasons why the term should be avoided altogether. First, most cyber-incidents happen during peacetime and not during a war or conflict. Second, while cyber-operations can have disruptive effects on critical infrastructure, economies, and national security, they fall short of the magnitude and intensity associated with conventional warfare. Third, a point that is discussed in more detail in Chapter 8, cyber-tools are not well suited if you need to create a targeted or large-scale, lasting, destructive effect at a precise point in time. Hence, their utility for most forms of warfare is limited.

If the term "cyber-war" is to be used anyway, it is helpful to make a distinction between two types: strategic cyber-war and operational cyber-war, as suggested by Martin Libicki (2009: 117). Strategic cyber-war refers to hypothetical conflicts where cyber-tools are employed as the primary or even standalone means of force. The concept of an "Electronic Pearl Harbor" falls into this category, depicting a scenario of a massive and unexpected cyber-attack on a nation's critical infrastructure that would draw the attacked state into a conflict with the attacking state. On the other hand, operational cyber-war refers to a whole range of CNOs in support of physical military operations. These operations are considered supportive in nature, as they occur within the context of conflicts that are primarily decided by traditional kinetic military actions.

According to the provided definitions, it is accurate to say that we have not yet experienced an instance of strategic cyber-war, and it is highly unlikely that we ever will. However, operational cyber-war, also called cyber-in-war, has become more prevalent over the years, reflecting the growing computerization of armed forces. An example can be seen in NATO's 1999 intervention against Yugoslavia. The widespread use of the internet for hacktivist activities by non-state actors during this conflict led to descriptions such as the "first war fought in cyberspace" or the "first war on the Internet." NATO and the United States tested their emergent InfOps doctrine. The US armed forces reportedly thought about hacking Slobodan Milosevic's bank accounts but refrained from it due to legal concerns (Dunn 2002: 151). Another often-cited example is the DDoS-attacks at the beginning of the Russian military campaign against Georgia in 2008 (Box 5.5).

In any conflict nowadays and in the future, cyberspace will play a role in the activities of state and non-state actors, way beyond the directly involved parties to the conflict. However, these activities involving cyberspace will be just one aspect of these conflicts, and most likely not the most important ones, rather than the sole focus. In conflicts where the success or failure of major participants is heavily reliant on computerized key activities throughout the course of events, we might consider using the term "cyber(ed) conflicts" (Demchak 2018). As the war in Ukraine shows, understanding the manifold uses and consequences of "cyber-in-war" at the strategic, operational, and tactical levels as well as understanding the role of private actors, or the impact of aggressive cyber-activities by non-state actors on international norms, will be an important task for future research.

> ## BOX 5.5 "CYBER-WAR" IN GEORGIA, 2008
>
> The Georgian attacks in 2008 started with the defacement campaign of the president's Saakashvili website, as well as with the DDoS-attacks on other government ministries' websites three weeks before the actual military campaign. Another wave of attacks, which included defacement of websites, was launched simultaneously with the invasion of Russian combat troops, with the aim to impair Georgian communications with the outside world and probably to spread chaos and fear.
>
> Although the attackers were predominantly anonymous civilians and some criminals from the notorious Russian Business Network, there was also an involvement of servers of the state-controlled telecommunications companies that helped to reroute the Georgian Internet traffic (Tiirmaa-Klaar et al. 2013: 21). How the synchronization occurred with military advances remains unclear. The attacks seem to have served their purpose by creating chaos and uncertainty in the Georgian government and disrupting the ability to communicate their message to the world, at least temporarily. Calling these attacks "cyber-war" does not describe their character, however.

Summary and Key Points

This chapter has provided an exploration of key cyber-threat categories. It is evident that the evolution of cyber-threats has been marked by a significant increase in the capabilities to exploit cyberspace for various threat-related activities. Non-state actors engaged in cyber-crime have grown more organized, specialized, and skilled, driven by the profitability of illicit activities. Similarly, state actors have invested in both offensive and defensive cyber-capabilities, although uncertainties persist regarding their true abilities and intentions. This trend, characterized as "more, better, worse," has been facilitated by technological advancements and the expanded digital landscape.

Categorizing cyber-incidents involves a sense-making process that is highly political due to the contested nature of identifying "markers" (or discursive anchors) and how they are perceived. Unlike terrorism, cyber-incidents do not generate media images that serve as performative elements aligned with the objectives of terrorism. That is why narratives play a crucial role in structuring information and shaping experiences, serving as integral components of cognitive sense-making processes (Homolar and Rodríguez-Merino 2019: 562). This chapter explored elements of the discursive anchors involved in the sense-making process. These anchors encompass factors such as the actors involved, their intent, the type of target, and the context in which the events unfold. In the case of conventional terrorism, it requires political actors to recognize and employ these markers. However, in the realm of cyber-incidents, the dynamics are more complex, involving a mix of political agents, private entities, and various hybrid arrangements that blur the boundaries between them. Understanding the extent of political agency and the interplay with private actors in the context of cyber-incidents is a critical aspect to be explored in the future.

The academic debate surrounding cyber-threat categories and their usefulness provides valuable insights into political practices, societal circumstances, and the establishment of laws and behavioral norms during specific periods. Exploring the different interpretations of similar incidents by various societal groups unveils intriguing research opportunities, inviting questions such as "who shapes this knowledge?" and "who holds the power to define?" Moreover, changes within these categories reflect a process of learning and evolving practices on both offensive and defensive fronts.

Notes

1. The question of necessary effects is often treated as a theoretical rather than an empirical question in the cyber-threats' literature.
2. Under the first, we find prohibited/illegal content such as child porn, as well as online scams, online intellectual property infringement, internet fraud, online harassment, and cyberstalking. They are excluded here because they do not appear in national security considerations.
3. The first figure is from Cybersecurity Ventures, the second from Statistica. com (accessed in March 2023) https://cybersecurityventures.com/cybercrime-damages-6-trillion-by-2021/, and www.statista.com/outlook/tmo/cybersecurity/worldwide#cost.
    Crime data has to be taken with a grain of salt because there is no commonly accepted way to measure its impact.
4. The issue with the label "terrorism" is apparent when we consider the activities of the Belarusian Cyber Partisans, a hacktivist collective that emerged in September 2020. This group is targeting the Belarusian government and is part of the Belarusian opposition movement. Lukashenko calls them "terrorists" whereas Western observers would consider this activism (Schrijver and Ducheine 2023).

References

Ablon, L., Libicki, M.C. and Golay, A.A. (2014). *Markets for Cybercrime Tools and Stolen Data: Hackers' Bazaar*. RAND Corporation.

Alperovitch, D. (2011). *Revealed: Operation Shady RAT: An Investigation of Targeted Intrusions into More Than 70 Global Companies, Governments, and*

Non-Profit Organizations During the Last Five Years. McAfee White Paper. Available at: https://icscsi.org/library/Documents/Cyber_Events/McAfee%20-%20Operation%20Shady%20RAT.pdf

Anderson, R., Barton, C., Böhme, R., Clayton, R., van Eeten, M.J.G., Levi, M., Moore, T. and Savage, S. (2013). Measuring the Cost of Cybercrime. In: Böhme, R. (ed.) *The Economics of Information Security and Privacy.* Springer, pp. 265–300.

Arquilla, J. and Ronfeldt, D.F. (1993). Cyberwar Is Coming! *Comparative Strategy* 12(2): 141–165.

Baezner, M. (2018). Hotspot Analysis: Regional Rivalry Between India-Pakistan: Tit-For-Tat in Cyberspace. CSS Cyber Defense Project. *Center for Security Studies*, August. Available at: https://css.ethz.ch/content/dam/ethz/special-interest/gess/cis/center-for-securities-studies/pdfs/Cyber-Reports-2018-04.pdf

Baezner, M. and Cordey, S. (2022). Influence Operations and Other Conflict Trends. In: Dunn Cavelty, M. and Wenger, A. (eds.) *Cyber Security Politics: Socio-Technological Transformations and Political Fragmentation.* Routledge, pp. 17–31.

Bitton, R. (2014). The Legitimacy of Spying Among Nations. *American University International Law Review* 29(5): 1009–1070.

Brenner, S.W. (2002). Organized Cybercrime? How Cyberspace May Affect the Structure of Criminal Relationships. *North Carolina Journal of Law & Technology* 4(1): 1–50.

Brown, G. (2016). Spying and Fighting in Cyberspace: What Is Which? *Journal of National Security Law & Policy* 8(3): 621–635.

Buchan, R. (2018). *Cyber Espionage and International Law.* Hart.

Buchan, R. (2019). Taking Care of Business: Industrial Espionage and International Law. *The Brown Journal of World Affairs* 26(1): 143–160.

Coleman, G. (2012). *Coding Freedom: The Ethics and Aesthetics of Hacking.* Princeton University Press.

Collin, B. (1997). Future of Cyberterrorism: Physical and Virtual Worlds Converge. *Crime and Justice International* 13(2): 15–18.

Conway, M. (2003). Hackers as Terrorists? Why It Doesn't Compute. *Computer Fraud & Security* 12: 10–13.

Conway, M. (2014). Reality Check: Assessing the (Un)Likelihood of Cyberterrorism. In: Chen, T., Jarvis, L. and Macdonald, S. (eds.) *Cyberterrorism: Understanding, Assessment and Response.* Springer, pp. 103–121.

Crenshaw, M. (2011). *Explaining Terrorism, Causes, Processes and Consequences.* Routledge.

Cristiano, F. (2019). Deterritorializing Cyber Security and Warfare in Palestine: Hackers, Sovereignty, and the National Cyberspace as Normative. *Cyber Orient* 13(1): 28–42.

Demchak, C. (2018). Three Futures for a Post-Western Cybered World. *Military Cyber Affairs* 3(1). https://doi.org/10.5038/2378-0789.3.1.1044

Denning, D. (2001). Activism, Hacktivism, and Cyberterrorism: The Internet as a Tool for Influencing Foreign Policy. In: Arquilla, J. and Ronfeldt, D.F. (eds.) *Networks and Netwars: The Future of Terror, Crime, and Militancy.* RAND Corporation, pp. 239–288.

Devanny, J., Martin, C. and Stevens, T. (2021). On the Strategic Consequences of Digital Espionage. *Journal of Cyber-Policy* 6(3): 429–450.

Dunn, M. (2002). *Information Age Conflicts: A Study on the Information Revolution and a Changing Operating Environment*. Zürcher Beiträge zur Sicherheitspolitik und Konfliktforschung, No. 64. Center for Security Studies.

Dunn Cavelty, M. and Jaeger, M.D. (2015). (In)Visible Ghosts in the Machine and the Powers that Bind: The Relational Securitization of Anonymous. *International Political Sociology* 9(2): 176–194.

FBI (2023). FBI Identifies Lazarus Group Cyber Actors as Responsible for Theft of $41 Million from Stake.com. *FBI National Press Office*, September 6. Available at: www.fbi.gov/news/press-releases/fbi-identifies-lazarus-group-cyber-actors-as-responsible-for-theft-of-41-million-from-stakecom

Fischerkeller, M.P. and Harknett, R.J. (2019). Persistent Engagement, Agreed Competition, and Cyberspace Interaction Dynamics and Escalation. *The Cyber Defense Review*, Special Edition, pp. 267–287. Available at: https://cyberdefensereview.army.mil/Portals/6/CDR-SE_S5-P3-Fischerkeller.pdf

Fleck, D. (2007). Individual and State Responsibility for Intelligence Gathering. *Michigan Journal of International Law* 28(3): 687–709.

Gerbaudo, P. (2017). From Cyber-Autonomism to Cyber-Populism: An Ideological Analysis of the Evolution of Digital Activism. *Triple C: Communication, Capitalism & Critique* 15(2): 477–489.

Giacomello, G. (2004). Bangs for the Buck: A Cost-Benefit Analysis of Cyberterrorism. *Studies in Conflict & Terrorism* 27(5): 387–408.

Gill, P., Corner, E., Conway, M., Thornton, A., Bloom, M. and Horgan, J. (2017). Terrorist Use of the Internet by the Numbers. *Criminology & Public Policy* 16(1): 99–117.

Grabosky, P. (2001). Virtual Criminality: Old Wine in New Bottles? *Social & Legal Studies* 10(2): 243–249.

Grabosky, P. (2013). Organised Crime and the Internet. *The RUSI Journal* 158(5): 18–25.

Guerrero-Saade, J.A. and Moriuchi, P. (2018). *North Korea Targeted South Korean Cryptocurrency Users and Exchange in Late 2017 Campaign*, No. CTA-2018-0116. Cyber Threat Analysis. Recorded Future.

Gülen, K. (2023). Cyber Espionage Remains a Real Threat to Both Governments and Businesses. *Dataconomy*, August 25. Available at: https://dataconomy.com/2022/11/cyber-espionage-examples-types-tactics/

Handler, S. (2022). *The Cyber Strategy and Operations of Hamas: Green Flags and Green Hats*. The Atlantic Council. Cyber Statecraft Initiative. Available at: www.atlanticcouncil.org/wp-content/uploads/2022/11/The-Cyber-Strategy-and-Operations-of-Hamas.pdf

Hardy, K. and Williams, G. (2014). What Is 'Cyberterrorism'? Computer and Internet Technology in Legal Definitions of Terrorism. In: Chen, T., Jarvis, L. and Macdonald, S. (eds.) *Cyberterrorism: Understanding, Assessment and Response*. Springer, pp. 1–24.

Hebdige, D. (2002). *Subculture: The Meaning of Style*. Routledge.

Homolar, A. and Rodríguez-Merino, P. (2019). Making Sense of Terrorism: A Narrative Approach to the Study of Violent Events. *Critical Studies on Terrorism* 12(4): 561–581.

Jarvis, L., Macdonald, S. and Nouri, L. (2014). The Cyberterrorism Threat: Findings From a Survey of Researchers. *Studies in Conflict & Terrorism* 37(1): 68–90.

Jordan, T. and Taylor, P.A. (2004). *Hacktivism and Cyberwars: Rebels With a Cause?* Routledge.

Kahn, H. (1965). *On Escalation: Metaphors and Scenarios.* Praeger.

Karagiannopoulos, V. (2018). *Living With Hacktivism: From Conflict to Symbiosis.* Palgrave Macmillan.

Karagiannopoulos, V. (2021). A Short History of Hacktivism: Its Past and Present and What Can We Learn From It. In: Owen, T. and Marshall, J. (eds.) *Rethinking Cybercrime: Critical Debates.* Palgrave Macmillan, pp. 63–86.

Koops, B.-J. (2010). The Internet and its Opportunities for Cybercrime. In: Herzog-Evans, M. (ed.) *Transnational Criminology Manual*, Vol. 1. WLP, pp. 735–754.

Kraemer-Mbula, E., Tang, P. and Rush, H. (2013). The Cybercrime Ecosystem: Online Innovation in The Shadows? *Technological Forecasting and Social Change* 80(3): 541–555.

Lavorgna, A. and Antonomoulos, G.A. (2022). Criminal Markets and Networks in Cyberspace. *Trends in Organized Crime* 25(2): 145–150.

Lawson, S. (2013). Beyond Cyber-Doom: Assessing the Limits of Hypothetical Scenarios in the Framing of Cyber-Threats. *Journal of Information Technology & Politics* 10(1): 86–103.

Lewis, J.A. (2002). *Assessing the Risks of Cyber-terrorism, Cyber War and Other Cyber Threats.* Center for Strategic and International Studies.

Libicki, M. (2009). *Cyberdeterrence and Cyberwar.* RAND Corporation.

Libicki, M. (2017). The Coming of Cyber Espionage Norms. In: Rõigas, H., Jakschis, R., Lindström, L. and Minárik, T. (eds.) *2017 9th International Conference on Cyber Conflict: Defending the Core.* NATO CCD COE Publications, pp. 1–17.

Lubin, A. (2020). The Liberty to Spy. *Harvard International Law Journal* 61(1): 185–243.

Makarenko, T. (2004). The Crime—Terror Continuum: Tracing the Interplay Between Transnational Organised Crime and Terrorism. *Global Crime* 6(1): 129–145.

Maschmeyer, L. (2023). Subversion, Cyber Operations, and Reverse Structural Power in World Politics. *European Journal of International Relations* 29(1): 79–103.

McCusker, R. (2006). Transnational Organised Cyber Crime: Distinguishing Threat From Reality. *Crime Law and Social Change* 46(4): 257–273.

Mihalache, A. (2002). The Cyber Space-Time Continuum: Meaning and Metaphor. *The Information Society* 18(4): 293–301.

Milan, S. (2015). Hacktivism as a Radical Media Practice. In: Atton, C. (ed.) *The Routledge Companion to Alternative and Community Media.* Routledge, pp. 550–560.

Morgan, F.E., Mueller, K.P., Medeiros, E.S., Pollpeter, K.L. and Cliff, R. (2008). *Dangerous Thresholds: Managing Escalation in the 21st Century.* RAND Corporation.

National Academy of Sciences (1991). *Computers at Risk: Safe Computing in the Information Age.* National Academy Press.

National Security Archives (2020). *USCYBERCOM After Action Assessments of Operation GLOWING SYMPHONY*. Available at: https://nsarchive.gwu.edu/briefing-book/cyber-vault/2020-01-21/uscybercom-after-action-assessments-operation-glowing-symphony

Ottis, R. (2008). Analysis of the 2007 Cyber Attacks against Estonia from the Information Warfare Perspective. In: *Proceedings of the 7th European Conference on Information Warfare and Security*, Plymouth. Academic Publishing Limited, pp. 163–168.

Pun, D. (2018). Rethinking Espionage in the Modern Era. *Chicago Journal of International Law* 18(1): 353–393.

Rid, T. (2020). *Active Measures: The Secret History of Disinformation and Political Warfare*. Farrar, Straus and Giroux.

Ryan, M. (2021). *Ransomware Revolution: The Rise of a Prodigious Cyber Threat*. Springer.

Schmid, A.P. (2011). The Definition of Terrorism. In: Schmid, A.P. (ed.) *The Routledge Handbook of Terrorism Research*. Routledge, pp. 39–98.

Schmid, A.P. and Jongman, A. (2008). *Political Terrorism* (3rd ed.). Transaction Books.

Schneier, B. (2007). *Schneier on Security: Cyberwar*. Available at: www.schneier.com/blog/archives/2007/06/cyberwar.html

Schrijver, P. and Ducheine, P. (2023). Cyber-Enabled Influence Operations: The Case of the Belarusian Cyber Partisans. *Militaire Spectator* 192(6). Available at: https://militairespectator.nl/sites/default/files/bestanden/artikelen/militaire_spectator_6_2023_schrijver.pdf

Schünemann, W. (2022). A Threat to Democracies? An Overview of Theoretical Approaches and Empirical Measurements for Studying the Effects of Disinformation. In: Dunn Cavelty, M. and Wenger, A. (eds.) *Cyber Security Politics: Socio-Technological Transformations and Political Fragmentation*. Routledge, pp. 32–47.

Segal, A. (2013). The Code Not Taken: China, the United States, and the Future of Cyber Espionage. *Bulletin of the Atomic Scientists* 69(5): 38–45.

Shandler, R. and Gomez, M.A. (2022). The Hidden Threat of Cyber-Attacks— Undermining Public Confidence in Government. *Journal of Information Technology & Politics* 20(4): 359–374.

Sharevski, F. and Kessel, B. (2023). Fight Fire with Fire: Hacktivists' Take on Social Media Misinformation. *arXiv preprint*. https://arxiv.org/abs/2302.07788

Singer, P. (2012). The Cyber Terror Bogeyman. *Brookings Commentary*. Available at: www.brookings.edu/articles/the-cyber-terror-bogeyman/

Skinner, C.P. (2014). An International Law Response to Economic Cyber Espionage. *Connecticut Law Review* 46(2014): 1165–1207.

Soesanto, S. (2022). *The IT Army of Ukraine: Structure, Tasking, and Ecosystem*. Cyberdefense Report. Center for Security Studies. Available at: https://css.ethz.ch/content/dam/ethz/special-interest/gess/cis/center-for-securities-studies/pdfs/Cyber-Reports-2022–06-IT-Army-of-Ukraine.pdf

Tabansky, L. (2012). Cybercrime: A National Security Issue? *Military and Strategic Affairs* 4(3): 117–135.

Temple-Raston, D. (2019). How the U.S. Hacked ISIS. *NPR*, September 26. Available at: www.npr.org/2019/09/26/763545811/how-the-u-s-hacked-isis

Tiirmaa-Klaar, H., Gassen, J., Gerhards-Padilla, E. and Martini, P. (2013). *Botnets*. Springer Briefs in Cybersecurity. Springer.

Traynor, I. (2007). Russia Accused of Unleashing Cyberwar to Disable Estonia. *The Guardian*, May 17. Available at: www.theguardian.com/world/2007/may/17/topstories3.russia

Volz, D. and Finkle, J. (2017). North Korea Links to 'WannaCry' Ransomware Attacks Suspected. *The Wire*, May16. Available at: https://staging.thewire.in/tech/north-korea-wannacry-ransomware-link

Wall, D.S. (2007). *Cybercrime: The Transformation of Crime in the Information Age*. Polity.

Weimann, G. (2004). *Cyberterrorism: How Real Is the Threat?* United States Institute of Peace Special Report, No 119. Available at: www.usip.org/sites/default/files/sr119.pdf

Whyte, C. (2020). Cyber Conflict or Democracy "Hacked"? How Cyber Operations Enhance Information Warfare. *Journal of Cybersecurity* 6(1): tyaa013.

Wilson, C. (2003). *Computer Attack and Cyber-Terrorism: Vulnerabilities and Policy Issues for Congress*, Congressional Research Report for Congress, RL32114, 17 October.

Work, J.D. (2019). The American Way of Cyber Warfare and the Case of ISIS. *New Atlanticist*, September 17. Available at: www.atlanticcouncil.org/blogs/new-atlanticist/the-american-way-of-cyber-warfare-and-the-case-of-isis/

Yen, A.C. (2003). Western Frontier or Feudal Society? Metaphors and Perceptions of Cyberspace. *Berkeley Technology Law* 17(4): 1207–1264.

Zetter, K. (2014). Sony Got Hacked Hard: What We Know and Don't Know So Far. *Wired*, December 3. Available at: www.wired.com/2014/12/sony-hack-what-we-know

6

INTERNATIONAL CYBER-SECURITY NORMS, PRACTICES, AND STRATEGY

In contrast to the 1990s, the cyber-security debate changed dramatically in the period after 2010. States, especially the already powerful ones, emerged as the biggest challengers to international stability, given their investment into offensive capabilities paired with their willingness to use cyber-means to reach political goals at the detriment of others. The growing importance of national security considerations related to the digital realm, with a sobering emphasis on geopolitical rivalries, ended an era of widespread "cyber-utopia" and led to a shift from laissez-faire politics toward calls for more state-centric forms of cyberspace governance (Mueller 2010; Dunn Cavelty 2015).

In the late 1990s, diplomatic endeavors were initiated with a primary focus on addressing the threat of cyber-warfare and preventing catastrophic "doom" scenarios. Their evolution and what they signify for international politics are discussed in the first subchapter. However, as cyberspace increasingly became a platform for unfriendly actions that operated below the threshold of traditional warfare, a significant portion of these activities occurred outside the purview of emerging and existing norms. The primary reason for this was that such activities were conducted during peacetime and in secrecy, predominantly by intelligence entities. Intelligence operations lack comprehensive regulation under international law. The latter part of this chapter delves into nondiplomatic state practices geared toward influencing adversary behavior, particularly focusing on the United States' strategic shift from deterrence to what it terms "persistent engagement."

DOI: 10.4324/9781003497080-6

Establishing Norms of Good Behavior Through Diplomatic Practices

In 2014, Joseph Nye published a policy paper introducing the concept of a "regime complex" to describe the existing ecosystem for managing global cyber-activities (Nye 2014). Using the fundamental principles of regime theory as developed by Krasner (1983), he characterized this complex as a diverse amalgamation of norms, institutions, and procedures, varying in scale and formality (Nye 2014: 7). This concept of the "regime complex" is relevant because it highlights the presence of an intricate network of overlapping international institutions and agreements that interact to govern state action in cyberspace, crisscrossing a large plethora of topics from the technical aspects of the internet, such as the domain name system (DNS) and technical standards, to the efforts that encompass security, human rights, and development (see also Pawlak 2019).

It is impossible to do justice to the entirety of this regime complex in just one chapter. Hence, I will focus mainly on the norms and processes at the level of the UN and particularly on its specialized organ known as the "First Committee." The primary aim of the chapter is to embed the diplomatic processes within the larger political contexts in which they happen. The First Committee is responsible for addressing disarmament, global challenges, and threats to peace that impact the international community, while actively seeking solutions to enhance the international security framework. Since it is a unique platform where nation-states convene and engage in discussions pertaining to international security, it enables the identification of significant areas of contention.

In international affairs, norms are typically defined as collective expectations regarding the appropriate conduct of actors (Finnemore 2017). Hence, even more important than understanding norms construction is the question whether or to what extent these norms seem to influence state behavior. This is the focus of the second subchapter.

High-Level Diplomatic Processes and Norms of "Good" Behavior

In 1998, the Russian Federation presented a Resolution to the UN General Assembly's First Committee on Disarmament and International Security due to concerns regarding the US military's emphasis on information dominance and warfare (Kavanagh et al. 2014: 11). The initial version of the Resolution suggested creating an "inventory of information technologies" to prevent their military application, which could be comparable to the use of weapons of mass destruction (Tikk-Ringas 2012: 3–4). After revisions, Resolution A/C.1/53/L.17/Rev.1 urged Member States to address information security issues, define unauthorized interference or misuse of information and telecommunications systems and resources, and develop international principles to enhance the security of global information and telecommunications systems. The General Assembly adopted it in January 1999 (A/RES/53/70), expressing concerns that these technologies and methods might be used in ways contradictory to the goals of international stability and security, potentially endangering the security of nations (United Nations General Assembly 1999).

The Resolution led to the establishment of the "UN Group of Government Experts (GGE) on Developments in the Field of Information and Communications Technologies in the Context of International Security," in short, UNGGE. Like other groups of a similar nature, the UNGGE was initially set up as a one-off forum. However, given the increasing politicization and militarization of the cyber-realm, it became a process with six iterations altogether to date and a spin-off process that is in its second round (The Open-Ended Working Group (OEWG), see further on). That makes it the longest-running ad hoc group of its kind within the UN system.

As the iterations progressed, there was a growing interest among the community of states. In the case of the fifth UN Group of Governmental Experts, "more than 40 countries competed for the available 25 seats, many of them newcomers to the process" (Tikk and Kerttunen 2017: 14). There was also an increasing professionalization of dedicated "cyber-diplomats" in some countries (Barrinha and Renard 2017), such as Michele Markoff from the United States and Andrey Krutskikh from Russia. The Permanent Five (China, France, Russia, the United Kingdom, and the United States) and Germany have been part of all UNGGEs. Estonia, Belarus, Brazil, and India were included four times. Most other States have participated in only one or two UNGGEs (see Table 6.1). Four sessions concluded with a consensus report, but two failed to reach consensus for reasons we will look at in more detail below.

The first UNGGE that commenced its work in 2004 failed to reach a consensus report. As noted by the Chair of the Group, "the members of

TABLE 6.1 Summary of UNGGEs

Year	2004–2005	2009–2010	2012–2013	2014–2015	2016–2017	2019–2021
Countries involved	15[1] Chair: Russia	15[2] Chair: Russia	15[3] Chair: Australia	20[4] Chair: Brazil	25[5] Chair: Germany	25[6] Chair: Brazil
Result	No consensus	Consensus	Consensus *International Law applies	Consensus *11 Norms	No consensus	Consensus

the GGE spoke different languages with respect to essential issues" (Krutskikh, quoted in Tikk-Ringas 2012: 7). Right from the outset, there were fundamental and enduring differences in how Russia, the United States, and other liberal democracies defined the scope of the issue (Giles 2012). In the UN processes, autocratic states emphasize technology *and* content under the label "information security," whereas liberal democracies wanted to keep the discussion focused on hacking technical systems only, using the label "cyber-security" (Giles and Hagestad 2013).

The fundamental differences come down to how permissible the relationship between cyberspace and individual freedom is seen to be. The Western perspective advocates for the free flow of information and knowledge, freedom of expression, protection of individual liberties, and cultural diversity as vital components of a democratic society (OECD 2011). Clashing with their tendency to prioritize the protection of their own "regime security" through information control, autocratic states perceive the rise of the internet governed by Western-defined mechanisms as a challenge, if not a threat to their sovereignty. Cyberspace is viewed as a platform for the dissemination of Western ideas and values that (deliberately) challenge and undermine their existing regimes (Zhang 2019). Hence, autocratic states seek greater government control over cyberspace and often also aim for some degree of decoupling from the "global" domain.

The second UNGGE convened after the cyber-incidents in Estonia (2007) and Georgia (2008), which caused a considerable international stir. In contrast to 2004, this guaranteed considerably more interest in the security dimensions of cyberspace. The process resulted in a short consensus report that recommended further dialogue, confidence building, stability, and risk reduction measures to address the implications of state use of ICTs, with a particular focus on critical infrastructures (United Nations General Assembly 2010). This basic agreement made it possible for the next GGE, convening post Stuxnet, to produce what was considered a milestone: its 2013 consensus report contained a strong affirmation of the application to existing international law to cybersecurity matters (United Nations General Assembly 2013). It stated that "international law, particularly the UN Charter, is applicable and essential" to the issue of cyber-security (para. 19). It also confirmed the applicability of "state sovereignty and the international norms and principles that flow from sovereignty" (para. 20) and hinted at the necessity for "respect for human rights and fundamental freedoms as set forth in the Universal Declaration of Human Rights and other international instruments" (para. 21).

The 2013 report was widely regarded as a success for Western governments with shared views. These governments consistently stressed that existing international law, such as the UN Charter and International

Humanitarian Law (IHL), already provided adequate guidance for state conduct during times of conflict, regardless of whether it occurred in the cyber-domain or elsewhere. Consequently, they argued against the need for additional treaties or frameworks in contrast to China and Russia. Both of these states advocate for *lex specialis*, proposing a "treaty" to ban cyber weapons, highlighting their concerns about Western-dominated international law. It is worth noting, however, that the 2013 report also represented a significant achievement for China and Russia, as it recognized the principle of sovereignty's relevance, a matter of particular importance to them (Tiirma-Klaar 2021).

The next UNGEE consensus report in 2015 managed to score the process's biggest achievement to date, by agreeing on 11 "general non-binding, voluntary norms, rules and principles for responsible behaviour of states" during peacetime (United Nations General Assembly 2015a: Section III). Eight are actions that states want to encourage, while three (norms numbers 3, 6, and 11) involve actions that countries should avoid:

1. Interstate cooperation on security
2. Consider all relevant information
3. Prevent misuse of ICTs in your territory
4. Cooperate to stop crime and terrorism
5. Respect human rights and privacy
6. Do not damage critical infrastructures
7. Protect critical infrastructure
8. Respond to requests for assistance
9. Ensure supply chain security
10. Report ICT vulnerabilities
11. Do no harm to emergency response teams

The possibility of consensus in the 2015 report was, to a large degree, facilitated by the avoidance of certain keywords and contentious concepts (Väljataga 2017). Although the report referred to "the principles of humanity, necessity, proportionality and distinction" (para. 28d), it notably did not mention IHL, from which these principles derive. The omission of IHL was an acknowledgment of China's stance that acknowledging *jus in bello* would legitimize the military use of cyberspace (Huang and Ying 2021; Tiirma-Klaar 2021: 20). Alas, IHL became the major stumbling block for the subsequent UN Group of Governmental Experts, which failed to produce a report in 2017. The opposition of Russia, China, and Cuba is primarily centered around the explicit application of international humanitarian law to cyber-operations (cf. United Nations General Assembly 2015b).

The breakdown of the norms process was met with widespread disappointment at the time, leading observers to describe it as the "death of the norms process" (Grigsby 2017) or "the end of an era" (Korzak 2017). The failure to build on the previous GGE's success was particularly disheartening as it unfolded amidst deteriorating geopolitical relationships among major powers. In response to this challenging environment and, some would say, vested interests, various private sector actors took the initiative to establish their own norms initiatives in 2017 and 2018. Notable efforts included Microsoft's Digital Geneva Convention (Smith 2017), Siemens' Digital Charter of Trust,[7] Telefonica's Digital Manifesto (Telefónica 2018), and Kaspersky's Global Transparency Initiative.[8] Although these initiatives garnered significant attention initially, they ultimately seemed to have had a limited impact on the behavior of states overall (Hurel and Lobato 2018; Gorwa and Peez 2020; Eggenschwiler 2022).

Contrary to initial concerns, however, high-level norms processes did not end. In 2021, two consensus reports were released, one by the sixth UN Group of Governmental Experts (United Nations General Assembly 2021a) and another by the newly established OEWG, which was initiated by Russia and open to all member states, running concurrently with the sixth GGE (Lauber and Eberli 2021). Though the split of the process caused concern, collectively, the consensus reports establish a normative framework with four pillars: the 11 norms, international law, confidence-building measures, and cyber capacity building (OEWG 2021: para. 7). While the future of the UNGGE remains uncertain at the time of writing, the OEWG was renewed for the period of 2021–2025 (A/RES/75/240) (cf. Paulus 2022). Furthermore, UN member states approved what is called a Programme of Action (PoA), a "permanent, action-oriented mechanism" to continue the discussion around responsible state behavior after the OEWG concludes in 2025 (United Nations General Assembly 2023).

In assessing the 2017 setback, it seems that the expectations following the 2015 success were simply too high. It is unrealistic to expect diplomatic processes to resolve major political issues and tensions, as they are inherently part of a broader power play (Henriksen 2016). The perceived "failure" in 2017 merely confirmed the well-known fact that significant differences of opinion exist among states regarding the application of international law (Tikk and Kerttunen 2017: 15). The GGE never had the mandate to create or dismiss existing international law, and no GGE report can alter the rights or obligations that already exist for states. Therefore, the GGE and its outcomes should be seen as reflections of the larger question of world order, like other international processes that bear relevance to cyber-governance.

Taking a broader perspective is essential for a comprehensive understanding of the ongoing dynamics in this field. While the Group of Governmental Experts (GGE) is widely regarded as a crucial process for negotiating norms, solely concentrating on activities within the First Committee of the UN General Assembly is limited in two significant ways. First, there are additional parallel activities taking place within the UN that hold importance and should be understood within their respective contexts. Second, norms are also developed and expressed through regional organizations and other avenues. Many of these efforts are driven by power dynamics and are rooted in the perception that the United States has utilized its technological superiority to establish network rules in its own favor (Zhang 2019).

A group of states, led by China and Russia, has been promoting a more state-centric approach to cyberspace since the late 1990s through various avenues (Raymond and Sherman 2024). One noteworthy effort is the "Code of Conduct on Information Security" that has been on the table since 1998 and was repeated by China and Russia in 2011, and again by the members of the Shanghai Cooperation Organisation in 2015 (McKune and Ahmed 2018).[9] The Code, which has been rejected by liberal democracies because it is seen as an attack against existing International Law and especially, human rights, emphasizes that a "multilateral," which means intergovernmental, system for Internet governance should be developed in contrast to the long-standing "multistakeholder" approach. Against the backdrop of an accelerating militarization of cyberspace, the defensive notion of "cyber-sovereignty"—one of the four principles articulated by Xi Jinping in 2017 in the "International Strategy of Cooperation on Cyberspace"—is attractive to many states far beyond China (Chen and Yang 2022; Gao 2022).

The desire to position states as the primary powers in cyberspace governance is further demonstrated by China's attempts to strengthen the International Telecommunication Union's (ITU's) role in Internet governance. The ITU was established on the premise that nation-states are the central actors in governance. Its mandate includes the development of technical standards that facilitate network and technology interconnection, as well as efforts to enhance global digital access. From 2014 to 2022, the ITU's Secretary-General position was held by Houlin Zhao, a Chinese national. During this period, the significance of controlling standard-setting processes gained attention, especially the ability to establish global standards for future technologies, such as 5G (Rühlig 2023). The vision of China's internet is "decentralized"—as in less dependent on Western mechanisms—and controllable top-down by national bodies (Hoffmann et al. 2020; Weyrauch and Winzen 2020). China's techno-politics is guided by a long-term strategy, encompassing two key aspects: First, it entails the development of its own technological capabilities to achieve self-reliance. Second, it involves building international consensus on the crucial question of "who will shape the rules, norms, and values of the internet" (Attrill and Fritz 2021: 3).

Cyber-norms also emerge and become institutionalized in various international forums, including regional ones, further contributing to ongoing contestation. For instance, discussions on cyber-norms have taken place within the African Union, the Association of Southeast Asian Nations (ASEAN), and the Shanghai Cooperation Organisation, among others (for a comprehensive but dated overview, refer to Kavanagh et al. 2014; cf. Weekes and Tikk-Ringas 2013; Tran Dai and Gomez 2018). Since 2014, China has organized its own event known as the "World Internet Conference" in Wuzhen. This initiative emerged partly in response to prominent multistakeholder meetings and conferences dominated by Western actors and involving private entities and civil society.[10] China's efforts reflect its desire to challenge Western dominance and shape the discourse on cyberspace governance in its own way.

From Norms Emergence to Norms Acceptance

Since 2014, the landscape of the "cyber regime complex" has undergone diversification, expansion, and increased contention, with various stakeholders pursuing distinct visions for the future of the internet. With such a wide range of approaches, ideas, and conflicting norms, it is pertinent to inquire: Which of the cyber-norms that have emerged from the UNGGE and other processes truly hold significance? In other words, do any of these norms genuinely influence state actions? To provide an answer, it is essential to first grasp the concept of norms and what they mean for international relations.

An international norm is understood as a "set of standards for the appropriate behavior of states" (Finnemore and Sikkink 1998: 893), connoting a collective moral judgment about what "proper" behavior is. According to the famous "norm life cycle," there are three stages norms need to go through until they begin to guide the action of states: norm emergence pushed by norm entrepreneurs, broad norm acceptance, which includes the so-called norm cascade, and finally internalization (Finnemore and Sikkink 1998: 896–901). Even if norms are contested, they "exist" if they are accepted by a large and influential enough community, and violators are held accountable (Finnemore 2017). Because they tend to develop as expectations and opinions in society about what is responsible and acceptable (and shape those expectations in turn), many norms change dynamically over time. Not least because of this, Martha Finnemore and Duncan Hollis have suggested that the outcome of norms processes may in fact be less important than the process by which they are formed (2016: 207; see also Kurowska 2019).

Norms can influence state action through two mechanisms. First, norms possess moral appeal, and states that consider themselves responsible members of the international community tend to endorse, adhere to, and promote these norms. Second, there may be potential costs associated with noncompliance, although it remains debatable whether nonbinding and voluntary norms create enough pressure to enforce compliance. Indeed, states exhibit greater reluctance to violate international law, as opposed to nonbinding norms (Schmitt and Vihul 2014). This is because international law can be enforced through coercion, while the diffusion of norms relies on the belief of norm-receiving states that following these norms is in their best interests (Chen and Yang 2022). Consequently, discussions within the UNGGE and related processes have predominantly focused on the applicability of international law and sought to establish acceptable thresholds for certain behaviors.

In the field of cyber-security, states agreed *that* international law applies from approximately 2013 onward. They do, however, not agree on *how* it applies.[11] This has led to a sizeable body of scholarly publications on cyber-operations and international law (i.e., Delerue 2020; Moynihan 2021; Mačák 2017, 2021), including the two Tallinn Manuals, a much-noticed scholarly restatement of international law as applied in the cyber-context (Schmitt 2013; Schmitt 2017). In contrast to legal scholars, international studies scholars are not as much interested in *how* international law might apply to cyberspace but are more interested in explaining *why* states have different opinions about international law and norms and how they behave politically because of it, both in diplomatic settings and in practice.

From a realist perspective, it is evident why most states are hesitant to adopt a clear stance on the application of international law in cyberspace. A position of ambiguity in this rapidly evolving, technologically driven domain provides strategic advantages (Roguski 2020). The big powers, however, have clear profiles that align with their larger aims and goals. The United States, as the dominant power in cyberspace, aims to preserve the post-war liberal world order by adhering to international law in a conservative manner (Henriksen 2019). Meanwhile, Russia acknowledges the applicability of international law to the cyber-domain, as demonstrated in the UNGGE discussions. Simultaneously, Russia, in collaboration with China, seeks to utilize the UN as a platform to develop new legally binding treaties due to perceived gaps in the current international legal framework to challenge America's dominance (Korzak 2021). China, on the other hand, follows an instrumentalist path in its relationship to international law in general (Wang and Cheng 2022) and often uses legal interpretations to counterbalance the dominant American posture in cyberspace and elsewhere.

The significance of cyber-norms, and whether they are merely political tools, is a subject of contrasting viewpoints. Taking an optimistic stance, a careful examination of cases and diplomatic developments suggests that cyber-norms do hold some degree of importance in guiding the behavior of states (Broeders et al. 2022). However, it is crucial to acknowledge that not all norms carry the same level of weight or influence at any given time. When analyzing state behavior in relation to cyber-operations, Norm 6, which emphasizes the avoidance of damage to critical infrastructure, appears to play a role in guiding decision-making processes, particularly in situations where multiple states possess the capability to carry out severe attacks. This observation aligns with discussions on thresholds, as explored in, that is, the Tallinn Manual. However, accurately measuring the impact of norms beyond their correlation with state-led cyber-incidents poses challenges without access to comprehensive records of decision-making processes. Experimental research methodologies could potentially address this limitation and provide further insights into the impact of cyber norms.

The alternative, more pessimistic perspective argues that the agreed-upon norms in cyberspace are inadequate and have not been effectively internalized, as evidenced by the aggressive practices of certain states. Indeed, cyber-norms also emerge through state practices outside of diplomatic processes. In particular, it is intelligence agencies that play a significant role in shaping practical norms governing acceptable cyber-espionage and other intelligence activities, which have profound implications for accepted state behavior in cyberspace (Georgieva 2020). Indeed, when examining the cyber-threat landscape and the types of attacks we see most, it becomes apparent that there is a substantial gap in the norms landscape: Neither the existing norms nor international law addresses peacetime espionage (Schmitt 2017: 25), which is the category under which most significant cyber-operations fall (Broeders et al. 2019: 2).

Several plausible explanations can account for why states engage in diplomatic negotiations for norms while simultaneously engaging in conducting aggressive operations below the threshold of war. First, it is possible, although unlikely, that the optimistic view is accurate, suggesting that the lack of internalization represents a transitional phase in the norms cycle. In this scenario, it is believed that over time, the norms will become stronger and more ingrained and will shape behavior more directly. Second, there may be diverging interests and irreconcilable tensions among different government bodies, such as the foreign ministry, military, and intelligence agencies. The lack of alignment among these entities can contribute to the inconsistent behavior observed. In this scenario, it could go either way: norms could become stronger or weaker, depending on power relationships within governments. Third, voluntary and nonbinding norms are highly unlikely to constrain the actions of powerful actors. This highlights the "Punishment Problem" (Kello 2021), where the absence of consequences for non-compliance diminishes the effectiveness of norms. In this scenario, norms processes are little more than a fig leaf. Fourth, states may strategically optimize their actions by focusing on activities that fall outside the scope of international agreements and carry a lower risk of escalation. This approach allows them to exploit loopholes and pursue activities that yield the greatest advantage, representing a form of "learning" based on available capabilities and resources.

Regardless of which explanation we lean toward, it is essential to focus on the broader strategic context that goes beyond diplomacy to understand the choices of state actors. To that end, we should shift our attention to state *practices*, emphasizing the importance of examining what states actually *do* rather than solely relying on their stated intentions in policy documents and international fora.

Shaping the Environment Through National Policies and Practices

We examine two aspects of such practices, with a focus on the United States due to the availability of literature on their reactions and policy documents. The first subchapter explores how international norms discussed in the UN and other fora can be viewed as part of the United States' overarching deterrence strategy. The second subchapter addresses the question that arises from the observation of aggressive activities falling below the threshold of war and what to do against them.

Changing the Cost-Benefit Calculus

The focus in diplomatic arenas is predominantly directed toward preventing large-scale destructive attacks that could potentially reach the threshold of an armed attack. That focus was a child of its time in many ways. First, it aligned with the prevailing fear of the threat posed by "cyberwar." Second, given the significance and potential damage to such scenarios, the discussions revolved around the applicability of the law of war in the cyberspace domain. The question of when a cyber-attack would be deemed an armed attack by another state and how to respond in such a situation was extensively deliberated in many publications, not least in the influential "Tallinn Manual on the International Law Applicable to Cyber Warfare" (Schmitt 2013). Published in 2013, this manual established, based on a severity of effect perspective, that any cyber-operation by a state resulting in significant damage or injuries to another state could be considered an international armed conflict and would therefore trigger the right to self-defense.

The prevention of such attacks aligns with the deterrence framework, which draws inspiration from the Cold War and the concept of mutually assured destruction (MAD). Deterrence has long been a central concept in the strategic posture of the United States. Initially developed to stabilize the Cold War between superpowers and reduce the likelihood of nuclear war, deterrence also aimed to dissuade potential adversaries from taking aggressive actions elsewhere in the world. The traditional understanding of successful deterrence involves three interrelated components known as the "3 Cs": capability, credibility, and communication (Haffa 2018). First, a defender must possess the necessary capabilities to inflict harm on an attacker in response to an attack (punishment). Additionally, they should have the ability to defend against an attack or deny the attacker the success of their attack (denial). Second, the challenger needs to believe that the defender is both willing and able to execute a retaliatory strike or effectively defend against an attack. Third, the defender must effectively communicate to the potential challenger what they can expect if they choose to initiate an attack. By effectively signaling their intentions and capabilities, the defender enables the challenger to make better-informed risk calculations.

A changing world order that moved from a bipolar to a unipolar world with a changing threat landscape after the end of the Cold War, led to a vibrant debate about the limits and promises of deterrence. While the concept did not necessarily become less important, it needed to be adapted to the changed circumstances and re(applied) to new challenges. Among other fields, it was also applied to cyberspace (Libicki 2009; Goodman 2010). While some scholars and policymakers claim that deterrence is not possible or very hard in cyberspace (Harknett and Nye 2017) others agree that it still has value, but the scope of the practical applicability of the tenets of deterrence to cyberspace is considerably more limited than in more traditional conventional and nuclear deterrence settings (Brantly 2020a; Soesanto and Smeets 2020/2021; Soesanto 2022).

Taking the specificities of cyber-threats and the domain into account, adapted concepts such as cumulative (Tor 2015) or punctuated cyber-deterrence emerged (Kello 2017), moving from an understanding of absolute deterrence to one that is cumulative and continuous in nature and works through decisive cyber-operations that signal that certain actions in cyberspace will not be tolerated. Other scholars suggest a focus on entanglement (Brantly 2020b), highlight that deterrence by denial is more important than deterrence by punishment (Borghard and Lonergan 2023) or champion the concept of cross-domain deterrence, which refers to the use of capabilities of one type to counter threats or combinations of threats of another type (Nye 2016/2017; Lindsay and Gartzke 2019). As one of the latest additions to the panopticon, the concept of "layered deterrence" as developed by the Cyberspace Solarium Commission suggests the use of "a whole-of-nation strategy that combines multiple instruments of power and focuses less on offense and more on defense based on positive national security objectives linked to long-term strategy" (Jensen 2020).

Despite the many conceptual adaptations, the prevailing consensus among scholars is that cyber-deterrence cannot be evaluated using the same criteria as nuclear deterrence (Nye 2017). The unique attributes of cyberspace, coupled with the diverse range of malicious actors driven by different motives, necessitate a flexible and multifaceted policy approach. Most importantly, striving for zero use in cyber-deterrence policies is both impractical and unnecessary (Daniel 2021: 153) since cyber-effects can be scaled, reversed, and exhibit a wide spectrum of impacts. Consequently, the establishment of and adherence to norms, or at least agreed-upon behavior, carry additional significance in this context (Lotrionte 2013). Establishing clear guidelines on what constitutes an armed attack in cyberspace and determining the conditions for escalation to other domains, such as employing conventional countermeasures, allow for a more credible threat of escalation and a clearer understanding of the costs associated with a cyber-attack (Libicki 2009; Stevens 2012). Policy documents also play a significant role in this regard, as they serve to articulate the United States' preparedness to utilize a range of tools to deter and respond to cyber-threats. The key to a good strategy is an appropriate "mix of passive and active actions" (McKenzie 2017: 3).

Agreed Competition and Persistent Engagement

Practices in cyberspace are constantly shifting and evolving, however. States engage in various behaviors, including conducting cyber-operations, developing military cyber-doctrines, and altering cyber-security policies, which in turn create new dynamics in the digital domain. Therefore, and in the absence of strong norms, the establishment of red lines often involves a process of trial and error, not least because the response to violations varies, with some red lines being met with consequences while others are not. This continuous interplay of actions and consequences serves as a parallel, messy process of norm-setting (Broeders and van den Berg 2020: 6). Optimally, this process would eventually lead to an equilibrium in the form of an "agreed competition," a situation that rests on a tacit understanding among key actors "what the 'agreed battle' is and is not, what the legitimate and illegitimate moves are, and what are 'within the rules' and what are escalatory moves" (Fischerkeller and Harknett 2019).

While there is no guarantee that such a state of agreement will ever be reached, it informs the way the USCYBERCOM thinks and communicates about its own strategy since 2018. Instead of expecting that the strategic behavior of states will be sufficiently influenced by diplomacy, norms, and deterrence, it defines its value around the idea of constant contact and friction. In the words of the Commander of USCYBERCOM: "Unlike the nuclear realm, where our strategic advantage or power comes from possessing a capability or weapons system, in cyberspace it's *the use* of cyber-capabilities that is strategically consequential" (Nakasone 2019: 4, my italics). The new concept that arose is called "persistent engagement," a strategy that is based on the idea that it is better to actively anticipate, search, and neutralize threats instead of hoping for them to be deterred.

This shift happens against the backdrop of a strong bureaucratic impetus of the USCYBERCOM to establish itself as "a brand-new military unified command" with a clearly offensive mandate (Lindsay 2021: 261; Smeet and Lin 2019) as well as the aforementioned changes in the threat landscape. With the increasing significance of activities "under the threshold of war," some scholars, among them the initial scholar in residence at the USCYBERCOM, began to question the credibility and effectiveness of deterrence approaches (Harknett et al. 2010; Harknett and Goldman 2016; Fischerkeller and Harknett 2017; Sulmeyer 2018) and began championing a concept that was geared toward actively shaping the threat environment. In the US Department of Defense (DoD) 2018 Cyber Strategy, the notion of "defend forward" features as the new strategic concept for the cyber-domain. Presenting cyberspace as a domain of constant contact and strategic competition, it states DoD will, "disrupt or halt malicious cyber activity at its source, including activity that falls below the level of armed conflict" (US DoD 2018: 1). The belief is that "[t]hrough persistent action and competing more effectively below the level of armed conflict, we can influence the calculations of our adversaries, deter aggression, and clarify the distinction between acceptable and unacceptable behavior in cyberspace" (US Cyber Command 2018: 6).

There are many open questions, not least about how to measure the success of this new strategy (Healey et al. 2020). Like the early cyberwar debate in the 1990s, the discussions about the policy and its consequences happen among a relatively small group of US scholars, not least on blogs such as Lawfare (Harknett 2018; Miller and Pollard 2019; Schneider 2019; Maschmeyer 2020) and War on the Rocks (Fischerkeller 2020).

Critics of the concept argue, among other things, that the US could be perceived as acting aggressively and unilaterally in cyberspace, which could lead to countermeasures and retaliation by other countries (Healey 2019). Another concern is that persistent engagement could be too resource intensive: The United States may not have the capacity to sustain persistent engagement activities at the scale necessary to effectively deter and disrupt malicious cyber-activity (Schneider 2019, 2020).

Some also question the effectiveness of persistent engagement, arguing that it may not actually deter or disrupt malicious activity, so that a posture of greater restraint might ultimately be more effective in reducing the frequency and intensity of adversary cyber-operations (Healey and Caudill 2020). Finally, critics argue that persistent engagement could undermine international norms and cooperation in cyberspace (Klimburg 2020). By engaging in offensive cyber-operations, the United States could be seen as violating the norms of behavior established by the international community and could discourage other countries from working with the United States on cybersecurity issues, also because most European military cyber-organizations will not be able to increase their operational capacities to such a degree that they can navigate "seamlessly, globally, and continuously," as persistent engagement demands (Smeets 2020).

BOX 6.1   THE US CYBER COMMAND IN ACTION

Not a lot is known about the cyber-operations conducted by the USCYBER-COM (see also Graff 2020; Smeets 2022). In 2016, the Obama administration announced a cyber-campaign against the Islamic State, ISIS, part of which became known as "Operation Glowing Symphony" (see also Box 5.4). Another operation that was never officially confirmed were the actions to prevent the Russian Internet Research Agency (IRA) from interfering with the 2018 midterm elections (Nakashima 2019; also, Buchanan 2019).

Among other things, according to unnamed US officials, USCYBERCOM sent Russian trolls and hackers messages using emails, pop-ups, texts, and direct messages, and blocked internet access to the IRA (Greenberg 2019a). Other news reports about an operation to plant malware in Russian electric utilities (Sanger and Perlroth 2019) are disputed. Some observers assume that the US officials who leaked Cyber Command's Russian grid hacking to the *New York Times* may in fact have intended to signal to Russia that it could turn off the lights in Moscow, without having to do so, not least because the National Security Council expressed no concerns about the report's publication (Greenberg 2019b).

Overall, it is always difficult to evaluate the impact of a single policy, and USCYBERCOM is by far not the only relevant actor in charge of acting against cyber-threats. Cyber-threats are multifaceted due to the involvement of various actors, each with distinct capabilities and motivations. Therefore, addressing this intricate landscape of threats requires a comprehensive approach encompassing both offensive and defensive countermeasures across the public and private sectors.

Indeed, a pragmatic strategy such as the "layered cyber-deterrence" framework can provide a coherent structure. This framework acknowledges the diversity of actors and tactics at play, offering a robust way to manage these challenges. Its essence lies in achieving a desired end state characterized by a diminished likelihood and impact of high-consequence cyber-attacks. This goal is achieved through the strategic implementation of three interconnected pillars: shaping behavior, denying benefits, and imposing costs (Buchanan 2020; King and Gallagher 2020). In the evolving landscape of cyber-threats, the effectiveness of any framework is contingent upon collaboration and synergy among various stakeholders, transcending national and organizational boundaries.

Summary and Key Points

This chapter highlighted the interplay between diplomacy, state-driven strategies, and state policies and practices, especially by intelligence agencies, in addressing (and creating) cyber-threats. It underscored the broader geopolitical context and the significance of cyber-norms as guiding principles for state behavior in cyberspace. In many ways, what we see in the realm of cyber-norms is indicative of a larger context. As the chapter illustrated, changing cyber-norms reflect broader global trends, which includes attempts by authoritarian powers to establish new norms.[12]

This chapter underscored how international (multilateral) diplomacy and state-driven (unilateral) strategies for addressing cyber-threats have often coevolved. Various incidents have drawn attention to the pressing nature of cyber-security concerns but have also highlighted *how* states are using this space against each other. Traditional frameworks of international law, designed for contemplating matters of war and peace, offered some utility, such as discussing "thresholds" that might trigger the right to self-defense. However, they offered limited normative guidance in elucidating what actions are permissible and prohibited below the threshold of war. Most importantly, intelligence agencies shaped practical norms, especially regarding cyber-espionage and covert action.

Sovereign states regard intelligence activities as essential components of their national security and foreign policy and consider intelligence gathering a legitimate means of protecting their interests. Hence, they are reluctant to cede control over these activities to international regulations or agreements. Intelligence agencies operate in a gray area where activities are deliberately ambiguous, and states can maintain plausible deniability about their involvement. This ambiguity makes it difficult to attribute specific actions to a state with the level of certainty required for legal proceedings. Furthermore, intelligence activities are inherently secretive and discretionary, which makes it challenging to establish enforceable rules and mechanisms for monitoring compliance.

Not least because of how some of their key strategic rivals were using cyberspace against them, the United States has switched from a strategy of deterrence to a strategy of persistent engagement. The idea behind persistent engagement is to actively and continuously engage with potential adversaries in cyberspace to detect, respond to, and mitigate threats before they can cause significant harm. It is rooted in the understanding that cyberspace is a dynamic and evolving environment, and a proactive approach is essential to effectively protecting networks, systems, and critical infrastructure from cyber-threats. Whether this strategy is effective remains to be seen.

Notes

1. Apart from the permanent five of the UN Security Council (China, France, Russia, the United Kingdom, the United States): Belarus, Brazil, Germany, India, Jordan, South Korea, Malaysia, Mali, Mexico, Russia, South Africa
2. Apart from the permanent five of the UN Security Council (China, France, Russia, the United Kingdom, the United States): Belarus, Brazil, Estonia, Germany, India, Israel, Italy, South Korea, Qatar, Russia, South Africa
3. Apart from the permanent five of the UN Security Council (China, France, Russia, the United Kingdom, the United States): Argentina, Australia, Belarus, Canada, Egypt, Estonia, Germany, India, Indonesia, Japan
4. Apart from the permanent five of the UN Security Council (China, France, Russia, the United Kingdom, the United States): Belarus, Brazil, Colombia, Egypt, Estonia, Germany, Ghana, Israel, Japan, Kenya, Malaysia, Mexico, Pakistan, the Republic of Korea, Spain
5. Apart from the permanent five of the UN Security Council (China, France, Russia, the United Kingdom, the United States): Australia, Botswana, Brazil, Canada, Cuba, Egypt, Estonia, Finland, Germany, India, Indonesia, Japan, Kazakhstan, Kenya, Mexico, the Netherlands, Senegal, Serbia, South Korea, Switzerland
6. Apart from the permanent five of the UN Security Council (China, France, Russia, the United Kingdom, the United States) Australia, Brazil, Estonia, Germany, India, Indonesia, Japan, Jordan, Kazakhstan, Kenya, Mauritius, Mexico, Morocco, the Netherlands, Norway, Romania, Singapore, South Africa, Switzerland, Uruguay.
7. www.charteroftrust.com/
8. www.kaspersky.com/transparency-center

9. Russia is also pushing for a formal negotiation process for a new international treaty to combat cybercrime in the UN Third Committee (Korzak 2021), rejecting the Council of Europe's Budapest Convention (Costigan 2021). In March 2023, Russia issued a new draft for a UN international convention on cybersecurity.
10. Notable examples include the Internet Governance Forum (IGF), which is convened annually by the United Nations Secretary-General, the World Summit on the Information Society (WSIS) hosted by the ITU, the "London Process" (a series of conferences since 2011, also known as the Global Conference on Cyberspace), the "Seoul Conference on Cyberspace" (2013), the "Paris Call for Trust and Security in Cyberspace" (launched in 2018), and the Dutch-led "Global Commission on the Stability of Cyberspace (GCSC)" (active from 2019 to 2021).
11. Two noteworthy resources are the Cooperative Cyber Defence Centre of Excellence (CCDCOE) Cyberlaw Project: https://cyberlaw.ccdcoe.org/wiki/Main_Page and the *Official Compendium of Voluntary National Contributions on the Subject of How International Law Applies to the Use of Information and Communications Technologies*, compiled as part of the 2021 UNGGE process: https://front.un-arm.org/wp-content/uploads/2021/08/A-76-136-EN.pdf (also see United Nations General Assembly 2021b).
12. Numerous studies have explored recent shifts in the attitudes and behaviors of authoritarian major powers concerning the global order rooted in liberal, rule-based principles (cf. Ginsburg 2020; Paris 2020; Raymond and Sherman 2023).

References

Attrill, N. and Fritz, A. (2021). *China's Cyber Vision: How the Cyberspace Administration of China Is Building a New Consensus on Global Internet Governance.* Policy Brief. Report No. 52/2021. The Australian Strategic Policy Institute.

Barrinha, A. and Renard, T. (2017). Cyber-Diplomacy: The Making of an International Society in the Digital Age. *Global Affairs* 3(4–5): 353–364.

Borghard, E.D. and Lonergan, S.W. (2023). Deterrence by Denial in Cyberspace. *Journal of Strategic Studies* 46(3): 534–569.

Brantly, A.F. (ed.) (2020a). *The Cyber Deterrence Problem.* Rowman & Littlefield.

Brantly, A.F. (2020b). Entanglement in Cyberspace: Minding the Deterrence Gap. *Democracy and Security* 16(3): 210–233.

Broeders, D. and van den Berg, B. (eds.) (2020). *Governing Cyberspace: Behavior, Power, and Diplomacy.* Rowman & Littlefield.

Broeders, D., Boeke, S. and Georgieva, I. (2019). *Foreign Intelligence in the Digital Age. Navigating a State of "Unpeace."* The Hague Program for Cyber Norms Policy Brief, September. Available at: https://papers.ssrn.com/sol3/papers.cfm?abstract_id=3493612

Broeders, D., de Busser, E., Cristiano, F. and Tropina, T. (2022). Revisiting Past Cyber Operations in Light of New Cyber Norms and Interpretations of International Law: Inching towards Lines in the Sand? *Journal of Cyber Policy* 7(1): 97–135.

Buchanan, B. (2019). What to Make of Cyber Command's Operation Against the Internet Research Agency. *Lawfare*, February 28. Available at: www.lawfaremedia.org/article/what-make-cyber-commands-operation-against-internet-research-agency

Buchanan, B. (2020). *The Hacker and the State Cyber Attacks and the New Normal of Geopolitics*. Harvard University Press.

Chen, X. and Yang, Y. (2022). Contesting Western and Non-Western Approaches to Global Cyber Governance beyond Westlessness. *The International Spectator* 57(3): 1–14.

Costigan, S.S. (2021). Sovereign or Global Internet? Russia and China Press for Cybercrime Treaty. *Connections: The Quarterly Journal* 20(2): 9–13.

Daniel, M. (2021). Closing the Gap: Expanding Cyber Deterrence. In: Klimburg, A. (ed.) *New Conditions and Constellations in Cyber*. The Hague Centre for Strategic Studies, pp. 145–156.

Delerue, F. (2020). *Cyber Operations and International Law*. Cambridge University Press.

Dunn Cavelty, M. (2015). The Normalization of Cyber-International Relations. In: Thränert, O. and Zapfe, M. (eds.) *Strategic Trends 2015: Key Developments in Global Affairs*. Center for Security Studies, pp. 81–98.

Eggenschwiler, J. (2022). Big Tech's Push for Norms to Tackle Uncertainty in Cyberspace. In: Dunn Cavelty, M. and Wenger, A. (eds.) *Cyber Security Politics: Socio-Technological Transformations and Political Fragmentation*. Routledge, pp. 186–204.

Finnemore, M. (2017). Cybersecurity and the Concept of Norms. *Carnegie Endowment for International Peace*, November 30. Available at: https://carnegieendowment.org/files/Finnemore_web_final.pdf

Finnemore, M. and Hollis, D. (2016). Constructing Norms for Global Cybersecurity. *The American Journal of International Law* 110(3): 425–479.

Finnemore, M. and Sikkink, K. (1998). International Norm Dynamics and Political Change. *International Organization* 52(4): 887–917.

Fischerkeller, M.P. (2020). The Fait Accompli and Persistent Engagement in Cyberspace. *War on the Rocks*, June 24. Available at: https://warontherocks.com/2020/06/the-fait-accompli-and-persistent-engagement-in-cyberspace/

Fischerkeller, M.P. and Harknett, R.J. (2017). Deterrence Is Not a Credible Strategy for Cyberspace. *Orbis* 61(3): 381–393.

Fischerkeller, M.P. and Harknett, R.J. (2019). Persistent Engagement, Agreed Competition, and Cyberspace Interaction Dynamics and Escalation. *The Cyber Defense Review* (Special Edition 2019): 267–287.

Gao, X. (2022). An Attractive Alternative? China's Approach to Cyber Governance and Its Implications for the Western Model. *The International Spectator* 57(3): 15–30.

Georgieva, I. (2020). The Unexpected Norm-Setters: Intelligence Agencies in Cyberspace. *Contemporary Security Policy* 41(1): 33–54.

Giles, K. (2012). Russia's Public Stance on Cyberspace Issues. In: Czosseck, C., Ottis, R. and Ziolkowski, K. (eds.) *Proceedings of the 4th International Conference on Cyber Conflict*. CCD COE Publications, pp. 141–153.

Giles, K. and Hagestad, W. (2013). Divided by a Common Language: Cyber-Definitions in Chinese, Russian and English. In: Podins, K, Stinissen, J. and Maybaum, M. (eds.) *Proceedings of the 5th International Conference on Cyber-Conflict*. CCD COE Publications, pp. 1–17.

Ginsburg, T. (2020). How Authoritarians Use International Law. *Journal of Democracy* 31(4): 44–58.

Goodman, W. (2010). Cyber Deterrence: Tougher in Theory Than in Practice? *Strategic Studies Quarterly* 4(3): 102–135.

Gorwa, R. and Peez, A. (2020). Big Tech Hits the Diplomatic Circuit: Norm Entrepreneurship, Policy Advocacy, and Microsoft's Cybersecurity Tech Accord. In: Broeders, D. and van den Berg, B. (eds.) *Governing Cyberspace: Behavior, Power, and Diplomacy*. Rowman & Littlefield, pp. 263–284.

Graff, G. (2020). The Man Who Speaks Softly—and Commands a Big Cyber Army. *Wired*, October 13. Available at: www.wired.com/story/general-paul-nakasone-cyber-command-nsa/

Greenberg, A. (2019a). US Hacker's Strike on Russian Trolls Sends a Message—but What Kind? *Wired*, February 27. Available at: www.wired.com/story/cyber-command-ira-strike-sends-signal/

Greenberg, A. (2019b). How Not to Prevent a Cyberwar with Russia. *Wired*, June 19. Available at: www.wired.com/story/russia-cyberwar-escalation-power-grid/

Grigsby, A. (2017). The End of Cyber Norms. *Survival* 59(6): 109–122.

Haffa, R.P. (2018). The Future of Conventional Deterrence: Strategies for Great Power Competition. *Strategic Studies Quarterly* 12(4): 94–115.

Harknett, R.J. (2018). United States Cyber Command's New Vision: What It Entails and Why It Matters. *Lawfare*, March 23. Available at: www.lawfareblog.com/united-states-cyber-commands-new-vision-what-it-entails-and-why-it-matters

Harknett, R.J., Callaghan, J.P. and Kauffman, R. (2010). Leaving Deterrence Behind: Warfighting and National Cybersecurity. *Journal of Homeland Security and Emergency Management* 7(1): 1–24.

Harknett, R.J. and Goldman, E. (2016). The Search for Cyber Fundamentals. *Journal of Information Warfare* 15(2): 81–88.

Harknett, R.J. and Nye, J.S. (2017). Is Deterrence Possible in Cyberspace? *International Security* 42(2): 196–199.

Healey, J. (2019). The Implications of Persistent (and Permanent) Engagement in Cyberspace. *Journal of Cybersecurity* 5(1): tyz008.

Healey, J. and Caudill, S. (2020). Success of Persistent Engagement in Cyberspace. *Strategic Studies Quarterly* 14(1): 9–15.

Healey, J., Jenkins, N. and Work, J. D. (2020). Defenders Disrupting Adversaries: Framework, Dataset, and Case Studies of Disruptive Counter-Cyber Operations. In: Jančárková, T., Lindström, L., Signoretti, M., Tolga, I. and Visky, G. (eds.) *Proceedings of the 12th International Conference on Cyber Conflict*. CCD COE Publications, pp. 251–274.

Henriksen, A. (2016). Politics and the Development of Legal Norms in Cyberspace. In: Friis, K. and Ringsmose, J. (eds.) *Conflict in Cyber Space: Theoretical, Strategic and Legal Perspectives*. Routledge, pp. 151–164.

Henriksen, A. (2019). The End of the Road for the UN GGE Process: The Future Regulation of Cyberspace. *Journal of Cybersecurity* 5(1): tyy009.

Hoffmann, S., Lazanski, D. and Taylor, E. (2020). Standardising the Splinternet: How China's Technical Standards Could Fragment the Internet. *Journal of Cyber Policy* 5(2): 239–264.

Huang, Z. and Ying, Y. (2021). Chinese Approaches to Cyberspace Governance and International Law in Cyberspace. In: Tsagourias, N. and Buchan, R. (eds.) *Research Handbook on International Law and Cyberspace*. Edward Elgar Publishing, pp. 547–563.

Hurel, L.M. and Lobato, L. (2018). Unpacking Cyber Norms: Private Companies as Norm Entrepreneurs. *Journal of Cyber Policy* 3(1): 61–76.

Jensen, B. (2020). Layered Cyber Deterrence: A Strategy for Securing Connectivity in the 21st Century. *Lawfare*, March 11. Available at: www.lawfaremedia. org/article/layered-cyber-deterrence-strategy-securing-connectivity-21st-century

Kavanagh, C., Maurer, T. and Tikk-Ringas, E. (2014). *Baseline Review: ICT-Related Processes & Events Implications for International and Regional Security (2011–2013)*. ICT4Peace, Cyber Policy Process Brief. Available at: www.files.ethz.ch/isn/179768/Baseline%20Review%202014%20ICT%20Processes%20colprint.pdf

Kello, L. (2017). *The Virtual Weapon and International Order*. Yale University Press.

Kello, L. (2021). Cyber Legalism: Why It Fails and What to Do About It. *Journal of Cybersecurity* 7(1): tyab014.

King, A. and Gallagher, M. (2020). *Cyberspace Solarium Commission, Final Report*. Available at: https://drive.google.com/file/d/1ryMCIL_dZ30QyjFqFkkf10 MxIXJGT4yv/view?pli=1

Klimburg, A. (2020). Mixed Signals: A Flawed Approach to Cyber Deterrence. *Survival* 62(1): 107–130.

Korzak, E. (2017). UN GGE on Cybersecurity: The End of an Era? *The Diplomat*, July 31. Available at: https://thediplomat.com/2017/07/un-gge-on-cybersecurity-have-china-and-russia-just-made-cyberspace-less-safe/

Korzak, E. (2021). *Russia's Cyber Policy Efforts in the United Nations*. Tallinn Paper No. 11. Available at: https://ccdcoe.org/uploads/2021/06/Elaine_Korzak_ Russia_UN.docx.pdf

Krasner, S.D. (1983). *International Regimes*. Cornell University Press.

Kurowska, X. (2019). *The Politics of Cyber Norms: Beyond Norm Construction Towards Strategic Narrative Contestation*. EU Institute for Security Studies. Available at: https://eucyberdirect.eu/content_research/the-politics-of-cyber-norms-beyond-norm-construction-towards-strategic-narrative-contestation/

Lauber, J. and Eberli, L. (2021). From Confrontation to Consensus: Taking Stock of the OEWG Process. In: Klimburg, A. (ed.) *New Conditions and Constellations in Cyber*. The Hague Centre for Strategic Studies, pp. 31–39.

Libicki, M. (2009). *Cyberdeterrence and Cyberwar*. RAND Corporation.

Lindsay, J.R. (2021). Cyber Conflict vs. Cyber Command: Hidden Dangers in the American Military Solution to a Large-Scale Intelligence Problem. *Intelligence and National Security* 36(2): 260–278.

Lindsay, J.R. and Gartzke, E. (eds.) (2019). *Cross-Domain Deterrence. Strategy in an Era of Complexity*. Oxford University Press.

Lotrionte, C. (2013). A Better Defense: Examining the United States' New Norms-Based Approach to Cyber Deterrence. *Georgetown Journal of International Affairs* 14: 75–88.

Mačák, K. (2017). From Cyber Norms to Cyber Rules: Re-Engaging States as Law-Makers. *Leiden Journal of International Law* 30(4): 877–899.

Mačák, K. (2021). Unblurring the Lines: Military Cyber Operations and International Law. *Journal of Cyber Policy* 6(3): 411–428,

Maschmeyer, L. (2020). Persistent Engagement Neglects Secrecy at Its Peril. *Lawfare*, March 4. Available at: www.lawfaremedia.org/article/persistent-engagement-neglects-secrecy-its-peril

McKenzie, T.M. (2017). *Is Cyber Deterrence Possible? Perspectives on Cyber Power*. Air University Press.

McKune, S. and Ahmed, S. (2018). Authoritarian Practices in the Digital Age: The Contestation and Shaping of Cyber Norms Through China's Internet Sovereignty Agenda. *International Journal of Communication* 12. Available at: https://ijoc.org/index.php/ijoc/article/view/8540

Miller, J.N. and Pollard, N.A. (2019). Persistent Engagement, Agreed Competition and Deterrence in Cyberspace. *Lawfare*, April 30. Available at: www.lawfaremedia.org/article/persistent-engagement-agreed-competition-and-deterrence-cyberspace

Moynihan, H. (2021). The Vital Role of International Law in the Framework for Responsible State Behaviour in Cyberspace. *Journal of Cyber Policy* 6(3): 394–410.

Mueller, M. (2010). *Networks and States: The Global Politics of Internet Governance*. MIT Press.

Nakashima, E. (2019). U.S. Cyber Command Operation Disrupted Internet Access of Russian Troll Factory on Day of 2018 Midterms. *The Washington Post*, February 27. Available at: https://www.washingtonpost.com/world/national-security/us-cyber-command-operation-disrupted-internet-access-of-russian-troll-factory-on-day-of-2018-midterms/2019/02/26/1827fc9e-36d6-11e9-af5b-b51b7ff322e9_story.html

Nakasone, P.M. (2019). An Interview with Paul M. Nakasone. *Joint Forces Quarterly* 92(1): 4–9.

Nye, J.S. (2014). *The Regime Complex for Managing Global Cyber Activities*. The Global Commission on Internet Governance. Paper Series: No. 1, May. Available at: www.cigionline.org/static/documents/gcig_paper_no1.pdf

Nye, J.S. (2016/2017). Deterrence and Dissuasion in Cyberspace. *International Security* 41(3): 44–71.

OECD (2011). *OECD Council Recommendation on Principles for Internet Policy Making*. December 13. Available at: https://web-archive.oecd.org/2014-04-08/89234-49258588.pdf

Paris, R. (2020). The Right to Dominate: How Old Ideas About Sovereignty Pose New Challenges for World Order. *International Organization* 74(3): 453–489.

Paulus, A. (2022). *A Path to Progress at the UN Cybersecurity Forum*. Directions. Cyber Digital Europe. Blog Post. Available at: https://directionsblog.eu/a-path-to-progress-at-the-un-cybersecurity-forum/

Pawlak, P. (2019). The EU's Role in Shaping the Cyber Regime Complex. *European Foreign Affairs Review* 24(2): 167–186.

Raymond, M. and Sherman, J. (2024). Authoritarian Multilateralism in the Global Cyber Regime Complex: The Double Transformation of an International Diplomatic Practice. *Contemporary Security Policy* 45(1). https://doi.org/10.1080/13523260.2023.2269809

Roguski, P. (2020). *Application of International Law to Cyber Operations: A Comparative Analysis of States' Views*. The Hague Program for Cyber Norms Policy Brief, March. Available at: www.thehaguecybernorms.nl/research-and-publication-posts/application-of-international-law-to-cyber-operations-a-comparative-analysis-of-states-views

Rühlig, T. (2023). Chinese Influence through Technical Standardization Power. *Journal of Contemporary China* 32(139): 54–72.

Sanger, D.E. and Perlroth, N. (2019). U.S. Escalates Online Attacks on Russia's Power Grid. *New York Times*, June 15. Available at: https://www.nytimes.com/2019/06/15/us/politics/trump-cyber-russia-grid.html

Schmitt, M. (ed.) (2013). *Tallinn Manual on the International Law Applicable to Cyber Warfare*. Cambridge University Press.

Schmitt, M. (ed.) (2017). *Tallinn Manual 2.0 on the International Law Applicable to Cyber Operations*. Cambridge University Press.

Schmitt, M. and Vihul, L. (2014). *The Nature of International Law Cyber Norms*. Tallinn Papers No. 5. NATO Cooperative Cyber Defence Centre of Excellence. Available at: https://papers.ssrn.com/sol3/papers.cfm?abstract_id=2543520

Schneider, J. (2020). A Strategic Cyber No-First-Use Policy? Addressing the US Cyber Strategy Problem. *The Washington Quarterly* 43(2): 159–175.

Schneider, J.G. (2019). Persistent Engagement: Foundation, Evolution and Evaluation of a Strategy. *Lawfare*, May 10. Available at: www.lawfareblog.com/persistent-engagement-foundation-evolution-and-evaluation-strategy

Smeets, M. (2020). U.S. Cyber Strategy of Persistent Engagement & Defend Forward: Implications for the Alliance and Intelligence Collection. *Intelligence and National Security* 35(3): 444–453.

Smeets, M. (2022). A US History of Not Conducting Cyber Attacks. *Bulletin of the Atomic Scientists* 78(4): 208–213.

Smeets, M. and Lin, H. (2019). A Strategic Assessment of the U.S. Cyber Command Vision. In: Lin, H. and Zegart, A. (eds.) *Bytes, Bombs and Spies: The Strategic Dimensions of Offensive Cyber Operations*. Brookings Institution Press, pp. 81–104.

Smith, B. (2017). *The Need for a Digital Geneva Convention*, February 14. Available at: https://blogs.microsoft.com/on-the-issues/2017/02/14/need-digital-geneva-convention/

Soesanto, S. (2022). *Cyber Deterrence Revisited. Perspectives on Cyber Power*. Air University Press. Available at: www.airuniversity.af.edu/AUPress/Display/Article/2993347/cyber-deterrence-revisited/

Soesanto, S. and Smeets, M. (2020). Cyber Deterrence: The Past, Present, and Future. In: Osinga, F. and Sweijs, T. (eds.) *NL ARMS Netherlands Annual Review of Military Studies: Deterrence in the 21st Century—Insights from Theory and Practice*. Springer, pp. 385–400.

Stevens, T. (2012). A Cyberwar of Ideas? Deterrence and Norms in Cyberspace. *Contemporary Security Policy* 33(1): 148–170.

Sulmeyer, M. (2018). How the U.S. Can Play Cyber-Offense: Deterrence Isn't Enough. *Foreign Affairs*, March 22. Available at: www.foreignaffairs.com/articles/world/2018-03-22/how-us-can-play-cyber-offense

Telefónica (2018). *A Manifesto for a New Digital Deal*. Available at: https://perma.cc/9RXC-JE3D

Tiirma-Klaar, H. (2021). The Evolution of the UN Group of Governmental Experts on Cyber Issues from a Marginal Group to a Major International Security Norm-Setting Body. In: Klimburg, A. (ed.) *New Conditions and Constellations in Cyber*. The Hague Centre for Strategic Studies, pp. 14–28.

Tikk, E. and Kerttunen, M. (2017). *The Alleged Demise of the UN GGE: An Autopsy and Eulogy*. Cyber Policy Institute. Available at: https://cyber-peace.

org/wp-content/uploads/2018/11/Tikk-Kerttunen-2017-The-Alleged-Demise-of-the-UN-GGE-An-Autopsy-and-Eulogy.pdf

Tikk-Ringas, E. (2012). *Developments in the Field of Information and Telecommunication in the Context of International Security: Work of the UN First Committee 1998–2012*. ICT4Peace, Cyber Policy Process Brief. Available at: www.files.ethz.ch/isn/167403/Eneken-GGE-2012-Brief.pdf

Tor, U. (2015). 'Cumulative Deterrence' as a New Paradigm for Cyber Deterrence. *Journal of Strategic Studies* 40(1–2): 92–117.

Tran Dai, C. and Gomez, M.A. (2018). Challenges and Opportunities for Cyber Norms in ASEAN. *Journal of Cyber Policy* 3(2): 217–235.

United Nations General Assembly (1999). 53rd Session. Developments in the Field of Information and Telecommunications in the Context of International Security (A/RES/53/70) [Resolution]. Adopted on the Report of the First Committee (A/53/576). Available at: https://undocs.org/A/RES/53/70

United Nations General Assembly (2010). 65th Session. Group of Governmental Experts on Developments in the Field of Information and Telecommunications in the Context of International Security: Note by the Secretary-General (A/65/201) [Report]. Available at: https://undocs.org/A/65/201

United Nations General Assembly (2013). 68th Session. Group of Governmental Experts on Developments in the Field of Information and Telecommunications in the Context of International Security: Note by the Secretary-General (A/68/98) [Report].

United Nations General Assembly (2015a). 70th Session. Developments in the Field of Information and Telecommunications in the Context of International Security (A/RES/70/237) [Resolution]. Adopted on the Report of the First Committee (A/70/455). Available at: http://undocs.org/A/RES/70/237

United Nations General Assembly (2015b). 70th Session. Group of Governmental Experts on Developments in the Field of Information and Telecommunications in the Context of International Security: Note by the Secretary-General (A/70/174) [Report]. Available at: https://undocs.org/A/70/174

United Nations General Assembly (2021a). Report of the Group of Governmental Experts on Advancing Responsible State Behaviour in Cyberspace in the Context of International Security. UN Doc. A/76/135, July 14. Available at: https://undocs.org/A/76/135

United Nations General Assembly (2021b). Official Compendium of Voluntary National Contributions on the Subject of How International Law Applies to the Use of Information and Communications Technologies by States Submitted by Participating Governmental Experts in the Group of Governmental Experts on Advancing Responsible State Behaviour in Cyberspace in the Context of International Security Established Pursuant to General Assembly Resolution 73/266. Available at: http://undocs.org/A/76/136

United Nations General Assembly (2023). 78th Session. Programme of Action to Advance Responsible State Behaviour in the Use of Information and Communications Technologies in the Context of International Security (A/C.1/78/L.60/REV.1). Available at: https://undocs.org/A/C.1/78/L.60/REV.1

US Cyber Command (2018). *Achieve and Maintain Cyberspace Superiority: Command Vision for U.S. Cyber Command*, March 23. Available at: https://assets.

documentcloud.org/documents/4419681/Command-Vision-for-USCYBER-COM-23-Mar-18.pdf

US Department of Defense (2018). *Summary: Department of Defense Cyber Strategy.* Available at: https://media.defense.gov/2018/Sep/18/2002041658/-1/-1/1/CYBER_STRATEGY_SUMMARY_FINAL.PDF

Väljataga, A. (2017). Back to Square One? The Fifth UN GGE Fails to Submit a Conclusive Report at the UN General Assembly. *CCDCOE Blog.* Available at: https://ccdcoe.org/incyder-articles/back-to-square-one-the-fifth-un-gge-fails-to-submit-a-conclusive-report-at-the-un-general-assembly

Wang, J. and Cheng, H. (2022). China's Approach to International Law: From Traditional Westphalianism to Aggressive Instrumentalism in the Xi Jinping Era. *The Chinese Journal of Comparative Law* 10(1): 140–153.

Weekes, B. and Tikk-Ringas, E. (2013). *Cyber Security Affairs: Global and Regional Processes, Agendas and Instruments.* ICT4Peace, Cyber Policy Process Brief. Available at: www.files.ethz.ch/isn/167404/processbrief_2013.pdf

Weyrauch, D. and Winzen, T. (2020). Internet Fragmentation, Political Structuring, and Organizational Concentration in Transnational Engineering Networks. *Global Policy* 12(1): 51–65.

Zhang, B. (2019). Cyberspace and International Humanitarian Law: The Chinese Approach. In: Linton, S., McCormack, T. and Sivakumaran, S. (eds.) *Asia-Pacific Perspectives on International Humanitarian Law.* Cambridge University Press, pp. 323–337.

7

CYBER-INCIDENTS

A Conceptualization

As the previous chapters have shown, the evolution of cyber-security politics is predicated on cyber-incidents. It is therefore essential to explore their key characteristics in more details. A cyber-incident can be defined as an event that produces actual or potential adverse effects on an information system, network, or the information stored within them.[1] This definition encompasses events that occur within computer systems as well as those originating externally but exerting significant influence on the targeted machine, for instance, the destruction of a server using a physical hammer. Incidents that occur due to deliberate human actions are called "cyber-attacks." Beyond this focus on computers as physical objects as targets, the definition can be expanded to encompass events or rather a chain of events that also impact the semantic realm, such as influence operations, as well as events that indirectly influence cyber-security politics and practices, like 9/11, the Snowden revelations, or the Arab Spring uprisings.

Given the important position that cyber-incidents hold in the discourse, it is tempting to think of them as "drivers." While they often feel like "ruptures" and "wake up calls," seeing them in isolation leads down the slippery slope of technological determinism (Buzan and Hansen 2009: 54). Incidents do not occur in a political vacuum. What this chapter will highlight is that the meaning and ultimately importance of a cyber-incident gains in the debate are the outcome of discursive practices that occur in specific socio-political contexts (cf. Balzacq 2015). In other words, without sufficient attention to the larger context in which human actors made a choice to breach a system, we cannot fully understand the "power" that cyber-incidents have in shaping the debate.

DOI: 10.4324/9781003497080-7

From the viewpoint of "the victim"—the information system under attack in the first instance, and the owner of that system in the second—the adverse effect often manifests first as an unwanted performance of a computing device. In the IT-security community, this unwanted performance is expressed by the loss of either one or several of the following properties of data: its confidentiality, integrity, or availability—the so-called CIA triad. Yet, this unwanted performance alone is not sufficient to explain the increased salience of cyber-security topics in politics. Between the loss of confidentiality, integrity, or availability and socio-political effects lies a process that establishes the adverse effect in the target system or systems as relevant in a specific social and political context. A technical effect needs to be discursively linked to something with sufficient social or political value to become security politically relevant and accepted as such by the relevant audience, which also explains why only some cyber-incidents reach that stage while most others do not (Balzacq and Dunn Cavelty 2016).

It is not yet well researched what the discursive anchors are that need to be acknowledged and employed by technical and political actors to establish an adverse event as a cyber-incident that carries stable and accepted meaning within the cyber-discourse (Homolar and Rodríguez-Merino 2019). In contrast to other security-related events such as terrorist attacks or extreme weather events that are instantly recognizable through their destructive, violent effects, cyber-incidents are hardly ever associated with similar levels of destruction, leading to high levels of uncertainty about their larger meaning.

The uncertainties surrounding cyber-incidents encompass multiple layers and evolve throughout different phases. When an adverse effect is detected, an immediate priority arises to contain the incident and restore the affected system. Simultaneously, although with slightly less time sensitivity, it becomes crucial to assess the extent of the damage inflicted, such as data theft, deletion or modification of data, or unwanted encryption. Depending on available resources and the severity of the incident, victims may also seek to gather forensic evidence to identify the responsible parties, which can be utilized in legal proceedings or political actions in relevant contexts (Cichonski et al. 2012).

These different elements, which often overlap temporarily, can be collectively understood to be elements of an "attribution," which is the first subchapter's focus. Attribution—the process of identifying and assigning responsibility to individuals, groups, or entities responsible for a cyber-attack—has traditionally been perceived as a technological challenge, but it has emerged as a fundamentally political practice (Rid and Buchanan 2015). In fact, it lies at the core of enabling political action in response to cyber-incidents. Security concerns in the political realm revolve around human adversaries. In the second subchapter, we delve into the portrayal of hackers and hacker groups to understand the "who" behind cyber-incidents. The third subchapter focuses on the concept of "vulnerabilities," a weakness of an asset or group of assets that can be exploited by these threat actors. The fourth subchapter examines the methods employed to breach systems by exploiting vulnerabilities. We will end with a brief reflection on the other dynamics that are obscured by a focus on "incidents" and how to transcend them.

Attribution at the Heart of Cyber-Security Politics

Attribution connotes the process during which information is collected to understand the parameters of the cyber-incident. For decades, it was a commonly held assumption that attribution was unfeasible because online identities can be hidden, or false traces can be laid due to the architecture of cyberspace (see Box 7.1 on false flag operations). In policy circles, this "attribution problem" was considered highly problematic—without the ability to punish, one could not hope to deter. Worse, it was conjectured that cyber-weapons would become the preferred and often used weapon of choice in the future, not least because perpetrators would always have plausible deniability (Lindsay 2015; Lupovici 2016).

BOX 7.1 FAMOUS FALSE FLAG OPERATIONS

TV5 Monde: In April 2015, TV5 Monde, a French television network, was the victim of a cyber-attack. The attack resulted in the network's broadcasting being interrupted for several hours and their websites and social media accounts being compromised. Initially, there were suspicions that the Syrian army was behind the attack due to a group called the "Cyber Caliphate" claiming responsibility. However, it was later revealed that the attack was most likely carried out by a Russian hacker group known as APT28 or Fancy Bear, which is associated with the Russian government. The motive behind the attack remains a subject of speculation, but it was seen as part of wider cyber-operations conducted by state-sponsored actors targeting political and media organizations.

Olympic Destroyer: "Olympic Destroyer" was a cyber-attack that took place during the opening ceremony of the 2018 Winter Olympic Games held in Pyeongchang, South Korea. The main objective of the attack seemed to disrupt the opening ceremony and cause chaos. The malware targeted key components of the IT infrastructure, including timing and scoring systems, Wi-Fi networks, and other critical services. It did, however, not result in any long-term damage or compromise the integrity of the Games. The attackers intentionally included false indicators in the malware's code to mislead investigators. These false indicators pointed toward other threat actors, such as North Korea or China, potentially trying to divert attention from the true source. Relatively quickly, further investigations suggested that the attack was more likely the work of Russian threat actors.

In today's landscape, attribution is no longer considered the insurmountable challenge it was once believed to be, provided there is a willingness to allocate resources to the task. While uncertainties still exist, and there are numerous incidents that have not been attributed (Raiu 2022), persistent threat actors often exhibit patterns and behaviors repeatedly, and they leave traces in the form of identifiable tactics, techniques, and procedures (TTPs) (see Box 7.2). While it is relatively easy to misguide attributors along some technical elements (Skopik and Pahi 2020), it is costly and difficult to forge evidence convincingly across all technical artifacts and at scale.

BOX 7.2 TACTICS, TECHNIQUES, AND PROCEDURES (TTPs)

TTPs in cyber-security are used to describe the operational aspects of cyber-activities, whether they are offensive (performed by threat actors) or defensive (performed by organizations or security teams). Understanding TTPs is crucial for both detecting and mitigating cyber-threats, as it helps security professionals recognize and respond to specific attack patterns and trends. This knowledge can also inform the development of better cyber-security strategies and defenses (Johnson et al. 2016).

1. *Tactics*: Tactics are high-level strategies or approaches used to achieve a specific goal or objective in a cyber-operation. They provide a broad overview of the attacker's or defender's plan. For example, an attacker's tactic might be to gain unauthorized access to a target network, while a defender's tactic might be to monitor network traffic for signs of intrusion.
2. *Techniques*: Techniques are the specific methods or tools that are employed within a given tactic. These are the detailed steps taken to

implement a particular strategy. In the context of cyber-attacks, techniques often include exploiting software vulnerabilities, using phishing emails, employing malware, or conducting social engineering. Defenders also have techniques, such as implementing firewalls, intrusion detection systems (IDS), and patch management.

3. *Procedures*: Procedures are the step-by-step instructions or processes that guide the execution of a technique. They provide the necessary details for carrying out a particular method. For instance, in a phishing attack, the procedure might involve crafting a deceptive email, selecting targets, and deploying the email to victims. In cyber-security defense, procedures might outline how to respond to a security incident, such as isolating compromised systems and notifying affected parties.

Those who erroneously believed attribution would fail due to technical limitations failed to account for the significant influence of human factors on technology. Once the problem of attribution was recognized as crucial, entities with means began to invest in their attribution capabilities. This involved a combination of technical and nontechnical measures and methods drawn from the intelligence community to comprehend activities within computer networks. Not least, as the threat landscape evolved due to increased state-sponsored activities, a thriving industry of threat intelligence companies emerged, providing specialized services in this domain. Prominent examples include FireEye, Mandiant, and CrowdStrike. Notably, reports like the one published by Mandiant in 2013 on APT1, an APT group associated with China, significantly contributed to our understanding of tracing hostile threat activities (Mandiant 2013—more on APTs in the next section). Simultaneously, these reports underscored the political nature of threat intelligence, highlighting its broader implications beyond technical analysis (Egloff and Dunn Cavelty 2021). Subsequently, powerful actors like the United States began leveraging public attribution as a political tool to shape norms and standards in the cyber-security realm.

Attribution is based on the decision to allocate resources before any actual incident occurs because "computer network environments are not designed to support attribution of attackers" naturally (Wheeler and Larsen 2003: 4). Step one is the ability to detect an attack, which can be achieved through the implementation of IDS and other defensive measures. When evidence of a threat actor's activity on a network is discovered, several key questions arise: What is going on? What happened? How did the threat actor carry out their objectives within the network? What could have been those objectives, and were they accomplished? (Steffens 2020)

Rid and Buchanan's influential work on attribution in 2015 distinguishes between the "tactical" aspect of attribution (what occurred) and the "operational" aspect (how it happened) (Rid and Buchanan 2015). In some cases, the investigation aims to understand the attack's rationale and significance—the "who" and "why" aspects (Rid and Buchanan 2015: 10). It is possible to make a distinction between the attribution to a machine, to a person behind the machine, or to the organization responsible for initiating it in the first place, with mounting complexity and costs for the attribution process. This second phase might be followed by a third, when a political decision is made to communicate the findings of the forensic investigation either to a close group or to the public (Egloff 2020).

Public attribution, typically occurring as a final step, has emerged as a strategic tool employed by states to shape the geopolitical landscape and revive traditional notions of punishment. The act of publicly attributing cyber-attacks can take various forms, each serving distinct purposes (Egloff and Smeets 2023). Public attribution can have consequences such as indictments against individuals, as is the case with Chinese officials and Russian hackers, and the imposition of sanctions, as seen in cases involving Russia. Though the effectiveness of sanctions has often been questioned, restricting implicated individuals' international travel options will be a nuisance to them, even if not necessarily a deterrent. In addition to the punitive measures, public attribution serves a normative function by drawing boundaries and signaling that certain actions are unacceptable. Not least, by exposing operational details of the attackers' methods, it becomes more challenging for them to continue using the same tools effectively.

However, public attributions also pose trade-offs for the defending entity. One consideration is determining how much information to disclose about their own capabilities to make the attribution sufficiently credible. There is a risk that revealing too much could compromise their own intelligence capabilities in the future, as the attackers may alter their tactics and attack patterns in response. The "gain/loss ratio of public attribution" refers to weighing the intelligence and technical gains from disclosing information against the potential losses it may entail, which underscores the complex decision-making process involved in determining the extent of disclosure in public attributions (Egloff and Smeets 2023).

Early cases of attribution happened without the involvement of government entities, in private-led processes, often through a combination of technical information and the application of the "qui bono" logic, as commonly employed in criminal investigations. This logic is based on the question of "who benefits," which assumes that those who stand to gain the most are more likely to be the perpetrators. As we delve deeper into the study of cyber-incidents, it becomes increasingly evident that the "qui bono"-logic is not a bad yardstick. Two reasons support this perspective. First, cyber-incidents do not occur in isolation; they are employed as tools with specific aims in specific political contexts. In fact, they tend to arise almost exclusively within preexisting rivalries or enmities. Second, considering the substantial costs (and risks) associated with carrying out a high-level cyber-attack, it is reasonable to assume that those who benefit from such attacks are also the ones who have invested significant resources in executing them.

In more recent years, attribution processes have started to unfold within the realm of public-private assemblages, with private threat intelligence firms assuming increasingly significant roles (Collier 2018). Some of these transnational firms possess advanced forensic capabilities that surpass those of many nation-states. However, the attribution claims put forth by these firms may lack transparency and public legitimacy, raising concerns about their credibility. To comprehensively grasp the impact of cyber-incidents on cyber-security politics, it is crucial to closely examine attribution processes, since they determine the formation of public knowledge regarding cyber-incidents, including the level of certainty surrounding the identity of the perpetrators (Kuerbis et al. 2022).

It is also important to consider what is visible and what remains hidden from the public eye. The visibility of cyber-activities, particularly in Western contexts, is based on the reporting from Western (primarily US-based) threat-intelligence companies. The ability to see what is going on in networks is called "network visibility" and is based on "network telemetry," capabilities to collect, measure, and analyze data related to the behavior and performance of the network. It is this visibility that ultimately translates into political power: The ability to use cyberspace strategically—to use it in a targeted manner to achieve the affects you want—and knowing what is going on in as many networks as possible goes hand in hand.

The notion of "incidents" plays a role across all cyber-threat categories and is at the heart of the efforts to get a handle on the magnitude of the threat, which is connected to technical countermeasures, not least antivirus software. When computer viruses started to gain attention in the 1980s, the first antivirus software programs were developed, with the 1990s witnessing a rapid growth of the antivirus industry as the number of computer viruses increased. Antivirus companies develop and maintain vast databases of malware signatures. These signatures are unique patterns or characteristics that help identify known malware strains. When antivirus software detects a file or program matching a known signature, it is considered a positive detection or incident. Even though network defenses have greatly evolved since the early days of antivirus software to involve heuristic approaches and machine learning (ML), which do not look for a specific signature but "bad behavior" of systems, incidents are what these solutions flag (Egloff and Dunn Cavelty 2021). As part of what is known as "incident response," the malware can then be isolated and removed—it has been given visibility, which allows it to be traced, identified, deleted, counted, classified, etc. (Szor 2005; Slayton and Clarke 2020).

It was the publicly available work of threat intelligence companies, which themselves used methods and practices developed and employed by the Air Force and NSA, that gave us the ability to move away from singular incidents toward a broader threat picture. These companies began to leverage expertise, tools, and extensive datasets to attribute different activities to specific threat actors or groups. The key to doing this is what is called technical indicators, TTPs, and other metadata to build profiles of threat actors and their motivations (Hutchins et al. 2010). It soon became clear that, for attribution, focusing on individual incidents did not provide sufficient evidence to implicate specific state actors or organizations. Another concept that signals a move away from isolated incidents are "cyberspace operations" (Slayton 2021), which followed in the tradition of "information operations" (first mentioned around 1995—Department of the United States Air Force, Cornerstones of Information Warfare). In a military set-up, the term "operations" indicates the strategic, planned, and coordinated nature of the activities. Also, evaluating the impact of cyber-operations or campaigns requires analyzing the cumulative effects over time. Individual incidents may appear isolated or inconsequential, but when viewed as part of a broader campaign, their significance and potential harm become clearer (Harknett and Smeets 2022).

The Perpetrators

Clearly, not every cyber-incident is the same—not least because the objectives of the people behind it vary, which also influences the mode they choose to breach or affect the network. A label bestowed upon the actors behind cyber-incidents is "hacker." This term has a long history going back to at least the late 1950s and the MIT's Tech Model Railroad Club and has always carried an ambivalent meaning (Jordan 2017). For members of the Western computing community, "hacker" describes a member of a (more or less) distinct social group: someone who likes to explore things beyond their intended purpose, someone who knows how to write original programming code (Erickson 2003). A particular ethic (and therefore politics) used to be ascribed to this subculture: a belief in sharing, openness, and free access to computers and information; decentralization of government; and improvement of the quality of life through technologies (Levy 1984; Thomas 2002; Coleman 2012). However, the use of the term "hacker" for a wide variety of activities suggests a nonexistent homogeneity. For example, the distinctly Western, if not American, view does not apply to other parts of the world. Though good literature is sparse, the story of Chinese or Russian hackers is fundamentally different from Western accounts (Lindtner and Li 2012; Lindtner 2015; DeSombre and Byrnes 2018).

Since the skill set and tools used in "hacking" are "dual use," it became common to make a distinction between "good" and "bad" hackers, in part shaped by computer law that made some activity illegal and led to the prosecution of "hackers" as criminals (Nissenbaum 2004). A distinction between white, gray, and black hats later became common. The white hat connotes an ethical hacker because he attempts to improve the security of networks and is always careful not to break the law. With the rapid growth of the cyber-security industry, this type is now often labeled "IT security professionals" (Tanczer 2020). Black hats are driven by nefarious motives, such as financial gain or revenge. In the zone between are the gray hats: Depending on the context, they may sometimes violate laws, but they do not have the malicious intent that characterizes a black hat hacker. Aided by popular culture, the construction of a "hacker other," a technological genius enemy with different values who would act against the self-assigned ethics, was a consequence of such differentiations.

Hackers as antagonists took on different flavors over the years. After 9/11, for example, the debate started to focus on terrorist hackers (Bendrath et al. 2007), and from there it moved on to highly professional cyber-mercenaries, able to develop effective cyber-weapons and use them for whichever state paid the most (Maurer 2018). Popular media often romanticizes hackers, presenting them as solitary figures, eccentric geniuses (as seen in shows like Mr. Robot), operating from dimly lit basements. However, successful single actors are rare nowadays. The term "advanced persistent threats" (APTs), which was allegedly coined in 2006 by Colonel Greg Rattray of the US Air Force (van Otterloo 2015), represents a different type of hacking activity. The term APT was brought to the broader public's attention by Mandiant's 2013 "APT 1" report (Mandiant 2013).

Since then, the term APT has been used in different contexts. It is used to refer to specific actor groups, sometimes to describe the approach employed, and sometimes to denote a particular campaign. This ambiguity reflects the rapidly evolving nature of cyber-threats and the various interpretations within the cyber-security community. The most relevant characteristics of APTs are that they: (1) attack specific targets, (2) use sophisticated tactics, techniques and procedures, (3) constantly evolve their attack steps, (4) largely infiltrate a network, (5) perform repeating attack attempts, and (6) maintain long-term access to the target environment (Chen et al. 2014). These attacks are typically carried out by groups affiliated with states or "semi-state actors" (Egloff 2022).[2]

Some of the most notorious threat actors known today are compiled in Table 7.1. The sources of this knowledge are reports by corporate threat intelligence companies that are specialized in attributing to semi-state groups and a Google spreadsheet constantly changed by a group of dedicated threat analysts.[3] Given that threat intelligence companies are in competition with each other and might use slightly different methodologies based on different telemetry and data, these companies assign different names to the same or similar actors. For example, APT groups are numerically named by Mandiant, whereas Crowdstrike names APT groups by animals. A China APT group is designated with "Panda," Russian groups with "Bear," and Iran with "Kitten." There also tend to be subgroups associated with bigger groups, and groups that share toolsets. Because attribution of threat activities depends to a large degree on the ability to monitor activities in networks (the aforementioned "network visibility"), we have a lot of information on threat activities discovered on Western networks but almost no information on threat activities in strategic rivals' networks (see Table 7.2).

TABLE 7.1 A List of Prominent APTs

Name	Affiliated with	Known for
Lazarus (a.k.a. Hidden Cobra, Gods Apostles, Guardians of Peace, APT38, Whois Team, ZINC)	North Korea, operating since 2010	Sony Hack (2014) WannaCry (2017)
Equation Group (a.k.a. EQGRP, Housefly, Remsec, Tilded Team)	USA (Link to NSA's Tailored Access Operations (TAO) unit, operating since 2001)	Stuxnet (2010) Tools leaked by Shadow Brokers (2017)
Sandworm (a.k.a. Telebots, Electrum, Voodoo Bear, Iron Viking)	Russia, operating since 2009 (Russian military intelligence GRU unit 74455 sponsors Sandworm activity)	Power Outages in Ukraine (2015, 2016) NotPetya (2017)
Fancy Bear (a.k.a. APT28, Sofacy, Sednit, Strontium)	Russia, operating since 2010	DNC Hack (2016)
Cozy Bear (a.k.a. APT29, Dukes, Group 1000, Nobelium, SilverFish, StellarParticle, Dark Halo)	Russia, operating since 2008	DNC Hack (2016) Solar Winds (2020) (see Box 7.3)

(Continued)

TABLE 7.1 (Continued)

Name	Affiliated with	Known for
OilRig (a.k.a. APT34, Crambus, Helix Kitten, Twisted Kitten)	Iran, operating since 2012	Shamoon (2012)[4]
Homeland Justice (a.k.a. UNC2448, APT42, Crooked Charms)	Iran, operating since 2015	Attack on the Albanian government (2022)[5]
Turla Group (a.k.a. Snake, Venomous Bear, Group 88, Uroburos)	Russia, operating since (at least) 2004	Moonlight Maze (1999–2000) Epic Turla (2014–present)[6]
Comment Crew (a.k.a. APT1, Byzantine Hades, Comment Panda, Shanghai Group)	China, operating since 2006	Titan Rain (early to mid-2000s)[7] Ghost Net (2009)[8]
Unit 8200 (a.k.a. Duqu Group)	Israel, operating in cyberspace since at least 2010	Stuxnet (2010) Duqu (2011)

Source: This information is based on knowledge from September 2023.

TABLE 7.2 Number of Known/Listed APT Groups and Operations per Country

Number of identified APTs per country (September 2023)[9]	
China	126
Russia	37
North Korea	10
Iran	40
Middle East	25
Israel	4
NATO	7

All the threat actors on this list are clearly affiliated with nation-states because their operations are conducted within political contexts. This begs the question: Who is considered the most powerful or the most dangerous state in cyberspace? The answer to this question is not at all straightforward because there is no consensus on what cyber-power is or how it manifests (Dunn Cavelty 2018; cf. Maschmeyer 2023). There are attempts to measure "cyber-power" through indices such as *The National Cyber Power Index* (Voo et al. 2022) or an International Institute of Strategic Studies (IISS) study on state cyber-capacity (International Institute of Strategic Studies 2021; cf. Willett 2019 and Çifci 2022).

Harvard's *The National Cyber Power Index* uses 29 capability indicators, which results in the following list (from the state with the most cyber-power going to those with less): the United States, China, Russia, the United Kingdom, Australia, the Netherlands, South Korea, Vietnam, France, and Iran. The IISS study uses different indicators but also sees the United States as the strongest (by far), followed by Australia, Canada, China, France, Israel, Russia, and the United Kingdom. However, many questions remain about the notion of power that underlies these studies, not least because the ability to be a self-determined actor in cyberspace is derivative of a complicated interplay between offensive and defensive factors that include societal aspects (Klimburg 2011), which are context dependent and cannot be measured easily with indicators.

Also, knowing about the quantity of "cyber-power" a state possesses does not tell us much about whom to be concerned about. The level of threat emanating from another state depends on the type of relations we have with them to begin with. It also depends on the type of actions the other state may conduct against us or our allies. In "No Shortcuts," Max Smeets distinguishes between four types of state actors active in cyberspace, according to whether they have operational constraints and how high or low their resources are (2022a: 51):

- Loose Cannon (low constraints, high resources): Russia
- Trouble Maker (low constraints, low resources): North Korea
- Gentle Giant (high constraints, high resources): United States
- Paper Tiger (high constraints, low resources): most other (democratic) states

This way, a more fine-grained qualification with regard to the types of operations that are likely to be conducted is added. On the one hand, the quantity and quality of resources will determine the precision of operations and the likelihood of reaching strategic goals. On the other hand, the factor of constraint reflects the likelihood of conducting operations that do or do not confirm with international (humanitarian) law or whether they are ready to cause severe consequences for civilians. Of course, constraints and resources also interact. Because only if you spend a lot of resources on operations can you do high-level, targeted attacks (and thereby be constrained).

Vulnerabilities and Their Exploitation

While it is challenging to make broad generalizations about all types of cyber-incidents, there is a common factor that often marks the beginning of each one: the successful exploitation of a vulnerability. In Chapter 3, the significance of "vulnerabilities" as a key aspect of evolving threat perceptions was already emphasized. A vulnerability refers to a weakness present in an information system, system security procedures, internal controls, or implementation that could be exploited or triggered by a threat source.[10] In the realm of IT-security, vulnerabilities are generally classified into six types: hardware, software, network, personnel, physical, and organizational vulnerabilities. Each type represents a specific area where weaknesses or gaps may exist, creating potential entry points for attackers. When an attacker possesses knowledge of a vulnerability and possesses a viable attack vector, that vulnerability becomes an exploitable vulnerability. This means that the attacker—and here we no longer differentiate between state and non-state hackers—has identified a specific weakness and has the means to leverage it for unauthorized access, compromise, or other malicious activities.

Software vulnerabilities receive significant attention within the cybersecurity landscape due to their sheer quantity, and the industry offers numerous programs and tools dedicated to their discovery. In comparison, hardware vulnerabilities are relatively fewer in number. In fact, there are typically tens of thousands of software vulnerabilities for every hardware vulnerability identified. Although hardware vulnerabilities, such as the Intel Chip's vulnerability discovered in 2018, may require specialized knowledge to exploit, they present unique challenges when it comes to patching and mitigation. Unlike software vulnerabilities, which can often be addressed through patches or updates, fixing hardware vulnerabilities tends to be a more complex and time-consuming process. Hardware vulnerabilities may require modifications at the chip or hardware level, involving coordination with manufacturers and suppliers, as well as extensive testing before effective remedies can be implemented (Batelle Insider 2018).

The existence of numerous vulnerabilities is a reality in the software landscape, and new vulnerabilities are continually added with each software update. According to an often-cited source, on average, there are approximately 1–25 errors per 1,000 lines of code in software delivery, highlighting the potential for vulnerabilities (McConnell 2004: 499ff.). To address and track these vulnerabilities, public vulnerability databases play a crucial role. One of the most prominent databases is the CVE database (Common Vulnerabilities and Exposures), maintained by MITRE.[11] CVE serves as a reference for vulnerability scanners and contains a unique record for each discovered and reported vulnerability. As of January 2024, the CVE database lists over 220,000 records (which is an increase of 9,000 since September 2023).

However, it is important to acknowledge that many vulnerabilities remain unknown, undisclosed, or never receive a CVE number. The actual number of vulnerabilities may be significantly higher than what is recorded in public databases. However, not all the known vulnerabilities are exploitable, and only a fraction of the disclosed vulnerabilities (approximately 23%) has observed exploits. An even smaller percentage (around 5%) is actively exploited "in the wild," meaning they are being used by malware that can be found on the devices of ordinary users (Cyentia Institute and Kenna Security 2022: 7).

One significant reason why not all exploitable vulnerabilities are actively exploited is the "cost-benefit" logic that guides attackers. Each unpatched vulnerability holds a varying level of value for an attacker, who operates within limited time and resources. As a result, not all vulnerabilities are considered equally valuable or worth the effort to exploit. To aid in assessing the severity of vulnerabilities, the Common Vulnerability Scoring System (CVSS) exists as an open industry standard managed by the Forum for Incident Response and Security Teams (FIRST).[12] CVSS provides scores ranging from 0 to 10, indicating the severity of vulnerabilities (Mell et al. 2007). These scores categorize vulnerabilities into low, medium, high, and critical levels based on their potential impact.

Critical vulnerabilities, representing around 20% of all known vulnerabilities,[13] are the ones most likely to be targeted for exploitation. This is due to the significant harm they can cause if successfully exploited. Attackers prioritize vulnerabilities that offer higher potential gains, either in terms of the impact they can have on the target system, the data they can access or manipulate, or the potential for financial gain. In contrast, low- and medium-severity vulnerabilities may not be as attractive to attackers, as the potential benefits may not outweigh the investment of time, resources, and risk involved in exploitation.

Following the discovery and analysis of Stuxnet, significant attention was drawn to zero-day vulnerabilities, often surrounded by an air of myth. Zero-day vulnerabilities are exploitable vulnerabilities that are known to only a few individuals, and no public patch or fix has been released for them. This lack of public knowledge and available patches increases the likelihood of a successful exploit. A study conducted by RAND a few years ago indicates that zero-day vulnerabilities have an average lifespan of approximately 6.9 years (Ablon and Bogart 2017: 33). After one year, only around 5.7% of these vulnerabilities have been discovered by others (Ablon and Bogart 2017: 43). This suggests that the majority of zero-day vulnerabilities remain unknown and unaddressed for extended periods, leaving potential avenues for exploitation open (see also Roumani 2021).

The revelations made by Edward Snowden in 2013 also brought to our attention the inherent dilemma faced by certain governments with offensive cyber-programs, known as the "stockpile or disclose" dilemma. This dilemma revolves around the decision to either stockpile zero-day vulnerabilities, exploit them for their offensive capabilities, or to disclose them publicly so that they can be patched and fixed to the greater benefit of all. By leveraging zero-day vulnerabilities in current operating systems and hardware, governments can inject malware into strategically significant points of the internet infrastructure. However, this practice leaves those vulnerabilities unaddressed, potentially exposing key components of the information infrastructure to attacks (Leal and Musgrave 2023).

When a government becomes aware of an undisclosed vulnerability, whether through its own discovery programs (i.e., bug bounty programs), private contractors, or acquiring them from the market, they are faced with a decision on how to handle such vulnerabilities. They have the option to stockpile them for offensive purposes, sell them to other parties, or disclose them to the affected vendors or the public. To that end, the United States has implemented the Vulnerabilities Equities Process (VEP), which provides guidance to executive branch officials in determining whether to disclose or retain undisclosed vulnerabilities (Healey 2016; Willcockson 2021; Polley 2022). This process aims to strike a balance between national security interests and the need to protect critical systems and the general public. However, the dilemma goes beyond ethical considerations. Governments must weigh the strategic advantages of retaining undisclosed vulnerabilities for offensive purposes against the potential risks and consequences. There is a real-world impact on society if adversaries exploit these vulnerabilities before they are patched. The "EternalBlue" vulnerability serves as an example, highlighting the potential harm that can arise when critical vulnerabilities are not promptly addressed (Wilson 2022) (see Box 7.3).

BOX 7.3   ETERNALBLUE

Both the "NotPetya" (also known as "Petya," "ExPetr," "PetyaWrap," and other variants, attributed to Russia) and "WannaCry" (also known as "WanaCrypt0r" or "WanaCrypt," attributed to North Korea) cyber-attacks leveraged a specific vulnerability known as "EternalBlue." This vulnerability was part of a collection of exploits allegedly developed by the US NSA and leaked by a group known as the "Shadow Brokers" in April 2017. Both attacks had global consequences, affecting organizations, institutions, and individuals across multiple countries.

To end on a word of caution: Some researchers have warned against focusing too much on zero-days because it creates the impression that all attacks from well-organized groups need to be highly sophisticated. However, in most cases, low-level attacks like spear phishing are used. Some have argued that the number of zero-day exploits that are stockpiled by the USCYBERCOM is much lower than generally assumed (Healey 2016), potentially as low as fewer than ten. Recent data collection efforts show that 96% of all known cyber-attacks between states do *not* employ zero-days (EuRepoC 2023).

That said, 2021 saw the most use of zero-days yet (around 60 according to Google's Project Zero, in comparison to only 25 in 2020 and 20 in 2019),[14] a development mainly driven by criminal groups.[15] On the one hand, this increase may be a derivative of increased zero-day detection capabilities of groups like Google's Threat Analysis Group, Kaspersky's Global Research & Analysis Team, and Microsoft's Threat Intelligence Center (O'Neill 2019, 2021). On the other hand, the use of zero-days by the criminal groups shows that their level of skill is rising. For example, the average time to exploit software bugs has dropped significantly, from 42 days in 2020 to just 12 days in 2021 (Tung 2022). This 71% decrease in "time to known exploitation" indicates that hackers improved their ability to identify and exploit vulnerabilities. Such skill enhancement is likely driven by a combination of the competition among hacker groups, the money they have available to buy vulnerabilities, and the need to overcome stronger defense mechanisms, which force hackers to invest more resources into more complex exploit chains to achieve successful intrusions (O'Neill 2022).

The Anatomy of a Hack: Methods and Tools

Different types of attacks or operations and various tools employed to carry them out exist. Some tools are readily available as pre-built solutions, while others are custom-made, making them more valuable and costly. The term used for software tools employed in cyber-attacks is malware, which is a blend of "malicious" and "software." Its malicious nature refers to its ability to act against the will of computer or network owners. Examples of malware include viruses and worms, which are programs that replicate themselves with varying effects, as well as Trojan horses, which disguise themselves as benign applications but create a backdoor for hackers to later exploit and gain entry to the system. Spyware is designed to gather information about individuals or organizations without their consent, thus violating their privacy. Ransomware, on the other hand, encrypts a portion of a victim's data or locks people out of their computer system or network and demands payment for the data's release or restoration of access. Ransomware has gained significant attention since 2020 due to a sharp increase in highly disruptive incidents, such as the Colonial Pipeline ransomware attacks in 2021 (Box 7.4).

BOX 7.4   COLONIAL PIPELINE RANSOMWARE ATTACK, 2021

The Colonial Pipeline ransomware attack occurred in May 2021. Colonial Pipeline, one of the largest fuel pipeline operators in the United States, suffered a cyber-attack that led to the disruption of its operations. The attack was carried out by a cyber-criminal group known as DarkSide, which specializes in ransomware attacks. As a result, Colonial Pipeline was forced to shut down its operations temporarily to prevent further spread of the ransomware and protect the integrity of their systems.

The shutdown of the Colonial Pipeline had a significant impact on fuel supplies along the East Coast of the United States. The pipeline carries approximately 45% of the fuel consumed by the region, including gasoline, diesel, and jet fuel. The disruption caused fuel shortages, panic buying, and price increases in certain areas, leading to concerns about the availability and distribution of essential fuel resources.

In response to the attack, Colonial Pipeline engaged with law enforcement agencies and cyber-security experts to investigate the incident, contain the ransomware, and restore their systems safely. The company also paid a ransom of approximately US$4.4 million in Bitcoin to the attackers, although a portion of the ransom was later recovered by law enforcement.

During the early days of cyber-security, the focus revolved around viruses and worms, which drove much of the discussion. Creating these early viruses and worms did not demand extensive expertise or a team. In fact, some of the most well-known viruses, like "Morris Worm" (1981), "Melissa" (1999), and "ILOVEYOU" (2000), were developed by individuals. However, the threat landscape underwent a significant transformation: attacks became more personalized, groups started to organize, and motives turned criminal or political. Targeted attacks, which are aimed at specific individuals or groups, require a considerable amount of time to execute successfully. The more challenging it is to breach the target and achieve the desired impact, the more intricate the operation becomes. This complexity is reflected in the diverse range of tools and approaches employed to breach the targeted system. In essence, the more precise, controlled, and covert an attack, the greater the complexity of the entire operation.

As threats became more targeted, defensive strategies diversified. Instead of relying solely on antivirus software and firewalls, which primarily focus on keeping out known threats, new approaches emerged to detect intruders during an ongoing attack. For example, Lockheed Martin developed the "Cyber Kill Chain" methodology to illustrate the tactics employed by sophisticated threat actors when breaching a system (Lockheed Martin 2015). This methodology outlines seven distinct steps that well-organized entities typically follow for a successful operation: Reconnaissance, Weaponization, Delivery, Exploitation, Installation, Command & Control, and Actions on Objective (Hutchins et al. 2010).[16] In step one, attackers spend time identifying and getting to know their target. Often, so-called social engineering techniques are used here, whereby a human target is tricked into disclosing confidential information that helps the hacker gain access to the system. In step two, the attacker decides how to get into the network. The term "weaponization" refers to the process where tools—malware and delivery mechanisms—are built to attack the victims. For advanced attacks, malware can operate without detection, includes mechanisms to override the host IDS, can operate on its own without depending on remote command and control, and may even have the capability to re-infect the system if detected and removed. In the next four steps, the malware is delivered through delivery vectors such as email attachments, removable USB sticks, or websites; exploits a known weakness to breach the system; is installed so that the intruder has access to the system via remote access; and helps the attacker gain "command and control" over the breached system so that they can achieve their objectives, such as the exfiltration of data.

By adopting this methodology or similar ones (see, e.g., Caltagirone et al. 2013), defense strategies can be designed to think like advanced threat actors, thereby enhancing the overall security posture. One important focus that emerges from these models is the gathering of information about the adversary and their activities ("threat intelligence"). This approach emphasizes the need to proactively collect and analyze data on threats to better understand and mitigate risks. The market for advanced persistent threat protection has an estimated growth projection from US$5.2 billion in 2020 to $12.6 billion by 2025 (Markets and Markets 2020). Established antivirus companies like Symantec and Kaspersky have expanded their business models to incorporate advanced threat protection, while new companies such as Mandiant, FireEye, and CrowdStrike have emerged as key players in this market.

Digital information possesses certain characteristics that enable intruders to engage in various actions with potentially serious consequences. The impact of cyber-operations can vary depending on the value of the targeted information or the significance of the application for which the information is utilized. Consequently, the consequences of such actions can range in severity, impacting the affected individuals, organizations, or systems differently. The D5-Framework, derived from how the US Air Force defines its capabilities (US Air Force 2023: 4), provides a useful categorization for offensive cyber-operations beyond military conflicts. It encompasses five key objectives: deceive, degrade, deny, disrupt, and destroy:

1. *Deceive*: Involves manipulating or providing false information to make a target believe something that is not true. Deception tactics can be used to mislead adversaries, divert their attention, or create confusion.
2. *Degrade*: Aims to reduce the effectiveness or efficiency of a target system or its ability to collect information. By impairing or compromising the functionality of a system, the attacker seeks to hinder its normal operations.
3. *Deny*: Focuses on preventing adversaries from accessing targeted information, systems, or services. This objective aims to restrict their ability to gather intelligence, gain access, or utilize resources effectively.
4. *Disrupt*: Seeks to break or interrupt the flow of information, causing operational or functional disturbances. Disruption may involve blocking communication channels, interrupting critical services, or compromising network connectivity.
5. *Destroy*: Involves inflicting severe damage to a system, rendering it incapable of performing any function, or requiring substantial rebuilding to restore usability.

It is important to note that the D5-Framework primarily aligns with military missions and offensive cyber-operations. For a more comprehensive list, two activities often associated with intelligence activities also need to be considered: *Exploit*, the act of leveraging vulnerabilities or weaknesses in a system to gain unauthorized access for the purpose of collecting information or planting false/misleading data, and *Influence*, the objective of which is to influence adversary behavior to act favorably or in a desired manner, often through psychological or information warfare techniques (cf. Moore 2022).

Indeed, it is common for advanced attacks to involve an extended period of remaining undetected within the targeted network. This timeframe is known as "dwell time," and on average, it exceeded 200 days before discovery a few years ago (Stoneff 2018). During this period, the attacker aims to remain hidden as they explore the network to gain a deeper understanding of the target system. The decision to extend dwell time is often driven by several factors: First, the attacker may not possess complete knowledge of the target system initially and may need time to gather more information. By patiently observing, they can identify valuable assets, vulnerabilities, and potential avenues for further exploitation. Additionally, the objectives of the attack may evolve over time. As the attacker gains access and familiarizes themselves with the network, they may discover new opportunities or alter their initial goals based on the information obtained. Flexibility in objectives allows the attacker to adapt their strategy for maximum impact. However, there are risks associated with prolonged dwell time: Unintended exposure or detection of the attacker's presence during clandestine campaigns can lead to significant costs. For example, once specific malware or attack patterns are recognized by defensive systems, it becomes more challenging for the attacker to utilize the same tool kit in future operations.

It might already have become evident to the reader that advanced cyber-attacks require much more than just a piece of malware. A more accurate concept to use is "cyber-capabilities," which refers to "a combination of various elements that collectively enable adversaries to manipulate digital services or networks" (Egloff and Shires 2022: 3). Strategic cyber-capabilities are dependent on the target and must be tailored to specific configurations. The knowledge and expertise needed to cause specific types of failures, such as manipulating a centrifuge to spin out of control, must be acquired explicitly for that purpose. Due to the custom-built nature of malware, stockpiling up-to-date cyber-capabilities becomes more challenging once a conflict arises. Consequently, the "proliferation" of cyber-capabilities is not as straightforward as some have feared (Smeets 2022b). The complex nature of the cyber-security landscape underscores that not every vulnerability or zero-day exploit will be exploited. Targeting decisions are carefully considered, and the cost-benefit analysis plays a crucial role. Human actors, especially those operating within organizational contexts, evaluate their options and weigh the pros and cons before acting. This is a key point that we will revisit in Chapter 8.

Summary and Key Points

This chapter has provided a comprehensive exploration of cyber-incidents along the dimensions of actors, approaches, and vulnerabilities, as well as the question of attribution. Cyber-incidents have played a pivotal role in shaping international relations and security practices by revealing critical insights about adversaries, their capabilities, and intentions, triggering crucial reassessments of security measures and national cyber-strategies. However, we also acknowledged that cyber-incidents do not occur in isolation; their significance is intertwined with discursive practices within specific socio-political contexts. From the perspective of victims, adverse effects manifest as unwanted computing device performances, often involving the loss of data confidentiality, integrity, or availability. Yet, it is the process of linking these technical effects to social or political value that makes cyber-incidents security-politically relevant.

Many of these facets have only become known to us in the last few years, not least because of the knowledge accumulated in the threat intelligence space. It is paramount that cyber-security politics scholars engage with the procedures, methodologies, assumptions, and concepts that this highly specialized group of people use. If we do not, we will miss many nuances of the empirical reality of cyber-operations. These conversations happen largely in nonacademic literature and involve engaging with IT-security professionals.

Finally, it is necessary to reflect on the broader dynamics that a singular focus on cyber-incidents may obscure and emphasize the need to transcend this perspective for a deeper and more comprehensive understanding of cyber-security politics in our rapidly evolving digital world. For example, one of the lessons learned about the changing cyber-threat landscape after 2010 is that the focus on "incidents" is shortsighted and may be in part to blame for some of the misperceptions and blind spots that were revealed in the last decade. In fact, it is necessary to look beyond individual incidents to connect the dots and reveal the likely strategic objectives behind cyber-activities, a perspective that has largely come from threat intelligence.

Notes

1. See, for example, the Glossary from the NIST computer security resource center: https://csrc.nist.gov/glossary/term/cyber_incident.
2. The term "semi-state actors" recognizes the affiliation of these groups with specific states, while acknowledging their semiautonomous nature and potential involvement in cyber-operations (Egloff 2022).
3. This list is not comprehensive; it is contingent and subject to change when novel information is found: https://docs.google.com/spreadsheets/d/1H9_xaxQHp Waa4O_Son4Gx0YOIzlcBWMsdvePFX68EKU/edit#gid=1864660085
4. Shamoon, also known as Disttrack, is a type of destructive malware that has been involved in several high-profile cyber-attacks. It was first identified in 2012 when it targeted energy companies in the Middle East, particularly in Saudi Arabia. Shamoon is notable for its ability to cause significant damage to infected systems.
5. In July 2022, Iranian state cyber-actors—identifying themselves as "Homeland Justice"—launched a cyber-attack against the Government of Albania, which rendered websites and services unavailable. In September 2022, the same Iranian actors launched another wave of cyber-attacks, likely in retaliation for public attribution of the July attacks. In response, Albania decided to cut diplomatic ties with Iran and ordered Iranian diplomats and embassy staff to leave

in 24 hours (the first time a country has taken such a decision as a response to a cyber-operation).

6. The Epic Turla campaign is an ongoing operation that has targeted diplomatic and government entities in various countries, primarily in Eastern Europe and the Middle East. The group used a wide range of custom malware and techniques to infiltrate and maintain access to its targets.

7. "Titan Rain" is the code name given to a series of suspected cyber-espionage campaigns that occurred in the early to mid-2000s. These campaigns were attributed to state-sponsored Chinese hackers and aimed to infiltrate computer networks, primarily in the United States, to steal sensitive information.

8. The "GhostNet" campaign, also known as "GhostNet Cyber Espionage Network," was a large-scale and highly sophisticated cyber espionage operation that came to light in 2009. This campaign primarily targeted government and political organizations, particularly those in Southeast Asia.

9. Over 60 are unknown or not clearly attributed to one state.

10. https://csrc.nist.gov/glossary/term/vulnerability

11. https://cve.mitre.org/

12. www.first.org/cvss/

13. www.cvedetails.com/

14. "0day In the Wild" Google-docs Spread sheet: https://docs.google.com/spreadsheets/d/1lkNJ0uQwbeC1ZTRrxdtuPLCIl7mlUreoKfSIgajnSyY/edit#gid=0

15. Increased demand has an impact on zero-day prices: Zerodium's data indicated a rise of 1'150% for an Android exploit chain between 2016 and 2019: (see: AusCERT2021 Closing Keynote by Maddie Stone, https://www.youtube.com/watch?v=JImRRS4JJd8&t=1262s).

16. The Kill Chain is often criticized for its overly strong focus on malware, which neglects other attack types (Cycraft 2020; Engel 2014). Indeed, while the Cyber Kill Chain provides a structured framework for understanding the sequential steps of a cyber-attack, it may not perfectly capture the complexity and variation seen in all advanced attacks. However, it is generally acknowledged that privileged access to a system is a crucial prerequisite for conducting any advanced operation. Having privileged access allows attackers to manipulate the system, cover their tracks, compromise data, and clear logs in order to confuse or impede forensic investigations.

References

Ablon, L. and Bogart, A. (2017). *Zero Days, Thousands of Nights: The Life and Times of Zero-Day Vulnerabilities and Their Exploits*. RAND Corporation.

Balzacq, T. (2015). The 'Essence' of Securitization: Theory, Ideal Type, and a Sociological Science of Security. *International Relations* 29(1): 103–113.

Balzacq, T. and Dunn Cavelty, M. (2016). A Theory of Actor-Network for Cyber-Security. *European Journal of International Security* 1(2): 176–198.

Batelle Insider (2018). Hardware vs. Software Vulnerabilities. *Inside Batelle*. Blog. Available at: https://inside.battelle.org/blog-details/hardware-vs.-software-vulnerabilities

Bendrath, R., Eriksson, J. and Giacomello, G. (2007). From "Cyberterrorism" to "Cyberwar," Back and Forth: How the United States Securitized Cyberspace.

In: Eriksson, J. and Giacomello, G. (eds.) *International Relations and Security in the Digital Age*. Routledge, pp. 77–102.

Buzan, B. and Hansen, L. (2009). *The Evolution of International Security Studies*. Cambridge University Press.

Caltagirone, S., Pendergast, A. and Betz, C. (2013). *The Diamond Model of Intrusion Analysis*. US Department of Defense. Available at: https://apps.dtic.mil/dtic/tr/fulltext/u2/a586960.pdf

Chen, P., Desmet, L. and Huygens, C. (2014). A Study on Advanced Persistent Threats. In: *IFIP International Conference on Communications and Multimedia Security*. Springer, pp. 63–72.

Cichonski, P., Millar, T., Grance, T. and Scarfone, K. (2012). *Computer Security Incident Handling Guide. Recommendations of the National Institute of Standards and Technology*. Special Publication 800-61. Revision 2. Available at: http://dx.doi.org/10.6028/NIST.SP.800-61r2

Çifci, H. (2022). *Comparison of National-Level Cybersecurity and Cyber Power Indices: A Conceptual Framework*. Preprint from Research Square, October 17. Available at: https://doi.org/10.21203/rs.3.rs-2159915/v1

Coleman, G. (2012). *Coding Freedom: The Ethics and Aesthetics of Hacking*. Princeton University Press.

Collier, J. (2018). Cyber Security Assemblages: A Framework for Understanding the Dynamic and Contested Nature of Security Provision. *Politics and Governance* 6(2): 13–21.

Cycraft (2020). *CyCraft Classroom: MITRE ATT&CK vs. Cyber Kill Chain vs. Diamond Model, BUCERT*. Available at: https://medium.com/cycraft/cycraft-classroom-mitre-att-ck-vs-cyber-kill-chain-vs-diamond-model-1cc8fa49a20f

Cyentia Institute and Kenna Security (2022). *Prioritization to Prediction Volume 8: Measuring and Minimizing Exploitability*. Available at: https://library.cyentia.com/report/report_008756.html

DeSombre, W. and Byrnes, D. (2018). Thieves and Geeks: Russian and Chinese Hacking Communities. *Recorded Future*. Cyber Threat Analysis. Available at: https://go.recordedfuture.com/hubfs/reports/cta-2018-1010.pdf

Dunn Cavelty, M. (2018). Europe's Cyber-Power. *European Politics and Society* 19(3): 304–320.

Egloff, F.J. (2020). Public Attribution of Cyber Intrusions. *Journal of Cybersecurity* 6(1): tyaa012.

Egloff, F.J. (2022). *Semi-State Actors in Cybersecurity*. Oxford University Press.

Egloff, F.J. and Dunn Cavelty, M. (2021). Attribution and Knowledge Creation Assemblages in Cybersecurity Politics. *Journal of Cybersecurity* 7(1): tyab002.

Egloff, F.J. and Shires, J. (2022). Offensive Cyber Capabilities and State Violence: Three Logics of Integration. *Journal of Global Security Studies* 7(1): ogab028.

Egloff, F.J. and Smeets, M. (2023). Publicly Attributing Cyber Attacks: A Framework. *Journal of Strategic Studies* 46(3): 502–533.

Engel, G. (2014). Deconstructing The Cyber Kill Chain. *Dark Reading*. Available at: www.darkreading.com/attacks-breaches/deconstructing-the-cyber-kill-chain

Erickson, J. (2003). *Hacking: The Art of Exploitation*. No Starch Press.

EuRepoC (2023). *European Repository of Cyber Incidents, Data*. Version 1.1. Available at: https://eurepoc.eu/databases

Harknett, R.J. and Smeets, M. (2022). Cyber Campaigns and Strategic Outcomes. *Journal of Strategic Studies* 45(4): 534–567.

Healey, J. (2016). The US Government and Zero-Day Vulnerabilities: From Pre-Heartbleed to Shadow Brokers. *Journal of International Affairs*, November 1. Available at: https://jia.sipa.columbia.edu/news/us-government-and-zero-day-vulnerabilities-pre-heartbleed-shadow-brokers

Homolar, A. and Rodríguez-Merino, P. (2019). Making Sense of Terrorism: A Narrative Approach to the Study of Violent Events. *Critical Studies on Terrorism* 12(4): 561–581.

Hutchins, E., Cloppert, M. and Amin, R. (2010). *Intelligence-Driven Computer Network Defense Informed by Analysis of Adversary Campaigns and Intrusion Kill Chains*. White Paper. Available at: www.lockheedmartin.com/content/dam/lockheed-martin/rms/documents/cyber/LM-White-Paper-Intel-Driven-Defense.pdf

International Institute of Strategic Studies (2021). *Cyber Capabilities and National Power: A Net Assessment*. Available at: www.iiss.org/research-paper//2021/06/cyber-capabilities-national-power

Johnson, C., Badger, L., Watermire, D., Snyder, J. and Skorupka, C. (2016). *Guide to Cyber Threat Information Sharing*. NIST Special Publication 800-150. Available at: http://dx.doi.org/10.6028/NIST.SP.800-150

Jordan, T. (2017). A Genealogy of Hacking. *Convergence* 23(5): 528–544.

Klimburg, A. (2011). Mobilising Cyber Power. *Survival* 53(1): 41–60.

Kuerbis, B., Badiei, B., Grindal, K. and Mueller, M. (2022). Understanding Transnational Cyber Attribution: Moving from "Whodunit" to Who Did It. In: Dunn Cavelty, M. and Wenger, A. (eds.) *Cyber Security Politics: Socio-Technological Transformations and Political Fragmentation*. Routledge, pp. 220–237.

Leal, M.M. and Musgrave, P. (2023). Backwards from Zero: How the U.S. Public Evaluates the Use of Zero-Day Vulnerabilities in Cybersecurity. *Contemporary Security Policy* 44(3): 437–461.

Levy, S. (1984). *Hackers: Heroes of the Computer Revolution*. Anchor Press.

Lindsay, J.R. (2015). Tipping the Scales: The Attribution Problem and the Feasibility of Deterrence Against Cyberattack. *Journal of Cybersecurity* 1(1): 53–67.

Lindtner, S. (2015). Hacking with Chinese Characteristics: The Promises of the Maker Movement against China's Manufacturing Culture. *Science, Technology, & Human Values* 40(5): 854–879.

Lindtner, S. and Li, D. (2012). Created in China: The Makings of China's Hackerspace Community. *Interactions* 19(6): 18–22.

Lockheed Martin (2015). *Seven Ways to Apply the Cyber Kill Chain® with a Threat Intelligence Platform*. A White Paper Presented by: Lockheed Martin Corporation. Available at: www.lockheedmartin.com/content/dam/lockheed-martin/rms/documents/cyber/Seven_Ways_to_Apply_the_Cyber_Kill_Chain_with_a_Threat_Intelligence_Platform.pdf

Lupovici, A. (2016). The "Attribution Problem" and the Social Construction of "Violence": Taking Cyber Deterrence Literature a Step Forward. *International Studies Perspectives* 17(3): 322–342.

Mandiant (2013). *APT1: Exposing One of China's Cyber Espionage Units*. Available at: www.mandiant.com/sites/default/files/2021-09/mandiant-apt1-report.pdf

Markets and Markets (2020). *Market Research Report. Advanced Persistent Threat (APT) Protection Market*. Available at: www.marketsandmarkets.com/Market-Reports/advanced-persistent-threat-protection-market-7303302.html

Maschmeyer, L. (2023). Subversion, Cyber Operations, and Reverse Structural Power in World Politics. *European Journal of International Relations* 29(1): 79–103.

Maurer, T. (2018). *Cyber Mercenaries: The State, Hackers, and Power*. Cambridge University Press.

McConnell, S. (2004). *Code Complete: A Practical Handbook of Software Construction*. Microsoft Press.

Mell, P., Scarfone, K. and Romanosky, S. (2007). *A Complete Guide to the Common Vulnerability Scoring System Version 2.0*. FIRST Organisation. Available at: www.first.org/cvss/cvss-guide.pdf

Moore, D. (2022). *Offensive Cyber Operations: Understanding Intangible Warfare*. Hurst Publishers.

Nissenbaum, H. (2004). Hackers and the Contested Ontology of Cyberspace. *New Media & Society* 6(2): 195–217.

O'Neill, P.H. (2019). Inside the Microsoft Team Tracking the World's Most Dangerous Hackers. *MIT Technology Review*, November 6. Available at: www.technologyreview.com/2019/11/06/238375/inside-the-microsoft-team-tracking-the-worlds-most-dangerous-hackers/

O'Neill, P.H. (2021). 2021 Has Broken the Record for Zero-Day Hacking Attacks. *MIT Technology Review*, September 23. Available at: www.technologyreview.com/2021/09/23/1036140/2021-record-zero-day-hacks-reasons/

O'Neill, P.H. (2022). Wealthy Cybercriminals Are Using Zero-Day Hacks More than Ever. MIT Technology Review, April 21. Available at: www.technologyreview.com/2022/04/21/1050747/cybercriminals-zero-day-hacks/

Polley, L. (2022). *To Disclose, or Not to Disclose, That Is the Question: A Methods-Based Approach for Examining & Improving the US Government's Vulnerabilities Equities Process*. RAND Corporation.

Raiu, C. (2022). TOP 10 Unattributed APT Mysteries. Securelist by Kaspersky, October 7. Available at: https://securelist.com/top-10-unattributed-apt-mysteries/107676/

Rid, T. and Buchanan, B. (2015). Attributing Cyber Attacks. *Journal of Strategic Studies* 38(1–2): 4–37.

Roumani, Y. (2021). Patching Zero-Day Vulnerabilities: An Empirical Analysis. *Journal of Cybersecurity* 7(1): tyab023.

Skopik, F. and Pahi, T. (2020). Under False Flag: Using Technical Artifacts for Cyber Attack Attribution. *Cybersecurity* 3(8). https://doi.org/10.1186/s42400-020-00048-4

Slayton, R. (2021). What Is a Cyber Warrior? The Emergence of U.S. Military Cyber Expertise, 1967–2018. *Texas National Security Review* 4(1): 61–96.

Slayton, R. and Clarke, B. (2020). Trusting Infrastructure: The Emergence of Computer Security Incident Response, 1989–2005. *Technology and Culture* 61(1): 173–206.

Smeets, M. (2022a). *No Shortcuts: Why States Struggle to Develop a Military Cyber-Force*. Oxford University Press.

Smeets, M. (2022b). Cyber Arms Transfer: Meaning, Limits, and Implications. *Security Studies* 31(1): 65–91.

Steffens, T. (2020). *Attribution of Advanced Persistent Threats: How to Identify the Actors Behind Cyber-Espionage.* Springer.

Stoneff, C. (2018). *The Seven Steps of a Successful Cyber Attack.* Blog. Available at: www.beyondtrust.com/blog/entry/the-seven-steps-of-a-successful-cyber-attack

Szor, P. (2005). *The Art of Computer Virus Research and Defense.* Addison-Wesley.

Tanczer, L.M. (2020). 50 Shades of Hacking: How IT and Cybersecurity Industry Actors Perceive Good, Bad, and Former Hackers. *Contemporary Security Policy* 41(1): 108–128.

Thomas, D. (2002). *Hacker Culture.* University of Minnesota Press.

Tung, L. (2022). Hackers Are Getting Faster at Exploiting Zero-Day Flaws. That's Going to Be a Problem for Everyone. *ZDNet*, March 29. Available at: www.zdnet.com/article/hackers-are-getting-faster-at-exploiting-zero-day-flaws-thats-going-to-be-a-problem-for-everyone/

US Air Force (2023). *Cyberspace Operations.* Air Force Doctrine Publication 3-12. Available at: www.doctrine.af.mil/Portals/61/documents/AFDP_3-12/3-12-AFDP-CYBERSPACE-OPS.pdf

van Otterloo, S. (2015). An Overview of Advanced Persistent Threats. *ICT Institute.* Blog. Available at: https://ictinstitute.nl/advanced-persistent-threats/

Voo, J., Hemani, I. and Cassidy, D. (2022). *National Cyber Power Index 2022.* Belfer Center for Science and International Affairs, Harvard Kennedy School, September. Available at: www.belfercenter.org/sites/default/files/files/publication/CyberProject_National%20Cyber%20Power%20Index%202022_v3_220922.pdf

Wheeler, D.A. and Larsen, G.N. (2003). *Techniques for Cyber Attack Attribution.* Institute for Defense Analyses. IDA Paper P-3792. Available at: https://apps.dtic.mil/sti/pdfs/ADA468859.pdf

Willcockson, S.J. (2021). Revamping the Vulnerabilities Equities Process. *National Security Law Journal* 8(1): 123–161.

Willett, M. (2019). Assessing Cyber Power. *Survival: Global Politics and Strategy* 61(1): 85–90.

Wilson, M. (2022). The Ethics of Stockpiling Zero-Day Vulnerabilities. *Viterbi Conversations in Ethics* 6(1). Available at: https://vce.usc.edu/volume-6-issue-1/the-ethics-of-stockpiling-zero-day-vulnerabilities/

8

CYBER-OPERATIONS

Use and Utility

After the book discussed historical aspects of cyber-security politics and looked at different types of cyber-operations, this chapter turns to a critical appreciation of their use and utility in international politics. The aim is to first use available data to demonstrate which types of attacks are prevalent. What is confirmed is that cyber-doom, the big fear in the debate, is absent completely, while cyber-operations employed in peacetime and under the threshold of war dominate the picture. Most operations are related to espionage. Increasingly, state and non-state actors also seek to exert influence over the broader information sphere both before and during political disputes or conflicts, sometimes employing mildly disruptive attacks alongside these efforts.

The second part of this chapter then aims to explain these choices by state actors. Pulling together the knowledge about the difficulties attached to conducting targeted operations combined with their costs and risks, the chapter offers a framework that explains the prevalence of some attacks over others. It is the interplay between technological possibilities and political calculations that we need to consider. Third, we ask what the political utility of cyber-operations seems to be both in a conflict situation and in peacetime, not least using (preliminary) lessons derived from the war against Ukraine. Even though the war against Ukraine is likely an outlier, some of the long-standing assumptions the strategic community held about the value of cyber-operations in war need to be corrected.

DOI: 10.4324/9781003497080-8

Empirical Realities: Moving From "May Be" to "Evidence Shows"

The growing number of incidents with political significance in the last decade has led to several systematic data collections on politically motivated, state-attributable cyber-incidents.[1] While these undertakings vary in scope and quality, and only represent the reality of cyber-operations to a certain degree, they collectively enable us to gain a deeper understanding of how cyber-operations may serve states' political ambitions (Valeriano and Maness 2018; Valeriano 2022).

The first thing the data shows us is a significant surge in the number of incidents around 2018 (refer to Figure 8.1). Though different data sources contain different numbers of incidents, they all confirm this upward trend. This development also aligns with the observation that "the development of military cyber organizations became a truly global phenomenon in the ... period from 2014–2018" (Smeets 2022a: 27). To an unknown degree, it can also be attributed to heightened attention toward cyber-incidents and increased investments in advanced analytical capabilities.

According to COT website, a total of 34 countries conduct cyber-operations, with China, Russia, Iran, and North Korea accounting for 77% of all suspected operations in the past two decades.[2] However, due to significant information disparities and the absence of adequate attribution capabilities and public attribution statements in non-Western contexts, there is a lack of comparable data regarding the activities of Western cyber-commands on adversary networks (cf. Smeets 2022c).

What is considered a cyber-incident in these databases? This is a non-trivial question: As Healey observes (2021), the Russian SolarWinds intrusion could be "coded as a single campaign, an active intrusion into 110 organizations or a latent intrusion into 10,000." There is no common understanding on how to handle this issue or what the pros and cons of different options are. However, most data collections concentrate on aggregating a "cluster" of incidents aligning with the concept of "operations" (see Chapter 7), thus departing from the definition of incidents as single (isolated) events. These clusters of threat-activities typically acquire recognizable names in public-private attribution processes, like "Solar Winds" or "The Sony Hack." As scholars, we lack insights into the details of such attribution processes (Egloff and Dunn Cavelty 2021), and do not yet sufficiently understand the relationship between knowledge creation processes in technical communities and political implications.

An increase in the number of politically significant incidents serves as a strong indicator of heightened threat activity. However, quantitative measurements solely reflect the level of *effort* and not the actual *effects* of such

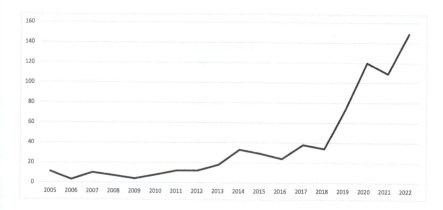

FIGURE 8.1 Number of Incidents per Year

Data Source: Council on Foreign Relations' "Cyber Operations Tracker" (COT) *www.cfr.org/cyber-operations/*

operations. This difference and the lack of literature on effects continue to be an issue for the entire cyber-security debate. Put differently: A "successful" intrusion does not signify much in political terms. The success and meaning of any operation can only be determined by the political or strategic effects that are achieved through that operation (Maschmeyer and Dunn Cavelty 2022), but the necessary discussion about how to measure the effects of cyber-operations across different dimensions is missing from the debate. We return to this problem in the last section of this chapter. The type of incident (crime, espionage, terrorism, etc.; see Chapter 5) provides some hints about the effects, since the categorization of the threat often aligns with the (attempted) actions by the attacker within the compromised network, but the categorization of incidents into threat categories is not sufficient to understand effects.

All available databases categorize approximately 60%–70% of cyber-operations as "espionage," with the primary effect being "data theft." Conversely, other types of operations, such as sabotage, denial of service, and data destruction, have a relatively minor presence (refer to Figure 8.2 for an illustration). This means that cyber-operations predominantly serve as a means for gathering intelligence, a trend that also holds true over time.

Furthermore, when considering the United States' four main adversaries—Russia, China, Iran, and North Korea—it becomes apparent that each of them uses cyberspace primarily for espionage purposes (refer to Figure 8.3): Russia (75%), China (98%), Iran (86%), and North Korea 61%).

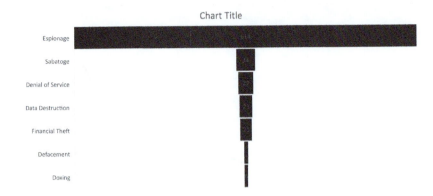

FIGURE 8.2 Incident Types (2000–2022)

Data Source: Council on Foreign Relations' "Cyber Operations Tracker" (COT) *www.cfr.org/cyber-operations/*

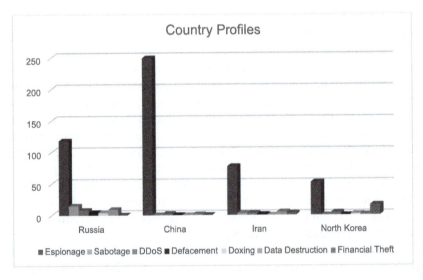

FIGURE 8.3 Type of Operations per Country

Data Source: Council on Foreign Relations' "Cyber Operations Tracker" (COT) *www.cfr.org/cyber-operations/*

While knowledge on the types of incidents provides insights into how cyberspace is primarily used, it does not provide a comprehensive understanding of the impact and severity of the incidents. To address this, the Dyadic Cyber Incident and Campaign Data (DCID) database uses a severity scale that ranges from 1 (least severe) to 10 (most severe) (Maness et al 2022: 8–9).[3] Clustered by severity (refer to Figure 8.4), the DCID data

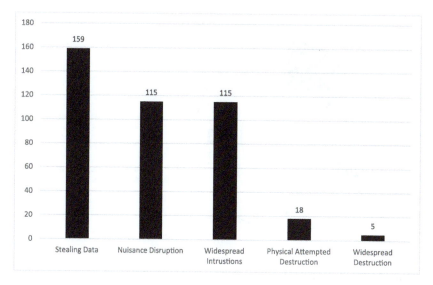

FIGURE 8.4   Impact/Severity of Cyber-Incidents

Data Source: Dyadic Cyber Incident and Campaign Data (DCID) database

has most incidents as severity 3 (39%), which corresponds to data theft, a finding that aligns with the prevalent use of cyber-operations for espionage purposes. Severity 2, indicating nuisance disruption, and severity 4, representing widespread intrusion, are tied for second place (28% each). There are only a few instances reaching severity 5, indicating attempted destruction (4%), and even fewer at severity 6, denoting widespread destruction (1%). These five cases of physical destruction involve Stuxnet (two entries because both the United States and Israel were involved), an alleged US operation that brought down North Korean missiles when testing (Houck 2018; Broad and Sanger 2017), and two instances of the Shamoon wiper malware (only data destruction). Notably, there are no recorded cases for severities 7 to 10, which include human death and widespread destruction.

The European Repository of Cyber Incidents (EuRepoC) database introduces an additional aspect by considering the distinction between long-term and short-term disruptions as an effect measure (Figure 8.5). According to the EuRepoC data, approximately 50% of incidents result in no disruption, while 36% lead to short-term disruptions. Only a small portion, around 7%, is associated with long-term disruptions lasting longer than 24 hours. Furthermore, the database identifies just three cases with geographically widespread effects, indicating that most disruptions remain local phenomena. It is important to note that these categories alone do not provide comprehensive information about the effects caused by such

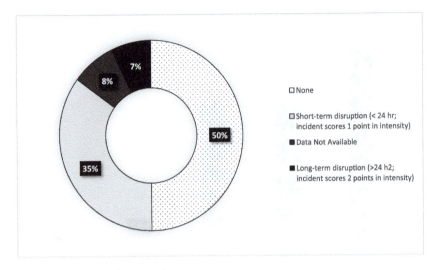

FIGURE 8.5 Type of Disruption

Data Source: European Repository of Cyber Incidents: (EuRepoC) database
https://eurepoc.eu/

disruptions. However, it is highly unlikely that small-scale, short-term disruptions will have significant and devastating effects that would affect a substantial portion of the population.

In sum, the empirical picture that emerges from the available data collections, however limited, is that cyber-operations are mainly used for espionage operations, and manifest predominantly as minor disruptions and nuisances. What is missing from this empirical reality are destructive, high-impact incidents, which were expected all throughout the 1990s and 2000s, despite the investment into cyber-capabilities by many states since. How can we explain this? And what does it signify?

The Determinants of Strategic Choice

There are several plausible explanations for why states mainly use cyberspace for espionage purposes and low-level threat activities. In line with its framework, the book argues that rather than looking for structural factors that explain all actions all the time, we should consider the interactions between technological opportunities and political constraints in specific contexts. In other words, technology constrains what you can achieve politically, whereas politics constrains what you will attempt to do technologically. Contrary to technologically deterministic explanations, the actions of states and other political actors are governed by more than just vulnerabilities in adversary networks and the existence of capabilities to exploit them (Lindsay and Gartzke 2017). Decisions to use cyber-capabilities against other states depend on "cost-benefit considerations" across multiple dimensions. To make this argument, the chapter discusses the differences between two types of cyber-capabilities, looks at the costs of developing and losing them, and finally discusses the trade-offs between costs and benefits.

Cyber-Capabilities: Two Ideal Types

As a first important step to understand the diverse utilization of cyber-operations by states, it is helpful to distinguish between two types of "cyber-capabilities."[4] These ideal types can be differentiated based on factors such as availability, cost, the level of skill (or organization complexity) needed to operate them, the barriers to entry, the precision with which they can be used, the (geographical) reach, and the speed of their deployment (see Table 8.1):

- The first type ("Generic") encompasses capabilities that are relatively inexpensive and require low levels of skill to plan and operate.
- The second type ("Elite") consists of capabilities that are costly and demand high levels of expertise. Sophisticated (as in targeted and precise) cyber-attacks always require significant resources, expertise, and specialized Type 2 capabilities.

Sophisticated threat actors can (and will) use Type 1 capabilities, but non-sophisticated threat actors cannot easily use Type 2 capabilities.[5] Table 8.1

TABLE 8.1 Cyber-Capabilities: Two Ideal Types

	Type 1: Generic	*Type 2: Elite*
Availability	Off-the-shelf	Custom-made
Costs	Low	High
Level of Skill	Low	High
Barrier to Entry	Low	High
Precision	Low	High
Reach	At scale	Limited targets
Deployment Speed	Fast	Slow
Typically Used for …	• DDoS-attacks[6] • Phishing Attacks[7] • SQL Injections[8] • Password Attacks[9] • Website Defacements	• Advanced Persistent Threat Campaigns[10] • Industrial Espionage • Targeted Supply Chain Attacks[11]

also contains examples of what the capabilities are mainly used for. If further explanations for these types of attacks are needed, they are given in the footnotes.

"Type 1 Generic" capabilities are available "off-the-shelf," meaning they are sold on the underground market or the dark web. They are commercially developed mostly by criminals or hacker groups and are designed to exploit known vulnerabilities or weaknesses in computer systems, networks, or software at scale (meaning they attempt to reach as many targets as possible). These tools often come with detailed instructions or user interfaces that simplify the process of launching attacks or deploying malware. Designed for optimal user-friendliness, they require low technical expertise to operate. Apart from single tools, "crime-as-a-service," package deals of criminal tools, services, or infrastructure sold by cyber-criminals to other individuals or groups in exchange for payment, are also available. The pricing for crime-as-a-service offerings varies depending on the specific service being provided, with some services being available on a subscription or pay-per-use basis (Manky 2013; Cherqi et al. 2018; Wade 2021). However, due to the inherent nature of software, networks, and their defenses, Type 1 tools are inadequate for targeted, covert operations because they are more likely picked up by standard defensive measures. That said, they are hard to attribute to one specific actor because they are used widely by different actors.

In contrast, "Type 2 Elite" capabilities are custom-made, and specifically developed and tailored to meet unique requirements and objectives. Custom-made cyber-capabilities are typically used in targeted attacks, such as state-sponsored espionage or sabotage operations. They are usually created by skilled and sophisticated threat actors for their own (often exclusive) use. Custom-made cyber-capabilities involve extensive research, development, and testing of targeted exploits and malware and are often designed to exploit zero-day vulnerabilities (previously unknown and unpatched security flaws) or employ advanced evasion techniques to bypass security measures. The more controlled and targeted an operation is—along the two dimensions of time and space—the more likely it is that specific political goals can be reached reliably. However, given that Elite capabilities are specific and tend to be used in different operations by the same actors, they can be attributed to specific threat actors.

There are three significant trade-offs, however (see also Maschmeyer's "subversive trilemma" (2021)):

- First, the more precise a cyber-capability is, the less it scales. In other words, the higher its destructive potential, the lower the number of targets it can hit (Rid and McBurney 2012: 6). The reason behind this trade-off is that the systems through which a destructive effect can be achieved are highly diverse. For example, Stuxnet was only able to manipulate a very specific type of system in place in Natanz.

- The second trade-off is between precision and availability. "Type 2 Elite" capabilities take considerable time to develop and test, since they must be tailored to the target and the desired effect (Smeets 2022b). Unlike a conventional attack, a precise and controlled cyber-operation is not something that can be "launched" upon the press of a button. The development of such a capability requires research and reconnaissance, exploit and malware development, testing and quality assurance, and operational planning. In general, this takes more time than planning conventional, kinetic operations where the capabilities are already available (McGhee 2016).

- The third trade-off is between the necessity for stealth and achieving effects quickly. For Type 2 operations, attackers must maintain access by remaining undetected to gather intelligence, understand the target's infrastructure, and carefully plan their actions to achieve the desired impact. In Jon Lindsay's words: "cyber campaigns are essentially long cons that need to trick people and machines for an extended period of time to be successful" (Lindsay 2023: 64). Also, the better the defenses in an attacked system, the more an attacker needs to invest upfront to avoid discovery. Only by operating stealthily, that is, by using advanced obfuscation methods or minimizing their footprint, attackers can evade detection by security systems, intrusion detection capabilities, or antivirus software, allowing them to maintain persistent access. This means that, first, pulling off advanced cyber-operations is much harder than is commonly assumed; and second, that not all imaginable scenarios can be pulled off.

A Look at the Costs of Cyber-Operations

In terms of costs, "Type 1 Generic" capabilities can range from relatively inexpensive to relatively expensive. Less advanced capabilities, such as basic exploit kits or simple malware, are very affordable, sometimes available for a few hundred dollars. On the other hand, more advanced capabilities with sophisticated features can command much higher prices, potentially reaching tens of thousands of dollars or more. The cost can also be influenced by factors such as the reputation of the tool or the seller, the rarity of the exploit or vulnerability being targeted, and the level of customer support provided. However, contrary to earlier beliefs that cyberspace would provide weak states with a cheap weapon to gain asymmetric advantage (Dossi 2020), affordable capabilities have limited coercive potential and often uncertain, even questionable strategic value.

"Type 2 Elite" capabilities, on the other hand, which have a higher strategic utility due to better control, require substantial resources encompassing financial, human, and technological investments. The considerable operational costs associated with certain cyber-operations are also noteworthy. Type 2 operations entail supplementary support functions, including intelligence gathering, reconnaissance, social engineering, or physical access to target environments. These support functions significantly contribute to the operation's success but necessitate additional resources and coordination that extend beyond the realm of cyberspace (Wilson et al. 2023). This point is crucial if we want to understand the use and utility of cyber-operations.

In "No Shortcuts," Max Smeets explains why there is a relative dearth of significant "cyber-effects operations" despite the proliferation of cyber-commands worldwide via a similar cost argument (2022a). According to Smeets, the absence of such operations is due to an *inability* to act in this domain rather than deliberate restraint. While launching a DDoS-attack using readily available internet capabilities (Type 1) is simple, Smeets shows how difficult it is to develop a functioning "military cyber-force" by running through five essential elements (PETIO-framework): people, exploits, toolset, infrastructure (for control and preparation), and organizational structure. In his opinion, the assumption that states that "go cyber" have already crossed the barriers to entry and possess Type 2 capabilities is incorrect (Smeets 2022a: 13). For the same reasons, it is also not a foregone conclusion that they will reach this kind of maturity in the future (cf. Slayton 2017).

Apart from the costs involved in building up and maintaining these capabilities, there is another crucial factor, that relates to the costs of *losing* capabilities. Indeed, engaging in cyber-operations carries an inherent risk for the attacker: the potentially permanent loss of their tools, techniques, or infrastructure in case the defender discovers the cyber-operation against the will of the attacker (Borghard and Lonergan 2019: 134). The risk of detection increases with higher operational complexity and a longer duration of the operation, due to an expanded digital footprint, an extended period of exposure, and the growing potential for operational mistakes.

The possible costs of a busted operation are varied. On the one hand, since "Type 2 Elite" capabilities often involve substantial financial investments in their development, acquisition, or customization, losing them results in the waste of these resources. Even worse, since the TTPs leveraged are now known to your adversaries, they might develop better defenses and countermeasures to mitigate future attacks. Developing or acquiring replacement tools necessitates taking such learning into account, which will result in higher costs for the attacker. On the other hand, the loss of "Type 2 Elite" capabilities will provide forensic evidence or indicators that can be used to attribute the cyber-operation back to the individuals or groups behind them. The more significant the damage or effect caused by a cyber-attack on a valuable target, the higher the likelihood of a reaction by the attacked state. The attacked state, considering its own readiness to condone further costs, has a range of options to react, including diplomatic protests, counter-operations in cyberspace, legal measures such as indictments, economic sanctions, or even military responses (van der Meer 2018). Particularly if the targeted state is the United States or one of its allies, or if the attack poses a threat to US interests, the aggressors must anticipate a high probability of attribution and counteraction. Of course, the ability to detect and attribute attacks is also dependent on capabilities.

Risk, Benefits, and Other Trade-Offs

It is crucial to reiterate that the mere availability of a capability does not guarantee its indiscriminate use—such is the nature of international relations. The decision to employ specific cyber-capabilities depends on various factors, including the adversary involved and the desired political objectives. Therefore, we can assume that aggressors assess the potential gains, the reactions of the attacked state or its allies, and the overall consequences before launching an attack. They may also have learned from past events, incorporating collective knowledge into their decision-making processes (Goldsmith 2003). Although the trade-offs and costs discussed above do not imply that causing extensive damage with cyber-capabilities is impossible, they do highlight the risks and expenses involved in (attempting) to do so. Consequently, the use of specific cyber-capabilities is constrained by political considerations.

To explain the use of specific capabilities in particular contexts, the book proposes a 2 x 2 table that considers two categories: The type of capability that is used (Type 1: Generic/Type 2: Elite) and the potential risks for the attacker (Low/High) (see Table 8.2 for descriptions and Table 8.3 for examples that align with these ideal types). The assumption is that "Type 1 Generic" capabilities always come with uncertain strategic gains, whereas "Type 2 Elite" capabilities guarantee a somewhat higher chance of reaching a goal. Whether an attack is low-risk or high-risk depends on several contextual factors. For example, the more critical the attack target is for the attacked state, the higher the risk of retaliation. Also, targeted attacks with "Type 2 Elite" capabilities with a clearly visible effect (i.e., "destruction") make it more likely that the toolset is lost, and they also make it more likely that a retaliatory measure will be taken.

TABLE 8.2 Type of Capabilities and Level of Risk

	Type 1: Generic	Type 2: Elite
Low Risk	Generic capabilities used at large have effects that are short-lived, diffuse, and hard to trace to a single entity. The potential gains are uncertain. The likelihood of retaliation or escalation is low.	Elite capabilities with a high degree of stealth have effects that are "silent" and hard to detect. The likelihood of losing the capabilities is low. The potential gains are high. The likelihood of retaliation or escalation is low.
High Risk	Generic capabilities used at large against (potentially) critical targets. The potential gains are uncertain. The likelihood of retaliation or escalation is potentially high because the effects are more likely to be considered grave.	Elite capabilities with high precision and stealth that can physically damage (or long-term disrupt) critical targets. The likelihood of losing the capabilities is high. The potential gains are high. Depending on attribution capabilities of attacked state, likelihood of retaliation and escalation is high.

TABLE 8.3 Examples and Frequency

	Type 1: Generic	Type 2: Elite
Low Risk	**Mild Disruptions** • DDoS-attacks and other mildly disruptive operations • Diffuse influence operations, misinformation at scale	**Espionage** • Targeted secret operations • Data breaches
High Risk	**Serious Disruptions and Hack & Leak** • Attacks that disrupt critical services (includes ransomware) • Targeted influence operations, esp. hack & leak	**Destructive Attacks** • Attacks that physically damage (or severely disrupt) critical infrastructures and services

Mild disruptions—generic/low risk (top left): Within this quadrant, we find activities such as DDoS-attacks and other mildly disruptive operations, as well as diffuse influence operations conducted through social media. These operations are characterized by their ease of execution, relatively low costs, and a lower likelihood of triggering substantial reactions

DDoS-attacks are predominantly employed by "hacktivists" or patriotic hackers (Ukraine is an exception to some degree; see further on). In that case, the activities are almost impossible to attribute to state actors for two main reasons: First, these activities rely on human behavior rather than the use of specific traceable malware. Second, these capabilities may not hold significant interest for states to utilize due to their fleeting effects. In other words, the impact or consequences resulting from these operations tend to be temporary or short-lived and diffuse. However, they tend to garner a lot of international (media) attention. Such attacks make the most sense if State A wants to cause (mild) chaos in State B or wants to express political disagreement. There is no comparable data for diffuse influence operations. Since the costs are low and attribution is hard, they seem to be an interesting option for state actors, even though the effects are hard to control, especially if the overall goal is just to create uncertainties and undermine trust in institutions.

Espionage—elite/low risk (top right): Within this quadrant, we find the majority of known, state-attributed cyber-operations. Indeed, cyberspace provides a relatively low-cost and covert means of conducting espionage activities in contrast to traditional methods of espionage, where human intelligence and physical surveillance can be risky, resource-intensive, and easily detected (Warner 2023). Espionage operations are less likely to be discovered than those that generate a visible effect, even though the capabilities used for espionage and covert operations are very similar (Lindsay 2023: 63). Hence, capabilities used in these kinds of operations are expected to have a longer lifespan. There is a risk of retaliation, but it is generally considered low because espionage activities are an accepted practice in international relations (within bounds). All in all, risks and benefits are well balanced here.

Serious disruptions and hack-and-leak operations—generic/high risk (bottom left): Within this quadrant, we have cyber-attacks that disrupt critical services (they are frequent in the criminal realm (ransomware) but rare in the political realm) and an emerging trend of targeted influence operations, particularly hack-and-leak operations. These operations still fall within the realm of relative ease in execution and have the potential for widespread impact. However, they come with a higher risk of retaliation and potential escalation compared to the first quadrant due to the nature of the targeted entities: critical infrastructures and critical services or processes (such as elections). There are no comparable datasets on influence operations, which makes it hard to reliably judge how frequent they are. However, there is a general unease in government circles about a possible increase in these types of operations. They seem an overall attractive, corrosive threat to our digitally dependent societies. Because these operations exploit existing vulnerabilities and simply amplify them, they are much harder to counter than technical risks (Maschmeyer 2023). Attribution, understanding the true intent behind operations, and isolating the effects of influence operations within broader contexts are very challenging (Bateman et al. 2021).

Destructive attacks—elite/high risk (bottom right): The absence of destructive attacks can be explained by the "unfavorable" cost-benefit balance in this quadrant. First, the evolving norms in cyberspace help to shape the strategic calculus of states. It is widely recognized in political circles that destroying an enemy state's critical infrastructures should be avoided unless there is a desire to engage in a full-scale conflict with them. Second, resorting to destructive cyber-operations requires careful consideration due to high political risks. Third, if the objective is to initiate a war, then traditional military means may be more appropriate and reliable in achieving the desired outcome. Cyber-capabilities, while efficient at causing minor disruptions and some limited damage, may not necessarily deliver the intended effect in the context of an all-out war. This also points to a lower strategic utility of cyber-capabilities in conflict situations.

Assessing the Strategic Utility of Cyber-Operations

Considering what we have learned about how they are mainly used, are cyber-operations really the big game changer that they are sometimes made out to be in international relations, or are their benefits and dangers overstated? Giving an answer to this question requires engaging further with their usefulness in reaching political goals. Unfortunately, our access to the necessary knowledge is limited. Ideally, we would be able to include the perspective of the attacked as well as the plans and goals of the attacker, which means we would need insights about the use of cyber-operations by the West (especially the United States) as well.

This lack of information notwithstanding, we can attempt to evaluate the strategic utility of cyber-operations based on available evidence and accumulated scholarly knowledge. To that end, the chapter looks at four elements. First, it returns to the question of "success" via "effects." Then, it considers their utility in the current international environment, which is shaped by strategic competition between the big powers since at least 2018. Second, we ask: What are they *not* useful for? Third, the book turns to conflict-settings and the theoretical utility of cyber-operations. Fourth, it looks at preliminary findings from the war against Ukraine, ongoing at the time of writing, as the first military conflict to incorporate such significant levels of cyber-operations on all sides, including noteworthy activities of non-state actors (Bateman 2022). What we find: While there is a very high level of cyber-activities accompanying the war, they have no observable effect on the military campaign and no effect on the political considerations of involved parties and allies. While that does not mean that they are irrelevant, it means that we must look closely at specific contexts and political decisions to understand the utility of cyber-operations.

Of Success, "Felt" Effects, and Cumulative Gains

Given that a cyber-incident is defined by the technical community as "an event that results in actual or *potentially* adverse effects on an information system, network, and/or the information residing therein," a hack can be considered a success as soon as it manages to breach a system (cf. Healey 2016: 47). From a technical standpoint, penetrating defensive barriers constitutes a victory for the attacking party, regardless of subsequent consequences. However, within a political and strategic context, the success of an operation executed by state actors must be evaluated in terms of how well it aligns with the political and strategic objectives driving the action and the extent to which these objectives are accomplished (Healey 2016: 45; see also Martino 2011; Denning 2015).

Therefore, to understand success, we would need to identify the primary political objective for which a state employed cyber-operations and evaluate to what degree that objective was attained (cf. Sullivan and Koch 2009: 708). This is a straightforward and little-contested observation. It also aligns with the documents the National Security Archive obtained about how the after-action review was done for the USCYBERCOM operation "Glowing Symphony" (National Security Archive 2020): "Success in Operation GLOWING SYMPHONY was assessed according to task accomplishment (whether elements of the operation are completed) and operational effectiveness (whether the operation has the impact desired). [document 1, page 2]."

Nonetheless, this evaluation presents formidable challenges for researchers. Given that attackers seldom disclose their intentions, researchers must rely on circumstantial evidence to make educated guesses. Moreover, the discovery of a malware implant or evidence of threat activity within a system does not always provide a clear understanding of the attacker's ultimate objectives, whether they were espionage, disruption, or other motives. Furthermore, the time lapses in detecting cyber-operations further compound the assessment process; attackers can clandestinely operate for extended durations, making it challenging to attribute specific consequences to a particular incident. The effects themselves may also unfold gradually, necessitating in-depth investigation and analysis to fully comprehend their ramifications (Libicki 2020: 202). In the case of Operation Glowing Symphony, we also have the observation that "[d]espite the high-priority placed on answering questions of effectiveness, the 30-Day Assessment reported difficulties in comprehensively assessing the overall impact to ISIS media" (National Security Archive 2020). This underscores the challenges faced by the attackers themselves in conducting such evaluations.

Nevertheless, comprehending the effects of cyber-operations remains a pivotal element in discerning success or failure. Notably, when these cyber-incidents result in effects that are "felt" or experienced by a substantial group of individuals or organizations, they tend to acquire political significance, potentially exerting an impact far beyond the realm of cyberspace. It is worth highlighting that these "felt" effects encompass cognitive impacts engendered through media coverage (Makridis et al. 2024). Although this facet of cyber-operations remains relatively under-researched, there are other domains, such as terrorism research, that have endeavored to comprehend the political and various effects (Laketa et al. 2021; Godefroidt 2022), providing avenues for future insights.

Historically, when examining the effects in the cyber-operations literature, the primary emphasis has been on their potential to inflict physical *destruction*. This focus can be attributed, at least in part, to the long-standing attention given to critical infrastructures as the referent object, often in conjunction with cyber-war and catastrophic scenarios (as discussed in Chapter 3). Nevertheless, it is noteworthy that Stuxnet remains the sole confirmed instance of an operation explicitly designed and successful in causing nonreversible physical damage.[12] As elaborated in Chapter 4, despite Stuxnet's significance, numerous questions persist regarding the cumulative effects of the malware, its unintended consequences, and its overall success. This ambiguity is exacerbated by secondary (reaction) effects that have ushered in a new era of cyber-competition.

When we shift our focus from destruction to *disruption*, a broader array of cases comes into consideration. Some of the most notable cyber-incidents, such as the DDoS-attacks in Estonia, the power grid attacks in Ukraine, WannaCry, or NotPetya, disrupted vital services, resulting in substantial economic damage, and thereupon eliciting political outrage. However, these cases also underscore the fact that the primary effect within the computer system provides only limited insight into the overall cumulative effects. Consequently, it does little to aid our comprehension of the political or strategic significance and repercussions of such incidents.

Political effects can manifest in diverse ways, including straining bilateral or multilateral relationships, potentially sparking retaliation or escalation, eroding trust, undermining international norms or agreements, or more broadly, influencing geopolitical dynamics (Agrafiotis et al. 2018

Egloff and Shires 2022). Cyber-operations can also exert a psychological impact on a population or targeted group (Shandler et al. 2023). They can contribute to deepening social divisions, eroding public confidence in institutions, or indirectly threatening social stability. While there are various approaches to measuring the economic effects of cyber-incidents (Dreyer et al. 2018), driven in part by the insurance industry's efforts to quantify cyber-risks, there remains a noticeable scarcity of literature concerning secondary or second-order consequences, especially those of a political nature.

However helpful the category of "felt" effects is to explain a connection between technical incidents and political consequences, there are many incidents where there is no "felt" effect or a substantially delayed one. For example, let us consider that we know that someone was in our networks for several months to conduct an espionage operation. We might also know that they were able to steal data. If we have good technical measures in place, we may know what kind of data they took. However, beyond this primary effect, what does this data theft signify in a broader context and from a longer-term perspective?

Significantly, the assessment of the impact of a cyber-breach hinges on multiple factors. First, it depends on whether, how, and when the adversary uses this data to create an adverse effect (and if we would be able to track this effect to the data breach). In addition, the policy reactions by the affected party also matter, not least when considering domestic audience costs (Egloff 2020) or the reputational damage that might arise from a mishandling of the incident (Makridis 2018). Furthermore, given that individual cyber-operations may be part of a larger campaign, a focus on the effects of single incidents is insufficient (Harknett and Smeets 2022). If a campaign spans five years, and throughout those five years, the attackers can gather data from a variety of different sources, the picture they can assemble—not least because of big data analytics—and the adversarial actions they might be able to take based on this picture should be considered when judging the strategic effects. Frankly, linking any such effects solely to cyber-operations is often not possible—perhaps creating the biggest difficulty for our understanding of effects and consequences.

Moreover, cyber-incidents happen within intricate geopolitical, technological, and social landscapes, rendering it difficult and, at times, impossible to attribute outcomes exclusively to the realm of "cyber." As shown in Chapter 4, the transition toward "strategic competition" provides an important backdrop for major power politics and the interplay between cyber-operations and this evolving environment (Fischerkeller and Harknett 2019). In this context, strategically consequential cyber-operations are characterized by their capacity to accrue cumulative gains, ultimately contributing to the desired effects. Again, this emphasis on cumulative gains complicates the endeavor to isolate the effects of cyber-operations. Strategic competition manifests in various arenas concurrently, rendering it inadvisable to isolate cyberspace as a distinct and insulated domain. Indeed, it is through its intricate entanglement with numerous facets of modern life that cyberspace exerts its multifaceted and complex impact.

What Are They (Not) Good For?

Another avenue to comprehend the utility of cyber-operations involves identifying their limitations. Scholarly research employing international relations theories to assess the effectiveness of cyber-operations has arrived at a consensus that they are ill-suited for coercion (Lindsay 2013; Borghard and Lonergan 2017), a concept known for its inherent challenges in the realm of international relations (Lonergan and Poznansky 2023). Indeed, a study conducted in 2018 noted that fewer than 5.2% of publicly disclosed cyber-operations led to concessions from their intended targets (Valeriano et al. 2018: 23), signifying that these operations had no easily discernible impact and failed to alter the behavior of the target entities. More recent data from the DCID database, upon which this observation is founded, paints an even more striking picture: a mere 2% of all known cyber-operations resulted in concessions, while a staggering 98% did not (Maness et al. 2022).

Furthermore, recent literature has delved into the question of whether cyber-operations tend to escalate conflicts, a concern frequently voiced in policy discussions. It has often been contended that the inherent ambiguities and uncertainties of cyberspace could exacerbate the security dilemma, potentially destabilizing situations (Buchanan 2017; see also Libicki and Tkacheva 2020). Beyond empirical observations in the real world, some scholars have employed experimental and survey methods to explore this issue, yielding findings that offer limited support for such concerns. These studies have revealed a prevailing reluctance to employ offensive cyber-capabilities, when provided with the choice, primarily due to apprehensions regarding the potential for escalation (Jensen and Bank 2016).

Additionally, studies using survey experiments have revealed a tendency toward willful *de*-escalation and evidence that cyber-operations are primarily seen as effective tools for "sub-crisis maneuvering" rather than instruments of full-scale escalation (Jensen and Valeriano 2019: 12). Other research casts doubt on the notion that a cyber-attack would be treated as equivalent to a comparable kinetic attack (Schneider 2018; Kreps and Schneider 2019; also, Borghard and Lonergan 2019). In line with this, Schneider et al. find that "cyber operations are primarily used to shape narratives as a complement to diplomacy prior to war and then as a support to military operations after war has escalated. Cyber operations, therefore, show an increasing and important amount of fizzle but not a lot of bang" (2022: 1).

Maschmeyer offers a convincing explanation for this limited utility through the concept of the "subversive trilemma," pointing out that severe operational constraints limit the strategic usefulness of cyber-operations to deliver a controllable effect at a particular time (Maschmeyer 2021; see also Lewis 2015). Because cyber-operations depend on secrecy to infiltrate a network and on the possibilities afforded by an adversary's systems, "subversive actors face a trilemma among speed, intensity, and control where an improvement in any of these variable(s) tends to produce a corresponding loss in the remaining one(s)" (Maschmeyer 2022). Compelling evidence for these trade-offs is found in Maschmeyer's analysis of Russia's cyber-operations against Ukraine between 2014 and 2018. As part of a larger subversive campaign, Russia carried out five major disruptive cyber-operations. However, even though the "power grid hack" in Ukraine in 2015 is often used as an example of Russia's cyber-prowess (see Box 8.1) and its readiness to go all out, a closer look at what was achieved reveals that it probably had very little strategic value. It took 19 months to develop, but even though the disruptive effect on the target was produced, it was neutralized within 6 hours. A second attempt in 2016 was neutralized within 75 minutes (Maschmeyer 2021).

BOX 8.1   SANDWORM'S POWER GRID HACK, 2015

The cyber-attack on Ukraine's power grid, attributed to the Russian state-sponsored hacking group known as "Sandworm," was a significant and high-profile incident. In late December 2015, hackers gained access to the computer systems of two regional electricity distribution companies in Ukraine. The attackers used malware to gain control of the power distribution management systems, which allowed them to manipulate circuit breakers and disrupt the flow of electricity. This resulted in power outages affecting several thousands of Ukrainian residents in the Ivano-Frankivsk region. The attack caused multiple substations to go offline for a maximum of 6 hours.

Ukrainian authorities, along with cyber-security firms and international organizations, launched investigations into the incident. They worked to remove the malware from compromised systems and to bolster cyber-security measures. Overall, the attack was seen as a significant escalation in the ongoing cyber-conflict between Russia and Ukraine. It further highlighted the potential for cyber-attacks to disrupt critical infrastructure and raised concerns about the vulnerability of such systems worldwide.

In retrospect, these cyber-operations failed to advance Russia's dual strategic goals of altering Ukraine's pro-Western foreign policy and eroding public support for such policies. It is plausible that Russia may have ceased attempting disruptive cyber-attacks against Ukraine after 2017 due to recognizing the relative ineffectiveness of these operations. According to this perspective, the primary threat posed by cyber-attacks is not an immediate catastrophic physical destruction, but rather the subtler, long-term, psychological, and societal harm they can inflict, such as eroding public trust in government (Maschmeyer 2023). The analogy of a termite infestation slowly eroding the foundations of our digital infrastructure underscores their potential for gradual yet significant—albeit challenging to quantify—effects (Schneider 2021). However, it is conceivable that such nebulous effects are not only sufficient but perhaps even advantageous or desired. Cyber-operations may help sow more ambiguity and uncertainty precisely because of the uncertainty surrounding their effects, optimizing the utility of activities that stay below the threshold of armed conflict in the protracted strategic competition often referred to as the "long game" (Paul et al. 2022).

Strategic, Operational, and Tactical Value in Conflict-Settings

Over a decade ago, Martin Libicki made a noteworthy observation stating that, "besides deterrence, norms, and taboos, one explanation for the lack of cyber warfare could be the severely limited strategic utility of cyber in war" (Libicki 2009: 117). This assertion stands out, especially given the prevailing belief in the potency of digital technologies in warfare within policy circles. The accumulation of evidence regarding the constraints of cyber-operations in conflict scenarios, including at the operational and tactical levels, continues to support this perspective, a point reinforced by the ongoing conflict in Ukraine.

A conflict environment certainly alters the strategic dynamics and some of the cost-benefit calculations that were discussed earlier. However, it does not fundamentally alter the inherent challenges associated with launching cyber-attacks or might in fact exacerbate them. In a conflict situation, the fear of retaliation by the adversary may diminish, as both parties are already engaged in a high-level conflict with destructive capabilities. One might assume that the use of destructive cyber-attacks against military targets would increase in such circumstances. However, this assumption overlooks the fact that these types of attacks are neither easy to execute nor straightforward to target and control, as we have previously established.

First, it is crucial to recognize that targeted cyber-attacks demand extensive planning over several months. Consequently, it is highly improbable for unforeseen physical conflicts to be immediately preceded by cyber-attacks. This encompasses the challenges associated with effectively initiating and deploying cyber-capabilities in unfamiliar or new environments (Work 2021). In addition, it is difficult to time an effect at the exact time it is needed.

Second concerning the fundamental elements of warfare, such as permanently disabling or degrading enemy conventional forces and occupying and controlling territories, cyber-operations are not effective (Libicki 2009: 59). The damage inflicted by cyber-attacks is often transient and reversible, necessitating additional resources to maintain their effects. Moreover, there is always an element of uncertainty regarding whether a disabled system may recover more swiftly than anticipated or whether the desired effect can be achieved at all (Schulze 2020: 190).

When there is an alternative option available to permanently destroy an asset instead of relying on a potentially unreliable cyber-capability, the preference for the former is considerably higher (Fink et al. 2014). This diminishes the strategic value of cyber-capabilities in the context of warfare (Smeets 2018; Borghard and Lonergan 2017: 477), and there are only a limited number of scenarios in which the use of cyber-attacks seems advantageous. For example, some experts contend that strategic cyber-operations could be particularly useful during the initial phases of a conflict because cyber-attacks tend to have their maximum impact when they catch adversaries off guard (Kostyuk and Zhukov 2017). Conversely, as a conflict prolongs and sustained cyber-attacks persist, the pool of undiscovered zero-day vulnerabilities (previously unknown software vulnerabilities) is likely to diminish, consequently reducing the expected effectiveness of cyber-operations (Schulze 2020: 188).

There is a noticeable gap in the examination of the operational and tactical employment of cyber-capabilities in the literature, with the focus primarily being on the strategic level. The operational level typically involves the planning and execution of military campaigns or large-scale organizational activities. This often involves activities like intelligence gathering or employing cyber-operations to disable specific systems, as exemplified in the cyber-elements of "Operation Orchard" in Syria in 2007 (Rid 2012: 19). However, it is important to note that strategic cyber-capabilities cannot be easily repurposed for tactical use at lower levels in the chain of command due to fundamental differences in the usage context (Metcalf and Barber 2014). Schulze has convincingly highlighted the challenges of integrating tactical cyber-operations into the traditional target cycle of conventional forces, primarily due to their lengthy planning and development phases (Schulze 2020: 191). In general, tactical units may find cyber-operations less suitable for their purposes. Existing studies, such as

Hollis (2011), emphasize InfOps (such as disseminating fake messages or employing malware/spyware to target individuals) as key use cases at the tactical level.

The Absence of Cyber-War in Ukraine: A Case Study

In what ways do these assumptions hold in the context of the war against Ukraine, which is ongoing at the time of writing? Before Russia's invasion of Ukraine in February 2022, a series of experts predicted the massive use of Russian offensive cyber-capabilities to "shock and awe" Ukraine's defenses and undermine their will to fight (Courtney and Wilson 2021; Healey 2022; but see Maschmeyer and Kostyuk 2022). Some seven suggested Russia need not invade because it could achieve the same outcomes by using a form of psychological warfare and "destructive cyber onslaught" (Giles 2021). Definitional problems aside, experts who expect cyber-war to be a go-to method keep underestimating the practical limitations of cyber-operations and consequently overestimating their strategic value, despite ample empirical evidence that cyber-attacks are not effective at coercive and destructive action.

The cyber-dimension in the war against Ukraine has fallen significantly below expectations. While the extent to which Russia may have been unable or unwilling to widely deploy high-level cyber-operations, and the impact of Ukrainian cyber-defenses supported by Western assistance, remains a subject of debate (Wilde 2022), it is evident that the actual cyber-operations have not matched the anticipated scale. In the first months of the conflict, there have been a series of hastily executed, poorly implemented, and outright failed cyber-operations by Russian threat actors (Maschmeyer and Dunn Cavelty 2022). Most of these operations have been characterized as "fast and easy" and low intensity, involving activities such as data wiping, website defacements, and DDoS-attacks. There have been a few instances of more complex cyber-attacks, but those that were attempted either failed or spiraled out of control. One notable example of failure was the attempt to trigger a power blackout in April 2022 using the same malware employed in 2016. This attempt was thwarted before it could be executed (O'Neill 2022). Another instance was the disruption of the Viasat satellite communications network, intended to sever Ukrainian military communications at the outset of the invasion. However, this operation failed to achieve a clearly measurable effect and instead resulted in unintended collateral damage, affecting the network's other European customers, including thousands of wind turbines in Germany (Box 8.2).

BOX 8.2   VIASAT HACK, 2022

The Viasat satellite hack on February 24, 2022, one hour before Russia invaded Ukraine, is the most impactful cyber-operation in the conflict to date. The purpose was most likely to disrupt Ukrainian military communication that relied on the KA-SAT satellite. Alternatively, the Viasat hack could have been an auxiliary attack in a wider information warfare/command-and-control warfare operation to increase Ukrainian dependency on more vulnerable land-line communications (Zettl-Schabath and Harnisch 2023).

The attackers gained access to the trusted management part of the KA-SAT network and then issued commands to overwrite part of the flash memory in modems with a wiper called "Acid Rain." The second phase of the attack was a DDoS-attack on Viasat servers. These modems were then unable to access the network but were not permanently damaged. There was also no direct effect on the satellite itself and its ground infrastructure. However, the attack had (likely) unintended consequences when it affected internet users and internet-connected wind farms in Germany.

The available evidence suggests a fluctuating pattern of cyber-attacks during the initial month of military operations, characterized by intense wiper-operations primarily targeting Ukrainian entities such as government institutions and telecommunication networks. Subsequently, there has been a decrease in the intensity of cyber-operations, with a notable decline in the number of cyber-attacks since July 2022 (Zettl-Schabath and Harnisch 2023; Bateman 2022). This observation aligns with the lack of successful coordination between Russian cyber-attacks and conventional military actions, as emphasized in a joint report by the Dutch General Intelligence and Security Service and the Military Intelligence and Security Service (Martin 2023; Fleming 2022; Defense Post 2022). In summary, there is no evidence that any of the cyber-operations sponsored by Russia or other cyber-activities related to the conflict, including the activities of hacktivist groups, have had a measurable impact on the course of the conflict. These cyber-operations have not provided observable tactical advantages, such as the sabotage of military equipment or disruption of enemy communications during battle, nor have they produced lasting effects on the overall trajectory of the conflict.

And yet, as several experts point out, the magnitude of the cyber-operations executed by Russia, Ukraine, and many other involved parties is unprecedented (Cattler and Black 2022; Umbach 2022; Microsoft 2022;

Grossman et al. 2023; Google 2023). This observation does not contradict the earlier discussion about the limitations and challenges associated with the utility of cyber-capabilities in the context of the conflict. To further discuss the utility of cyber-capabilities meaningfully, it is essential to make careful distinctions regarding the nature of cyber-operations being considered and the criteria used to measure "success." The term "offensive cyber-operations" or "cyber-effects operations," predominantly used by the United States, is not precise enough in this context. It fails to differentiate between the types of capabilities and the diverse goals and effects of different operations. Additionally, as previously noted, there is a general lack of discourse about the effects of cyber-operations, which further complicates the assessment of their strategic value.

First, some threat-intelligence professionals have criticized IR scholars for claiming that there is no cyber-war when there is so much cyber-activity. However, they focus exclusively on the quantity of incidents without linking them back to conflict dynamics or politics. The point is that while there is heightened cyber-activity, which includes attempts to damage critical infrastructures with cyber-means, these operations had no demonstrable effect on the overall battlespace dynamics (Willett 2022) and vice versa. This observation aligns with an earlier study by Kostyuk and Zhukov, which examined the use of both cyber and kinetic military operations in Syria (2013) and Eastern Ukraine. Their research similarly found no correlation between digital and kinetic attacks (Kostyuk and Zhukov 2017; also, Kostyuk and Gartzke 2022). This finding is not surprising, considering the timing difficulties inherent in cyber-operations, which can make it challenging to synchronize them with other military actions or to achieve measurable effects in the kinetic battlespace.

Second, a predominant element of the heightened cyber-activity during the conflict has been a "massive online 'information' battle for hearts and minds, comprehensibly amplified by private cyber-vigilante individuals and groups" (Willett 2022: 11). These activities conducted by hacker collectives are not a new phenomenon and have been observed in and around armed conflicts since at least the Kosovo conflict. However, what distinguishes the current situation is the Ukrainian government's active involvement in recruiting, training, and coordinating "thousands of individuals from both within and outside Ukraine to engage in sustained DDoS campaigns against Russian civilian infrastructure" (Soesanto 2023: 93). This represents a novel dimension in the conflict, the impact of which remains uncertain. While it is true that DDoS-attacks are typically characterized as minor disruptions with predominantly symbolic effects, the participation of civilians in attacks targeting the critical infrastructure of the enemy goes beyond the concept of self-defense and is likely to raise concerns related to norms of behavior in cyberspace, potentially causing additional tensions in this regard.

Third, the Ukraine War appears to challenge the conventional belief that the offense always holds the advantage in cyber-operations, suggesting that effective cyber-defense can make a difference (Beecroft 2022; however, see Kostyuk and Brantly 2022). While it is difficult to scientifically measure the impact of cyber-defenses, there have been notable efforts to enhance Ukraine's cyber-resilience. Beginning in early 2021, American companies have provided assistance to Ukraine by actively monitoring Russian cyber-activity, with Microsoft alone dedicating US$239 million in financial and technical support (Willett 2022: 15). Moreover, starting in December 2021, the USCYBERCOM deployed experts who collaborated with Ukrainian Cyber Command personnel to carry out defensive cyber-operations, contributing to the broader goal of bolstering cyber-resilience in critical networks (US Department of State 2022). Additionally, cyber-capabilities have played a significant role in intelligence collection for both sides of the conflict (Bateman 2022). Ukraine has received support from foreign countries in the form of remote intelligence, as well as analytical and advisory assistance (Martin 2022). These efforts underscore the growing recognition of the importance of cyber-defense and intelligence gathering in modern warfare.

In summary, the limitations observed in Russia's cyber-operations against Ukraine provide valuable insights that can shape our expectations for their future use in warfare (cf. Mueller et al. 2023). However, it is essential to exercise caution when generalizing these findings to other conflict settings, as each conflict possesses unique characteristics that may or may not be linked to cyber-operations (cf. Bommakanti 2023). Factors such as external support received by a nation in terms of IT-security and intelligence, the impact of learning from previous exposure to cyber-operations (e.g., Russia's actions since the Crimea annexation in 2014), and the maturity of offensive and defensive cyber-capabilities will all be crucial considerations in future conflicts. Nevertheless, drawing from 40 years of cyber-security politics and the knowledge available today, it is reasonable to assert with a high degree of confidence that, like any other strategic asset, the use of cyber-operations will be governed by political considerations, will be context-specific, and will primarily play a supporting rather than a decisive role in military operations.

Summary and Key Points

In this chapter, we explored the current landscape of cyber-operations in international politics, focusing on their use and utility. We started by examining prevalent types of cyber-attacks and dispelling the notion of cyber-doom, emphasizing that cyber-operations, particularly those in peacetime and below the threshold of war, are primarily related to espionage and, to a lesser degree, attempts to influence the information sphere. One of the biggest challenges is that we do not yet have good measures or understandings of the effects and success of cyber-operations, not least because it depends on the political and strategic goals of the attacker, and assessing their impact is complicated by factors like uncertainty about an attacker's intent and time delays in detection or manifestation of effects. Indeed, the effects of cyber-operations are crucial for determining their success or failure.

The second part of the chapter delves into the reasons behind state actors' choices in conducting cyber-operations. We considered the challenges, costs, and risks associated with targeted operations, offering a framework to explain the prevalence of certain types of attacks. Last, we evaluated the political utility of cyber-operations in both wartime and peacetime, drawing preliminary insights from the Ukraine conflict. In Ukraine, heightened cyber-activity has not demonstrated significant impact on the conflict's dynamics. Rather, the war to date confirms that cyber-operations utility is limited in war, particularly in causing permanent physical damage and controlling timing and effects. Therefore, cyber-operations are often used for InfOps, including intelligence gathering, rather than destruction.

We have come a long way in the last few decades. In contrast to an earlier, deep-seated belief that cyber-capabilities would become a low-risk "weapon" for the weak with which they might gain an asymmetric advantage, we have learned throughout the years that controlled, targeted attacks suitable to reach strategic goals are the opposite of cheap and easy to deploy. They require significant investments, it takes a lot of effort to control them, their effects are uncertain, and capabilities may only be used once in a specific timeframe. This chapter discussed the most important factors that are needed to understand their utility and their limitations. Not least because of the Ukraine War, many of the theoretical assumptions can now be approached with empirical evidence. Whether our insights will hold true in the future remains to be seen.

Notes

1. The data collections the book refers to are the following:
   - Significant Cyber Incidents by the Center for Strategic and International Studies (CSIS) since 2006 (pdf list); www.csis.org/programs/strategic-technologies-program/significant-cyber-incidents

- Council of Foreign Relations "Cyber Operations Tracker" (COT) since 2005 (dataset available for download) www.cfr.org/cyber-operations/
- The European Repository of Cyber Incidents (EuRepoC) since 2000 (dataset available for download) https://eurepoc.eu/
- The Dyadic Cyber Incident and Campaign Data (DCID) since 2000 (dataset available for download) https://drryanmaness.wixsite.com/cyberconflict/cyber-conflict-dataset

2. www.cfr.org/cyber-operations/ (May 2023)
3. The ten severity steps are:

   (1) Probing/packet sniffing without kinetic cyber ("Using cyber methods to breach networks but not utilize any malicious actions beyond that" (Maness et al. 2022: 9)).
   (2) Harassment, propaganda, denial, and nuisance disruption.
   (3) Stealing targeted critical information/data.
   (4) Widespread government, economic, military, or critical private sector network intrusion.
   (5) Single critical network infiltration and physical attempted destruction.
   (6) Single critical network infiltration and widespread destruction ("Critical stored information is destroyed or unrecoverable or functionality of the network must be limited to non-existent for a period of time" (Maness et al. 2022: 9)).
   (7) Minimal death as a direct result of cyber-incident.
   (8) Critical national economic disruption as a result of a cyber-incident.
   (9) Critical national infrastructure destruction as a result of a cyber-incident.
   (10) Massive death as a direct result of cyber-incident.

4. The book deliberately does not use the term "cyber-weapon" because it suggests characteristics that cyber-capabilities do not have, as will be explained in more detail below. As a reminder, "cyber-capabilities" refer to "a combination of various elements that collectively enable adversaries to manipulate digital services or networks" (Egloff and Shires 2022: 3) or the resources, skills, knowledge, operational concepts, and procedures to be able to have an effect in cyberspace (Uren et al. 2018).
5. Arguably, spyware employed politically is an unusual case, because of the specialized knowledge provided by commercial companies, falling somewhere in between the two types. It is not discussed in more detail here.
6. DDoS-attacks aim to overwhelm a target system, such as a website or network, by flooding it with an excessive amount of traffic. These attacks are easy to carry out using botnets, which are networks of compromised computers under the control of an attacker. The availability of DDoS-for-hire services has also made them more accessible.
7. Phishing attacks involve tricking individuals into revealing sensitive information, such as login credentials or personal data, by impersonating a legitimate entity through email, phone calls, or other means. Phishing attacks can be relatively simple to set up and execute, but their success largely depends on social engineering techniques and the gullibility of the targets.
8. SQL-injection attacks target websites or web applications that have vulnerabilities in their database query mechanisms. By exploiting these vulnerabilities, attackers can manipulate or extract data from the database. Successful SQL-injection attacks can grant unauthorized access to sensitive information or disrupt the functioning of a website.

9. Password attacks involve attempting to guess or crack passwords to gain unauthorized access to user accounts or systems. Techniques such as brute-force attacks (systematically trying all possible combinations) or dictionary attacks (using a pre-generated list of commonly used passwords) can be relatively simple to execute, particularly if the targeted user has weak or easily guessable passwords.
10. See Chapter 7 for details. Advanced Persistent Threats (APTs) are complex and highly targeted attacks typically carried out by well-funded and skilled adversaries, such as nation-state actors or advanced cyber-criminal groups. They involve a prolonged and stealthy intrusion into a target network, with the goal of stealing sensitive information or maintaining persistent access. APTs require significant resources, including advanced malware, exploits, and sophisticated command-and-control infrastructure.
11. Supply chain attacks involve compromising the software or hardware supply chain to gain unauthorized access or introduce malicious code into trusted products. Conducting successful supply chain attacks requires significant resources, intelligence gathering, and meticulous planning.
12. I make a distinction here between physical objects and data. Data is also a physical object but due to common storage practices, its destruction/deletion is mostly short-lived, whereas a destroyed centrifuge that needs replacement is not reversible.

Bibliography

Agrafiotis, I., Nurse, J.R.C., Goldsmith, M., Creese, S. and Upton, D. (2018). A Taxonomy of Cyber-Harms: Defining the Impacts of Cyber-Attacks and Understanding How They Propagate. *Journal of Cybersecurity* 4(1): tyy006.

Bateman, J. (2022). *Russia's Wartime Cyber Operations in Ukraine: Military Impacts, Influences, and Implications.* Carnegie's 'Cyber Conflict in the Russia-Ukraine War' Paper Series, December 16. Available at: https://carnegieendowment.org/2022/12/16/russia-s-wartime-cyber-operations-in-ukraine-military-impacts-influences-and-implications-pub-88657

Bateman, J., Hickok, E., Courchesne, L., Thange, I. and Shapiro, J.N. (2021). *Measuring the Effects of Influence Operations: Key Findings and Gaps from Empirical Research.* Carnegie's PCIO Baseline, June 28. Available at: https://carnegieendowment.org/2021/06/28/measuring-effects-of-influence-operations-key-findings-and-gaps-from-empirical-research-pub-84824

Beecroft, N. (2022). *Evaluating the International Support to Ukrainian Cyber Defense.* Carnegie's 'Cyber Conflict in the Russia-Ukraine War' Paper Series, November 3. Available at: https://carnegieendowment.org/2022/11/03/evaluating-international-support-to-ukrainian-cyber-defense-pub-88322

Bommakanti, K. (2023). *Beyond Cyber Fires and Ukraine: PLASSF Impact on a Sino-Indian Conventional War.* Observer Research Foundation Occasional Paper No. 409, September. Available at: www.orfonline.org/research/beyond-cyber-fires-and-ukraine/

Borghard, E.D. and Lonergan, S.W. (2017). The Logic of Coercion in Cyberspace. *Security Studies* 26(3): 452–481.

Borghard, E.D. and Lonergan, S.W. (2019). Cyber Operations as Imperfect Tools of Escalation. *Strategic Studies Quarterly* 13(3): 122–145.

Broad, W. and Sanger, D. (2017). U.S. Strategy to Hobble North Korea Was Hidden in Plain Sight. *New York Times*, March 4. Available at: https://www.nytimes.com/2017/03/04/world/asia/left-of-launch-missile-defense.html

Buchanan, B. (2017). *The Cyber-Security Dilemma: Hacking, Trust and Fear Between Nations*. Oxford University Press.

Cattler, D. and Black, D. (2022). The Myth of the Missing Cyberwar. *Foreign Affairs*, April 6. Available at: https://www.foreignaffairs.com/articles/ukraine/2022-04-06/myth-missing-cyberwar

Cherqi, O., Mezzour, G., Ghogho, M. and El Koutbi, M. (2018). Analysis of Hacking Related Trade in the Darkweb. In: *2018 IEEE International Conference on Intelligence and Security Informatics*, pp. 79–84.

Courtney, W. and Wilson, P.A. (2021). If Russia Invaded Ukraine. *The Rand Blog*, December 8. Available at: www.rand.org/blog/2021/12/expect-shock-and-awe-if-russia-invades-ukraine.html

Defense Post (2022). Russia Unexpectedly Poor at Cyberwar: European Military Heads. *Defense Post*, June 9. Available at: www.thedefensepost.com/2022/06/09/russia-poor-cyberwar/

Denning, D.E. (2015). Assessing Cyber War. In: Blanken, L., Rothstein, H. and Lepore, J. (eds.) *Assessing War: The Challenge of Measuring Success and Failure*. Georgetown University Press, pp. 266–284.

Dossi, S. (2020). On the Asymmetric Advantages of Cyberwarfare. Western Literature and The Chinese Journal *Guofang Keji*. *Journal of Strategic Studies* 43(2): 281–308.

Dreyer, P., Jones, T.M., Klima, K., Oberholtzer, J., Strong, A., Welburn, J.W. and Winkelman, Z. (2018). *Estimating the Global Cost of Cyber Risk: Methodology and Examples*. RAND Corporation.

Egloff, F.J. (2020). Public Attribution of Cyber Intrusions. *Journal of Cybersecurity* 6(1): tyaa012.

Egloff, F.J. and Dunn Cavelty, M. (2021). Attribution and Knowledge Creation Assemblages in Cybersecurity Politics. *Journal of Cybersecurity* 7(1): tyab002.

Egloff, F.J. and Shires, J. (2022). Offensive Cyber Capabilities and State Violence: Three Logics of Integration. *Journal of Global Security Studies* 7(1): ogab028.

Fink, K.D., Jordan, J. and Wells, J.E. (2014). Considerations for Offensive Cyberspace Operations. *Military Review* XCIV(3): 4–11.

Fischerkeller, M.P. and Harknett, J.R. (2019). *Persistent Engagement, Agreed Competition, Cyberspace Interaction Dynamics, and Escalation*. Institute for Defense Analysis.

Fleming, J. (2022). By Invitation: The Head of GCHQ Says Vladimir Putin Is Losing the Information War in Ukraine. *The Economist*, August 18. Available at: https://www.economist.com/by-invitation/2022/08/18/the-head-of-gchq-says-vladimir-putin-is-losing-the-information-war-in-ukraine

Giles, K. (2021). Putin Does Not Need to Invade Ukraine to Get His Way. *Chatham House Expert Comment*, December 21. Available at: www.chathamhouse.org/2021/12/putin-does-not-need-invade-ukraine-get-his-way

Godefroidt, A. (2022). How Terrorism Does (and Does Not) Affect Citizens' Political Attitudes: A Meta-Analysis. *American Journal of Political Science* 67(1): 22–38.

Goldsmith, B. (2003). Imitation in International Relations: Analogies, Vicarious Learning, and Foreign Policy. *International Interactions* 29(3): 237–267.

Google (2023). Fog of War: How the Ukraine Conflict Transformed the Cyber Threat Landscape. *Google Report*. Available at: https://services.google.com/fh/files/blogs/google_fog_of_war_research_report.pdf

Grossman, T., Kaminska, M., Shires, J. and Smeets, M. (2023). *The Cyber Dimensions of the Russia-Ukraine War*. Workshop Report, European Cyber Conflict Research Initiative, April. Available at: https://eccri.eu/wp-content/uploads/2023/04/ECCRI_REPORT_The-Cyber-Dimensions-of-the-Russia-Ukraine-War-19042023.pdf

Harknett, R.J. and Smeets, M. (2022). Cyber Campaigns and Strategic Outcomes. *Journal of Strategic Studies* 45(4): 534–567.

Healey, J. (2016). Winning and Losing in Cyberspace. In: Pissanidis, N., Rõigas, H. and Veenendaal, M. (eds.) *8th International Conference on Cyber Conflict*. NATO CCD COE Publications, pp. 37–49.

Healey, J. (2021). Understanding the Offense's Systemwide Advantage in Cyberspace. *Lawfare Blog*, December 22. Available at: www.lawfareblog.com/understanding-offenses-systemwide-advantage-cyberspace

Healey, J. (2022). Preparing for Inevitable Cyber Surprise. *War on the Rocks*, Blog. January 12. Available at: https://warontherocks.com/2022/01/preparing-for-inevitable-cyber-surprise/

Hollis, D. (2011). Cyberwar Case Study: Georgia 2008. *Small Wars Journal*, January 6. Available at: https://smallwarsjournal.com/jrnl/art/cyberwar-case-study-georgia-2008

Houck, C. (2018). Left-of-Launch Missile Defense: 'You Don't Want to Have Just One Solution to the Threat'. *Defense One*, January 24. Available at: www.defenseone.com/threats/2018/01/left-launch-missile-defense-you-dont-want-have-just-one-solution-threat/145438/

Jensen, B. and Banks, D. (2016). *Cyber Operations in Conflict: Lessons From Analytic Wargames*. Center for Long-Term Cybersecurity. Available at: https://cltc.berkeley.edu/cyber-operations/

Jensen, B. and Valeriano, B. (2019). *What Do We Know About Cyber Escalation? Observations from Simulations and Surveys*. Atlantic Council. Available at: www.atlanticcouncil.org/wp-content/uploads/2019/11/What_do_we_know_about_cyber_escalation_.pdf

Kostyuk, N. and Brantly, A. (2022). War in the Borderland Through Cyberspace: Limits of Defending Ukraine Through Interstate Cooperation. *Contemporary Security Policy* 43(3): 498–515.

Kostyuk, N. and Gartzke, E. (2022). Why Cyber Dogs Have Yet to Bark Loudly in Russia's Invasion of Ukraine. *Texas National Security Review*, Summer. Available at: https://tnsr.org/2022/06/why-cyber-dogs-have-yet-to-bark-loudly-in-russias-invasion-of-ukraine/

Kostyuk, N. and Zhukov, Y.M. (2017). Invisible Digital Front: Can Cyber Attacks Shape Battlefield Events? *Journal of Conflict Resolution* 63(2): 317–347.

Kreps, S. and Schneider, J. (2019). Escalation Firebreaks in the Cyber, Conventional, and Nuclear Domains: Moving Beyond Effects-Based Logics. *Journal of Cybersecurity* 5(1): tyz007.

Laketa, S., Fregonese, S. and Masson, D. (2021). Introduction: Experiential Landscapes of Terror. *Conflict and Society: Advances in Research* 7(1): 1–8.

Lewis, J.A. (2015). 'Compelling Opponents to Our Will': The Role of Cyber Warfare in Ukraine. In: Geers, K. (ed.) *Cyber War in Perspective: Russian Aggression against Ukraine.* NATO CCD COE Publications, pp. 39–47.

Libicki, M.C. (2009). *Cyberdeterrence and Cyberwar.* RAND Corporation.

Libicki, M.C. (2020). Correlations between Cyberspace Attacks and Kinetic Attacks. In: Jančárková, T., Lindström, L., Signoretti, M., Tolga, I. and Visky, G. (eds.) *2020 12th International Conference on Cyber Conflict.* NATO CCD COE Publications, pp. 199–213.

Libicki, M.C. and Tkacheva, O. (2020). Cyberspace Escalation: Ladders or Lattices? In: Stevens, T., Floyd, K. and Pernik, P. (eds.) *Cyber Threats: Horizon Scanning and Analysis.* NATO CCD COE Publications, pp. 60–73.

Lindsay, J.R. (2013). Stuxnet and the Limits of Cyber Warfare. *Security Studies* 22(3): 365–404.

Lindsay, J.R. (2023). Hidden Dangers in the US Military Solution to a Large-Scale Intelligence Problem. In: Chesney, R. and Smeets, M. (eds.) *Deter, Disrupt, or Deceive: Assessing Cyber Conflict as an Intelligence Contest.* Georgetown University Press, pp. 60–85.

Lindsay, J.R. and Gartzke, E. (2017). Coercion through Cyberspace: The Stability-Instability Paradox Revisited. In: Greenhill, K.M. and Krause, P.J.P. (eds.) *The Power to Hurt: Coercion in Theory and in Practice.* Oxford University Press, pp. 179–203.

Lonergan, E. and Poznansky, M. (2023). Are We Asking Too Much of Cyber? *War on the Rocks*, May 2. Available at: https://warontherocks.com/2023/05/are-we-asking-too-much-of-cyber/

Makridis, C. (2018). Do Data Breaches Damage Reputation? Evidence from 45 Companies Between 2002 and 2018. *Journal of Cybersecurity* 7(1): tyab021.

Makridis, C., Lennart, M. and Smeets, M. (2024). If It Bleeps It Leads?—Media Coverage on Cyber Conflict and Misperception. *Journal of Peace Research* 61(1). https://doi.org/10.1177/00223433231220

Maness, R.C., Valeriano, B., Hedgecock, K., Jensen, B.M. and Macias, J.M. (2022). *The Dyadic Cyber Incident and Campaign Dataset, version 2.0.* Available at: https://drryanmaness.wixsite.com/cyberconflcit/cyber-conflict-dataset

Manky, D. (2013). Cybercrime as a Service: A Very Modern Business. *Computer Fraud & Security* (6): 9–13.

Martin, A. (2022). UK Government Confirms Its Intel Agency Is Helping to Defend Ukraine. *The Record*, November 1. Available at: https://therecord.media/uk-government-confirms-its-intel-agency-is-helping-to-defend-ukraine

Martin, A. (2023). Dutch Intelligence: Many Cyberattacks by Russia Are Not Yet Public Knowledge. *The Record*, February 22. Available at: https://therecord.media/dutch-intelligence-russia-cyberattacks-many-not-yet-public-knowledge

Martino, R.A. (2011). *Leveraging Traditional Battle Damage Assessment Procedures to Measure Effects from a Computer Network Attack.* Air Force Institute of Technology.

Maschmeyer, L. (2021). The Subversive Trilemma: Why Cyber Operations Fall Short of Expectations. *International Security* 46(2): 51–90.

Maschmeyer, L. (2022). Infiltrate, Exploit, Manipulate: Why the Subversive Nature of Cyber Conflict Explains Both Its Strategic Promise and Its Limitations. *Lawfare*, July 12. Available at: www.lawfaremedia.org/article/infiltrate-exploit-manipulate-why-subversive-nature-cyber-conflict-explains-both-its-strategic

Maschmeyer, L. (2023). Subversion, Cyber Operations, and Reverse Structural Power in World Politics. *European Journal of International Relations* 29(1): 79–103.

Maschmeyer, L. and Dunn Cavelty, M. (2022). Goodbye Cyberwar: Ukraine as Reality Check. Center for Security Studies. *Policy Perspectives* 10(3).

Maschmeyer, L. and Kostyuk, N. (2022). There Is No Cyber 'Shock and Awe': Plausible Threats in the Ukrainian Conflict. *The War on the Rocks*, February 8. Available at: https://warontherocks.com/2022/02/there-is-no-cyber-shock-and-awe-plausible-threats-in-the-ukrainian-conflict/

McGhee, J. (2016). Liberating Cyber Offense. *Strategic Studies Quarterly* 10(4): 46–63.

Metcalf, A.O. and Barber, C. (2014). Tactical Cyber: How to Move Forward. *Small Wars Journal*, September 14. Available at: https://smallwarsjournal.com/jrnl/art/tactical-cyber-how-to-move-forward

Microsoft (2022). An Overview of Russia's Cyberattack Activity in Ukraine. *Digital Security Unit*, Special Report, April 27. Available at: https://query.prod.cms.rt.microsoft.com/cms/api/am/binary/RE4Vwwd

Mueller, G.B., Jensen, B., Valeriano, B., Maness, R.C. and Maciaset, J.M. (2023). *Cyber Operations During the Russo-Ukrainian War: From Strange Patterns to Alternative Futures*. Center for Strategic and International Studies.

National Security Archives (2020). *USCYBERCOM After Action Assessments of Operation GLOWING SYMPHONY*. Available at: https://nsarchive.gwu.edu/briefing-book/cyber-vault/2020-01-21/uscybercom-after-action-assessments-operation-glowing-symphony

O'Neill, P.H. (2022). Russian Hackers Tried to Bring Down Ukraine's Power Grid to Help the Invasion. *MIT Technology Review*, April 12. Available at: www.technologyreview.com/2022/04/12/1049586/russian-hackers-tried-to-bring-down-ukraines-power-grid-to-help-the-invasion/

Paul, C., Schwille, M., Vasseur, M., Bartels, E.M. and Bauer, R. (2022). *The Role of Information in U.S. Concepts for Strategic Competition*. RAND Corporation.

Rid, T. (2012). Cyber War Will Not Take Place. *Journal of Strategic Studies* 35(1): 5–32.

Rid, T. and McBurney, P. (2012). Cyber-Weapons. *RUSI Journal* 157(1): 6–13.

Schneider, J. (2021). The Cyber Apocalypse Never Came. Here's What We Got Instead. *Politic*, July 27. Available at: www.politico.com/news/magazine/2021/07/27/cyber-apocalypse-russia-china-warfare-500787

Schneider, J.G. (2018). What War Games Tell Us About the Use of Cyber Weapons in a Crisis. *Net Politics, Council on Foreign Relations*, June 21. Available at: www.cfr.org/blog/what-war-games-tell-us-about-use-of-cyber-weapons-crisis

Schneider, J.G., Schechter, B., and Shaffer, R. (2022). A Lot of Cyber Fizzle but Not a Lot of Bang: Evidence about the Use of Cyber Operations from Wargames. *Journal of Global Security Studies* 7(2): ogac005.

Schulze, M. (2020). Cyber in War: Assessing the Strategic, Tactical, and Operational Utility of Military Cyber Operations. In: Jančárková, T., Lindström, L., Signoretti, M., Tolga, I. and Visky, G. (eds.) *2020 12th International Conference on Cyber Conflict*. NATO CCD COE Publications, pp. 183–197.

Shandler, R., Gross, M.L. and Canetti, D. (2023). Cyberattacks, Psychological Distress, and Military Escalation: An Internal Meta-Analysis. *Journal of Global Security Studies* 8(1): ogac042.

Slayton, R. (2017). What Is the Cyber Offense-Defense Balance? Conceptions, Causes, and Assessment. *International Security* 41(3): 72–109.

Smeets, M. (2018). The Strategic Promise of Offensive Cyber Operations. *Strategic Studies Quarterly* 12(3): 90–113.

Smeets, M. (2022a). *No Shortcuts: Why States Struggle to Develop a Military Cyber-Force*. Oxford University Press.

Smeets, M. (2022b). Cyber Arms Transfer: Meaning, Limits, and Implications. *Security Studies* 31(1): 65–91.

Smeets, M. (2022c). A US History of Not Conducting Cyber Attacks. *Bulletin of the Atomic Scientists* 78(4): 208–213.

Soesanto, S. (2023). Ukraine's IT Army. *Survival* 65(3): 93–106.

Sullivan, P.L. and Koch, M.T. (2009). Military Intervention by Powerful States, 1945–2003. *Journal of Peace Research* 46(5): 707–718.

Umbach, F. (2022). Russia's Cyber Fog in the Ukraine War. *GIS Reports (blog)*, June 16. Available at: www.gisreportsonline.com/r/russia-cyber/

Uren, T., Hogeveen, B. and Hanson, F. (2018). Defining Offensive Cyber Capabilities. *Australian Strategic Policy Institute Report*. Available at: www.aspi.org.au/report/defining-offensive-cyber-capabilities

US Department of State (2022). *U.S. Support for Connectivity and Cybersecurity in Ukraine*. Fact Sheet. Office of the Spokesperson, May 10. Available at: www.state.gov/u-s-support-for-connectivity-and-cybersecurity-in-ukraine/

Valeriano, B. (2022). The Need for Cybersecurity Data and Metrics: Empirically Assessing Cyberthreat. *Journal of Cyber Policy* 7(2): 140–154.

Valeriano, B. and Maness, R.C. (2018). How We Stopped Worrying about Cyber Doom and Started Collecting Data. *Politics and Governance* 6(2). Available at: www.cogitatiopress.com/politicsandgovernance/article/view/1368

Valeriano, B., Jensen, B.M. and Maness, R.C. (2018). *Cyber Strategy: The Evolving Character of Power and Coercion*. Oxford University Press.

van der Meer, S. (2018). *State-Level Responses to Massive Cyber-Attacks: A Policy Toolbox*. Clingendael Policy Brief. Available at: www.clingendael.org/sites/default/files/2018-12/PB_cyber_responses.pdf

Wade, M. (2021). Digital Hostages: Leveraging Ransomware Attacks in Cyberspace. *Business Horizons* 64(6): 787–797.

Warner, M. (2023). The Character of Strategic Cyberspace Competition and the Role of Ideology. In: Chesney, R. and Smeets, M. (eds.) *Deter, Disrupt, or Deceive: Assessing Cyber Conflict as an Intelligence Contest*. Georgetown University Press, pp. 43–59.

Wilde, G. (2022). *Cyber Operations in Ukraine: Russia's Unmet Expectations*. Carnegie's 'Cyber Conflict in the Russia-Ukraine War' Paper Series. December 12.

Available at: https://carnegieendowment.org/2022/12/12/cyber-operations-in-ukraine-russia-s-unmet-expectations-pub-88607

Willett, M. (2022). The Cyber Dimension of the Russia–Ukraine War. *Survival* 64(5): 7–26.

Wilson, B., Goughnour, T., McKernan, M., Karode, A., Tierney, D., Arena, M.V., Vermeer, M.J.D., Perez, H. and Levedahl, A. (2023). *A Cost Estimating Framework for U.S. Marine Corps Joint Cyber Weapons*. RAND Corporation.

Work, J.D. (2021). *Rapid Capabilities Generation and Prompt Effects in Offensive Cyber Operations*. Available at: https://osf.io/preprints/socarxiv/esx6m

Zettl-Schabath, K. and Harnisch, S. (2023). One Year of Hostilities in Ukraine: Nine Notes on Cyber Operations. *Spotlight Article*, April. Available at: https://strapi.eurepoc.eu/uploads/One_Year_of_Hostilities_in_Ukraine_59f3e36897.pdf?updated_at=2023-04-20T12:19:26.189Z

9

THE POLITICS OF CYBER-SECURITY NOW AND IN THE FUTURE— CONCLUDING REMARKS

Cyber-security has never been more important. As societies become more dependent on digital platforms for communication, commerce, and essential services, the potential disruptive impact of cyber-threats has grown exponentially. In this era of rapid technological evolution, the significance of sufficient cyber-security extends beyond mere protection of individual and organizational interests—it becomes a linchpin for ensuring the resilience, stability, and trustworthiness of our digital ecosystems and, in turn, many of society's key functions.

In this dynamic field, a nuanced understanding of the politics surrounding cyber-security becomes indispensable for at least three reasons. First, cyber-security concerns are inherently intertwined with geopolitical dynamics and power struggles. State actors play a decisive role in shaping cyberspace and its use, influencing policies, and determining rules of engagement. One of the key challenges for them is to navigate the oxymoron of advancing their strategic objectives in the digital realm while at the same time mitigating the potential destabilizing effects of their cyber-activities on international relations. Second, the governance of cyberspace involves finding an acceptable balance between state authority, industry practices, and societal expectations. Political decisions regarding the regulation and oversight of digital technologies impact not only national (and sometimes international) security but also individual privacy, freedom of expression, and economic interests. Third, the politics of cyber-security necessarily extend beyond national borders. Investing into diplomatic dimensions is essential for fostering international cooperation, building alliances, and establishing norms that promote responsible behavior in

DOI: 10.4324/9781003497080-9

cyberspace. Without them, the international community faces heightened risks of tensions amplified by cyber-issues, a further erosion of trust among nations, and the potential for destabilizing cyber-activities.

This book has offered a comprehensive understanding of the broader political context within which cyber-security has gained prominence. It looked at a variety of notable cyber-incidents, explaining the insights they provide into otherwise hidden state capabilities and practices. Furthermore, it explored how these incidents have influenced threat perceptions and shaped countermeasures. Throughout its pages, the book emphasized the importance of acknowledging the symbiotic relationship between technological advancements and political dynamics, underscoring their combined influence. With this, the fallacy of perceiving digital technologies as a quasi-material force with a revolutionary, one-sided impact on society is remedied. Such deterministic perspectives tend to lead to overly alarmist accounts about the disruptive nature of new technologies.

From the book's chapters, eight key insights emerge, which are discussed below. Afterward, the conclusion looks at the validity of these insights in the coming years and explores six trends that are likely to impact the shape and study of cyber-security politics in the future.

Eight Key Insights

The impact of technologies is not autonomous; rather, it depends on how humans utilize them in specific contexts. This interdependence emphasizes the need to avoid overlooking technological path-dependencies and constraints that arise at the intersection of technology and human life. Technologies are not isolated entities; they are embedded within intricate global socio-technical systems, shaping and being shaped by broader societal elements. The eight key insights that emerge from this book's pages are a result of such co-shaping dynamics:

(1) *Cyber-security is like other political issues*: Despite rapid technological innovation, cyber-security fundamentally resembles other political issues, due to enduring principles rooted in social, political, and cultural structures.
(2) *Cyber-power is interconnected*: Cyber-power is increasingly intertwined with strategic competition, favoring the already strong who can leverage other power resources.
(3) *Secret activities shape cyber-security politics*: The secret practices of intelligence actors have been more important in shaping the norms space than open, diplomatic norms processes.

(4) *Threat intelligence companies play a pivotal role in knowledge creation*: Threat intelligence companies play a pivotal role in knowledge creation, but their role and the biases they carry are insufficiently understood.

(5) *Technology and politics constrain each other*: Technology constrains political possibilities, and politics constrains technological use, explaining why some types of cyber-operations are more prevalent than others.

(6) *Possible cyber-operations depend on available capabilities*: The nature of cyber-operations is contingent on available cyber-capabilities. Capabilities for a targeted, controlled effect are costly and challenging to develop and maintain.

(7) *The effects of cyber-operations are hard to measure and isolate*: The impact of cyber-activities is hard to isolate; their significance lies in interconnectedness and secondary impact, making the assessment of effects challenging.

(8) *Cyber-doom is debunked*: Contrary to the notion of cyber-doom, cyber-operations predominantly occur in peacetime, posing long-term, psychological, and societal threats rather than immediate catastrophic destruction.

1. Cyber-Security Is Like Other Political Issues

The first insight emphasizes that despite the rapid pace of technical innovation, cyber-security is fundamentally akin to other political issues. Regardless of shifts in the scale, scope, and speed of information flows and digital computations, enduring principles rooted in social, political, and cultural structures persist. The politics of cyber-security emerges from the interplay between digital technologies, political processes, and the interpretation of incidents. A crucial task for policymakers is to strike an optimal balance between national security-focused politics and conventional approaches to address cyber-threats. This involves defining roles and responsibilities for bureaucratic units and other stakeholders (Dunn Cavelty and Egloff 2019).

It is essential to recognize that the ongoing political discourse about cyber-security is only partially stable. This discourse evolves in response to the emergence of prominent cyber-incidents, each revealing gaps in our understanding and challenging existing paradigms. These incidents play a transformative role in shaping not only our responses but also the very foundations of our comprehension of cyber-security, highlighting the need for continuous adaptation and improvement in our strategies and policies based on what we learn. However, the book also underscored that cyber-incidents do not happen in a political vacuum. Without adequate consideration of the broader context in which human actors decide to compromise a system, we do not understand the power that cyber-incidents hold in shaping threat perceptions and countermeasures.

2. Cyber-Power Is Interconnected

The second insight highlights that cyber-power is contingent on and interconnected with existing power resources in other domains, which favors the already strong. Economic strength is a significant determinant of power. Major technology companies and their human capital that shape the digital environment through their products and services are a key source of power. When cyber-attacks escalated in persistence, targeting, cost, and disruption, governments responded by investing into their ability to shape cyberspace. Many reasserted their own power position vis-à-vis or alongside companies. As governments became more involved in cyberspace to safeguard their national interests, a connection emerged between technological innovation and strategic competition. This strategic competition encompassed not only traditional military dimensions but also economic, technological, and information domains, all of which intersect within the cyber-security landscape. Given that digital technologies are dual-use, impacting both the global economic and military balance, states perceive them as strategic resources (Mazarr et al. 2022).

Powerful states typically have robust resource bases, including economic strength, technological capabilities, and military prowess. This abundance of resources provides them with the means to invest in strategic initiatives, research and development, and the acquisition of advanced technologies. These states also tend to be at the forefront of technological innovation. They have advanced research and development institutions, strong educational systems, and a conducive environment for innovation, allowing them to stay ahead in emerging fields such as cyber-security, artificial intelligence (AI), and space technologies. However, against the backdrop of an escalating technology competition, the most powerful states are incentivized to influence the innovation process and the proliferation of new technologies in their narrow national interests. This intensifying technology race not only shapes national threat perceptions but also contributes to the formulation of doom scenarios and zero-sum thinking. "The concept of "weaponized interdependence" arose in this context (Farrell and Newman 2019). Additionally, it fosters an environment where states may prioritize short-term gains over cooperative global efforts, potentially hindering international collaboration on shared challenges such as cyber-security.

3. Secret Activities Shape Cyber-Security Politics

The third insight underscores a shift in the perception of cyberspace, initially seen as a potential battleground for military and terrorist entities, toward its emergence as the preferred arena for intelligence activities and actors. The unique features of cyberspace, including anonymity, global reach, and adaptability, make it an ideal environment for intelligence agencies to conduct covert operations, collect information, and exert influence on a global scale (Rid 2020). This transformation in the role of cyberspace for intelligence purposes required significant investments and coincided with a geopolitical shift from a post-9/11 focus on terrorism to a renewed emphasis on great power rivalry (Buchanan 2020).

In the realm of intelligence, maintaining secrecy is paramount, as the discovery of their activities can result in the loss of valuable capabilities. Understanding the role intelligence actors (and APTs) play in shaping norms of state behavior requires insights derived from (cyber-)incidents such as the Snowden Revelations or the Shadow Broker Leaks (see Chapter 4), which unveiled covert practices to the world. These revelations become crucial for experts and scholars seeking to unravel the intricacies of intelligence activities and their impact on the evolving landscape of cyberspace (Chesney and Smeets 2023). Open norms processes are important but have remained semi-successful in changing the behavior of states.

The importance of intelligence activities means that "leaks" play a crucial role in research related to cyberspace and intelligence activities, and will likely do so in the future. However, the use of leaked information raises ethical considerations. Researchers must navigate issues such as privacy, national security concerns, and the potential harm caused by the disclosure of sensitive information. Ethical research practices require careful consideration of the implications of using leaked data, ensuring that the benefits of the research outweigh potential harms. Researchers should also be mindful of the legal implications of handling classified or stolen information (Boustead and Herr 2020).

4. Threat Intelligence Companies Play a Pivotal Role in Knowledge Creation

Apart from (state) intelligence agencies, private threat intelligence companies also occupy a pivotal role in producing and providing knowledge about cyber-threats in political contexts. These commercial entities specialize in collecting, analyzing, and interpreting vast amounts of data to provide organizations with actionable insights into the world of cyber-threats. Among their crucial responsibilities is the task of attribution—unraveling the identities and motivations behind cyber-incidents. The forensic capabilities of some of the bigger transnational firms are more advanced than those of many states (Egloff and Dunn Cavelty 2021).

The commercial orientation of threat intelligence companies introduces a layer of complexity in their role, particularly in attribution processes. Operating as profit-driven businesses, these entities are motivated by revenue, prompting concerns in some quarters regarding transparency and potential conflicts of interest. The reliance on threat intelligence reporting, while providing valuable insights, presents challenges for researchers. One significant concern is the inability to observe the entirety of conflictual cyber-interactions (Egloff and Smeets 2023). The information available represents a biased sample, though its exact extend remains uncertain, highlighting malicious activities in cyberspace that are closely linked to the political and economic interests of Western states and threat intelligence firms (Maschmeyer et al. 2021).

As the negotiation of cyber-security extends to the global level, it becomes imperative to recognize and understand how different regions and cultures perceive the interplay between technology and politics in cyberspace. Moreover, gaining insights into how ideas of cyber-threats manifest in various regions is crucial. The dominance of Western perspectives in the current cyber-security discourse underscores the need for a more inclusive and comprehensive understanding that encompasses diverse global viewpoints and experiences (Mhajne and Henshaw 2024).

5. Technology and Politics Constrain Each Other

The fifth insight underscores the reciprocal relationship between technology and politics in the realm of cyber-security. On the technological front, variables such as vulnerabilities, potential manipulations in machines or networks, and the perceived societal value of a targeted entity collectively define the realm of possibilities. Simultaneously, in the political domain, the axiom "not everything that can be done is done" prevails. Mere possession of cyber-capabilities does not guarantee their utilization; instead, these capabilities are regarded as tools in the strategic toolbox. Their deployment is contingent on their alignment with specific strategic or political objectives.

The decision-making process regarding cyber-operations is context-dependent, involving a meticulous evaluation that considers factors such as potential risks versus anticipated gains, the specific cyber-dimension involved, and alternative courses of action. This nuanced understanding emphasizes that technological capabilities do not operate in isolation; their effectiveness and utilization are intricately tied to the broader political landscape and strategic considerations. This insight is one of the most important to understand the use and utility of cyber-operations now and in the future.

6. Possible Cyber-Operations Depend on Available Capabilities

The sixth insight underscores that the nature of cyber-operations is contingent upon the available cyber-capabilities, emphasizing that those capable of generating a targeted, controlled effect are neither cheap nor easy but rather costly and challenging to develop (Smeets 2022). The concern that "cyber-weapons" could enable weaker entities (including non-state actors) to gain an asymmetric advantage against conventional superpowers necessitates a nuanced examination. Achieving destructive and material (irreversible) effects in the cyber-realm proves to be a formidable challenge, demanding significant investments in human, organizational, and technical resources that are only available to state actors.

While the term "cyber-weapon" is frequently used as an analogy, it can evoke misleading images and expectations on the level of policy. Unlike physical objects such as guns or bombs that can be stored and deployed for a lasting impact, cyber-capabilities are highly context-dependent and short-lived (Smeets 2018). The commencement of a cyber-operation does not yield immediate effects; instead, the process unfolds over an extended period. The time between initiation and success, involving activities like system infiltration or manipulation attempts, often spans months, with preparatory phases extending even further. Importantly, success is not guaranteed, and its achievement depends on the targeted system and its defenses, which may not be fully known at the operation's outset. This inherent uncertainty underscores that not all cyber-operations are strategically advantageous in a military campaign. Success is contingent on factors that evolve during the operation, emphasizing the complexity and unpredictability of cyber-activities in a military context.

7. The Effects of Cyber-Operations Are Hard to Measure and Isolate

The seventh insight highlights that the impact of cyber-activities and their overall significance cannot easily be isolated; it is the interconnectedness that holds significance. As an example, evaluating the consequences of a cyber-breach involves different considerations. First, the adversary's utilization of breached data and the timing of that use profoundly influences the outcome, and tracking such effects proves challenging. Additionally, the affected party's policy responses, especially considering domestic audience costs and reputational damage, play a crucial role in shaping the incident's impact. Although economic costs stemming from disruptions are relatively easier to measure, a comprehensive assessment of the incident's broader consequences requires tracing effects through secondary consequences and over time.

Moreover, focusing solely on individual cyber-incidents is insufficient, as they may be part of larger campaigns spanning years. The cumulative data gathered and the potential adversarial actions over time, facilitated by big data analytics, necessitate a broader perspective on cumulative effects when assessing strategic effects (Harknett and Smeets 2022). However, linking these effects exclusively to cyber-operations often proves challenging, posing a significant obstacle to understanding consequences. The transition to "strategic competition" as a geopolitical framework further complicates matters. This complexity arises from the entanglement of cyberspace with various facets of modern life, challenging attempts to compartmentalize it as a distinct and isolated domain.

8. *Cyber-Doom Is Debunked*

The notion of impeding cyber-doom is debunked. Cyber-operations predominantly occur in peacetime and below the threshold of war. These operations, often centered on espionage and influencing the information sphere, are characterized by uncertainty regarding their actual impact. Contrary to immediate catastrophic physical destruction, the primary threat of cyber-attacks most likely lies in subtler, long-term, psychological, and societal harm, eroding public trust in government.

Cyber-operations are perceived as capable of causing challenging-to-quantify yet destabilizing effects. However, the alleged asymmetrical vulnerability of democracies is marked by a lack of knowledge about the real consequences of disinformation. The nebulous nature of these effects may be advantageous or even intentional, creating ambiguity and uncertainty. Since the effectiveness of foreign disinformation and propaganda relies on exploiting preexisting social distrust and political grievances, a comprehensive counterstrategy is essential, combining technological fortification, strategic communication initiatives, and societal resilience efforts (Dunn Cavelty et al. 2023).

Predictions for the Future

In considering the relevance of these insights for the future, the expectation leans toward continuity of the observed patterns and relationships. In their essence, human behavior, societal structures, and economic and political dynamics remain constant over time. Societies' organization, governance, and interactions are likely to maintain a certain degree of continuity even amid technological evolution. This anticipation is grounded in the recognition that institutional inertia, cultural norms, and established practices often resist rapid and radical shifts. Political systems and societal structures, constructed on accumulated experiences, tend to adapt gradually rather than undergo abrupt transformations. That said, there are five trends that we can expect with some certainty. All will have an impact on the politics of cyber-security in the future:

(1) *Cyber-security will become (even) more important*: The global digital transformation will intensify cyber-security concerns. These developments will create new demands for technical and organizational research that needs to be better integrated with approaches from the social and political sciences.

(2) *Power disparities will grow*: Concerns about cyber-security exclusivity are driven by disparities in resources and technological capabilities. The digital divide will likely widen, leading to an uneven distribution of cyber-security preparedness and the potential exposure of certain groups to cyber-risks.

(3) *Cyber-threats will continue to evolve (and surprise us)*: The dynamism of cyber-threats is intricately tied to actor dynamics, economic factors, and continuous innovation in the cyber-underground.

(4) *States will regulate more*: Digital transformations and increasing vulnerabilities of digital systems will prompt governments to play a proactive role in shaping cyber-security through national and international regulatory interventions.

(5) *Fragmentation in cyberspace will increase*: The pursuit of digital sovereignty within the context of strategic competition is likely to lead to geopolitical fragmentation within cyberspace with unclear consequences to date.

1.   Cyber-Security Will Become (Even) More Important

The trajectory of cyber-security concerns is expected to intensify with the global progression of digital transformation. This transformation involves an increased digitization and automation of technical processes across societal and economic domains. As complex systems interconnect, cyber-security is set to play an expanded role in politics. As these technical systems become tighter coupled and integrate more aspects of society and economy, cyber-security concerns will inevitably expand to more policy fields at both the national and international levels. These developments will create new demands for technical and organizational research that needs to be better integrated with approaches from the social and political sciences.

Looking at emerging technologies, AI and ML are poised to be pivotal in strengthening cyber-security defenses. The real-time pattern detection and anomaly identification capabilities of AI and ML hold promise for enhancing adaptability and responsiveness in security measures. Additionally, the eventual advent of quantum computing, though quite a while off yet realized, presents a dual challenge and opportunity. While quantum computers pose a potential threat to existing encryption methods, ongoing efforts focus on developing quantum-resistant encryption to safeguard digital communications. Following a familiar pattern of previous tech-hypes, emerging technologies are often considered revolutionary with game-changing qualities for security. Scholars of technological change convincingly show that such transformations are far from straightforward (cf. Lindsay 2023/2024). Indeed, this book demonstrated that the anticipated revolutionary changes promised by cyberspace in the realm of warfare did not materialize in the ways initially envisioned.

2. Power Disparities Will Grow

The trajectory of the digital transformation is likely to be marked by challenges, disparities, and uneven progress. The integration of digital technologies into various aspects of society will inevitably encounter obstacles, including resistance, regulatory complexities, and debates surrounding issues like privacy and security. The process will be far from uniform, with different regions and sectors facing distinct hurdles and experiencing varying paces of change. One significant concern is the potential emergence of cyber-security exclusivity, driven by disparities in resources and technological capabilities. The digital divide, which already reflects uneven access to technology, may widen the gap in cyber-security preparedness. This disparity goes beyond merely identifying vulnerabilities; it extends to the capacity of different entities to effectively counter cyber-threats. The uneven distribution of resources may result in certain groups or communities being disproportionately exposed to cyber-risks, exacerbating existing inequalities (Calderaro and Craig 2020).

The manifestation of these disparities can be observed not only in a power ranking based on cyber-capabilities but also in the ability to counteract and mitigate cyber-threats. Societies that are already under pressure will become more likely targets for cyber-attacks, including influence operations. This lack of equitable distribution in cyber-security benefits underscores the importance of addressing the digital transformation with a focus on inclusivity and a commitment to mitigating potential negative consequences for vulnerable populations.

3. Cyber-Threats Will Continue to Evolve (and Surprise Us)

The story of cyber-security politics is also a story of cyber-incidents that destabilize previously held assumptions. The dynamism of cyber-threats and their capacity to surprise us is intricately tied to the complex interplay of actor dynamics and economic factors. The profit motive has been a powerful driver in the history of cyber-security, with cyber-crime emerging as a lucrative industry. The promise of financial gains incentivizes threat actors to innovate continually, developing new attack methods and tools to exploit vulnerabilities. This innovation is further fueled by competition within the cyber-underground, where actors strive to outpace security measures through the creation of more advanced and sophisticated techniques. This cyber-marketplace operates on principles of supply and demand, propelling the continuous evolution of cyber-threats as actors seek to meet the demand for novel and more effective tools.

Nation-states engage in cyber-attacks for various reasons, including intelligence gathering, geopolitical influence, and strategic advantage. State-sponsored threat actors often possess substantial resources and advanced capabilities, allowing them to develop and deploy sophisticated cyber-tools. While nation-states engaging in cyber-attacks are not guided by direct economic motives in the same way cyber-criminals are, economic considerations also influence state-sponsored cyber-activities. The investment made by states in the development, enhancement, and maintenance of their cyber-capabilities is driven by an expectation of a tangible return on investment (ROI), albeit in a strategic and geopolitical sense rather than a traditional economic one. The ROI in the context of cyber-capabilities for nation-states is measured in terms of achieving strategic objectives, ensuring national security, and gaining a competitive edge on the global stage. It is therefore likely that in the future, the question of how to measure the success of cyber-operations will become more important.

4. States Will Regulate More

As societies globally continue to undergo digital transformations, governments are poised to play an increasingly proactive role in shaping cyber-security through regulatory interventions. One pivotal area of focus already is the protection of critical infrastructure, encompassing sectors vital to national functioning such as energy, transportation, health care, and finance. Regulations stipulate cyber-security standards, necessitate comprehensive incident response plans, and mandate regular audits to ensure the resilience of these essential systems. Other areas of regulation will be related to the responsible handling of personal information by organizations or will be about supply chain security, which will focus on enhancing the cyber-security posture of suppliers and service providers, potentially incorporating supply chain risk assessments, security standards for vendors, and increased transparency in supply chain practices. Not least, the increasing frequency and severity of cyber-attacks have spurred discussions on the need for clearer regulations regarding software security and accountability.

The effectiveness of these regulations will hinge on their adaptability to evolving circumstances, international collaboration, and the delicate balance between security imperatives and the imperative for ongoing innovation. Close collaboration between governments and private entities is likely to remain crucial for effective cyber-security, as the private sector plays a significant role in critical infrastructure and technological innovation. Overall, researchers will need to pay more attention to regulatory mechanisms (beyond law) in their cyber-security research (van Eeten 2017; Clark-Ginsberg and Slayton 2019).

5. Fragmentation in Cyberspace Will Increase

The concept of digital sovereignty, within the context of strategic competition, is poised to usher in transformative changes that reverberate across diplomatic, economic, and strategic domains. As nations strive to assert control over their digital infrastructures, a notable consequence is the potential for geopolitical fragmentation within cyberspace. This pursuit of sovereignty carries the inherent risk of creating isolated digital ecosystems, raising concerns about the hindrance of international cooperation, information sharing initiatives, and coordinated responses to cyber-threats. The collaborative fabric of global cyber-security efforts may face further unraveling due to these emerging dynamics.

A significant impact of the digital sovereignty drive is the emergence of distinct regulatory frameworks tailored by nations to their unique political, economic, and cultural contexts. This trend toward regulatory customization may result in regulatory divergence, posing challenges to cross-border data flows, collaborative cyber-defense initiatives, and the establishment of universally accepted global cyber-norms. Normative disputes are likely to intensify in the aftermath of digital sovereignty pursuits (Raymond and Sherman 2023).

Furthermore, the pursuit of digital sovereignty may lead to the formation of regional cyber-security blocs. Countries with shared approaches to digital governance could align their strategies, contributing to a fragmented global cyber-security landscape. The emergence of these blocs introduces new dynamics that have the potential to reshape traditional alliances and partnerships that historically defined the global approach to cyber-security. The geopolitical implications of digital sovereignty, therefore, extend beyond national borders, shaping the evolving landscape of cyber-security governance (Mueller 2017).

Conclusion

This comprehensive exploration into the realm of cyber-security politics has highlighted the interplay between technology, politics, and society. The persistence and evolution of cyber-threats underscore the urgent need for continuous adaptation and learning, emphasizing the importance of pulling together theoretical knowledge from diverse disciplines to enable a better comprehension of the multifaceted issues at hand. As the demand for knowledge rises, a transdisciplinary collaboration between scholars and practitioners might become increasingly crucial.

In navigating the uncharted waters of the digital era, the pursuit of knowledge becomes more closely intertwined with the quest for resilient, adaptive, just, and inclusive cyber-futures. As this book concludes, let it not just mark the end of a discussion but serve as a catalyst for ongoing dialogues, shared insights, and collective action. May it contribute to shaping a digital landscape that reflects the best of our combined capabilities and shared aspirations.

References

Boustead, A.E. and Herr, T. (2020). Analyzing the Ethical Implications of Research Using Leaked Data. *PS: Political Science & Politics* 53(3): 505–509.

Buchanan, B. (2020). *The Hacker and the State Cyber Attacks and the New Normal of Geopolitics*. Harvard University Press.

Calderaro, A. and Craig, A.J.S. (2020). Transnational Governance of Cybersecurity: Policy Challenges and Global Inequalities in Cyber Capacity Building. *Third World Quarterly* 41(6): 917–938.

Chesney, R. and Smeets, M. (eds.) (2023). *Deter, Disrupt, or Deceive: Assessing Cyber Conflict as an Intelligence Contest*. Georgetown University Press.

Clark-Ginsberg, A. and Slayton, R. (2019). Regulating Risks Within Complex Sociotechnical Systems: Evidence from Critical Infrastructure Cybersecurity Standards. *Science and Public Policy* 46(3): 339–346.

Dunn Cavelty, M. and Egloff, F. (2019). The Politics of Cyber-Security: Balancing Different Roles of the State. *St Antony's International Review* 5(1): 37–57.

Dunn Cavelty, M., Eriksen, C. and Scharte, B. (2023). Making Cyber Security More Resilient: Adding Social Considerations to Technological Fixes. *Journal of Risk Research* 26(7): 801–814.

Egloff, F.J. and Dunn Cavelty, M. (2021). Attribution and Knowledge Creation Assemblages in Cybersecurity Politics. *Journal of Cybersecurity* 7(1): tyab002.

Egloff, F.J. and Smeets, M. (2023). Publicly Attributing Cyber Attacks: A framework. *Journal of Strategic Studies* 46(3): 502–533.

Farrell, H. and Newman, A.L. (2019). Weaponized Interdependence: How Global Economic Networks Shape State Coercion. *International Security* 44(1): 42–79.

Harknett, R.J. and Smeets, M. (2022). Cyber Campaigns and Strategic Outcomes. *Journal of Strategic Studies* 45(4): 534–567.

Lindsay, J.R. (2023/2024). War Is from Mars, AI Is from Venus: Rediscovering the Institutional Context of Military Automation. *Texas National Security Review* 7(1). Available at: https://tnsr.org/2023/11/war-is-from-mars-ai-is-from-venus-rediscovering-the-institutional-context-of-military-automation/

Maschmeyer, L., Deibert, R.J. and Lindsay, J.R. (2021). A Tale of Two Cybers—How Threat Reporting by Cybersecurity Firms Systematically Underrepresents Threats to Civil Society. *Journal of Information Technology & Politics* 18(1): 1–20.

Mazarr, M.J., Beauchamp-Mustafaga, N., Blank, J., Charap, S., Chase, M.S., Grill, B., Grossman, D., Massicot, D., Moroney, J.D.P., Morris, L.J., Noyes, A., Pezard, S., Rhoades, A.L., Shih, A., Stalczynski, M., Shostak, M., Thaler, D.D. and Walker, D. (2022). *Security Cooperation in a Strategic Competition*. RAND Corporation.

Mhajne, A. and Henshaw, A. (2024). *Critical Perspectives on Cybersecurity: Feminist and Postcolonial Interventions*. Oxford University Press.

Mueller, M. (2017). *Will the Internet Fragment? Sovereignty, Globalization and Cyberspace*. Polity.

Raymond, M. and Sherman, J. (2023). Authoritarian Multilateralism in the Global Cyber Regime Complex: The Double Transformation of an International Diplomatic Practice. *Contemporary Security Policy* 45(1).

Rid, T. (2020). *Active Measures: The Secret History of Disinformation and Political Warfare*. Farrar, Straus and Giroux.

Smeets, M. (2018). A Matter of Time: On the Transitory Nature of Cyberweapons. *Journal of Strategic Studies* 41(1–2): 6–32.

Smeets, M. (2022). *No Shortcuts: Why States Struggle to Develop a Military Cyber-Force*. Oxford University Press.

van Eeten, M. (2017). Patching Security Governance: An Empirical View of Emergent Governance Mechanisms for Cybersecurity. *Digital Policy, Regulation and Governance* 19(6): 429–448.

INDEX

Note: Page numbers in *italics* indicate a figure and page numbers in **bold** indicate a table on the corresponding page.

crime: crime-as-a-service 162;
organized 42, 83; prevention 108,
121n9
criminal: activities 26, 55, 83–85;
groups 68, 144 (*see also*
cyber-criminal); investigation 134;
tools 162 (*see also* cyber-tools)
critical infrastructure: attacks against
84, 87, 95–96, **166**, 167, 170,
173, 178; destruction 23, 33, 64;
financial sector 88; protection
40–41, 43–44, 108, 113, 199–200
critical infrastructure protection (CIP)
19, 41
Crypto Wars 47
CryptoLocker 84
Cuba 108
Cuckoo's Egg 36
cyber-: Caliphate 131; coercion 24,
112, 172; criminal 26, 35, 83, 145,
182n10, 199; deterrence 24, 116,
119; diplomats 106; doom 11, 60,
79, 155, 180, 191, 196; influence
operations 68, 92–93; Kill Chain
146, 150n16; norms 111, 113, 119,
200; power 8, 17, 39, 139–140,
192; prefix uses 17, 49; resilience
179; terrorism 12, 45, 79–80, 94;
vigilante 178; weapon 24, 58, 131,
137, 195
cyber-attack: defense systems 146;
hack-and-leak 12, 56, 65, 68,
92, 167; methodology 146;
motivation 16, 83, 87, 119, 136,
194; prevention/protection 22,
43–44, 114–115; targeted 37, 39,
42, 56–59, 63–64, 85–88, 90,
140, 162, 165, 180; trade-offs and
costs 21, 48, 63, 68, 116, 134–135,
162–165, 173
cyber-capabilities: definition 148;
generic and elite 161–163, **166**;
investment in 11, 24, 39, 160;
offensive and defensive 60, 97, 117,
176, 179; risks and benefits 165;
strategic utility 168, 175, 178, 191,
194–195
cyber-crime: activity characteristics
80, 83; lucrative industry 97, 199;
protection policy 43–44; Russian
connection 85; state sponsored
85–86

cyber-espionage: as acceptable
intelligence gathering 113, 119;
engagement 23; famous cases 91,
150n7; illicit use of computers
89–90; protection policy 32; state/
semi-state actors **81**
cyber-incident: definition 3, 33, 129,
169; identifying markers 97–98; not
isolated incidents 72; occurrences
of 44–45, 55–56, 79, 92, 129,
140, 156; parameters 131–133;
perpetrators 136, 148; ramifications
4, 12, 18, 25, 135, 149, *159*, 171;
technology 68, 72, 130
cyber-operation: application of
humanitarian law 108, 113, 115,
140; definition 3; evolution of
12–13, 25–26; feeling the effects 60,
80, 92, 156–157, 168, 170–172,
178, 180, 191; levels of secrecy 56,
58–59, 62; limitations 18, 37, 48,
59, 61, 113, 163, 172–173, 176,
178–179; main countries involved
156–157; military dimension
64–65, **82**, 116; narratives 97,
172; offensive 118, 147; political
utility 155–156, 164, 168–169,
172, 175–176, 195; primary
objective identification 57–58,
72, 80, 131–133, 146–147, 169;
psychological effects 39, 171, 174,
176; strategic utility 164, 168, 174,
terrorist collaborations 83, 95; use
and utility 155
cyber-security: conflicting notions/
ideas 46, 111; debates 8, 11, 20,
23, 32, 40, 43, 49, 64, 71, 198;
dilemma 3, 142–143, 172; field
of study 5, 8, 10–12, 18, 23, 47,
64, 72, 112, 149, 190; gray zone
65, 137; international 2, 4, 46,
105, 189; landscape 56, 141, 148,
192, 201; negligence 1; pertinent
examples 6–8, 18, 26; politics of
16, 20, 23–25, 27, 32–33, 45, 55,
72, 89, 93, 129, 155, 179; relative
flexibility 18; stability 22, 84, 104,
106, 189, 191; strategic competition
56, 63–64, 117, 168, 174, 190,
192, 196–197
cyber-threat: addressing hostile
factors 33, 37–38, 40, 43, 45;

For Product Safety Concerns and Information please contact our EU
representative GPSR@taylorandfrancis.com Taylor & Francis Verlag GmbH,
Kaufingerstraße 24, 80331 München, Germany

Printed and bound by CPI Group (UK) Ltd, Croydon, CR0 4YY

08/06/2025
01897008-0002